Representing the Nonprofit Organization

REPRESENTING THE NONPROFIT ORGANIZATION

MARILYN E. PHELAN
Professor of Law
Texas Tech University School of Law

CALLAGHAN & COMPANY
3201 Old Glenview Road/Wilmette, Illinois 60091

Copyright © 1987 by Callaghan & Company
All Rights Reserved

"This publication is designed to provide accurate and authoritative information in regard to the subject matter covered. It is sold with the understanding that the publisher is not engaged in rendering legal, accounting, or other professional service."—From a Declaration of Principles jointly adopted by a Committee of the American Bar Association and a Committee of Publishers.

TABLE OF CONTENTS*

CHAPTER 1 *Creation of a Nonprofit Corporation*
- § 1:01. Organization of a Nonprofit Corporation.
- § 1:02. Articles of Incorporation.
- § 1:03. —Form for Articles of Incorporation.
- § 1:04. —Purpose Clause.
- § 1:05. Corporate Name.
- § 1:06. —Form for Application for Reservation of Corporate Name.
- § 1:07. Registered Office and Agent.
- § 1:08. —Form for Statement of Change of Registered Office or Registered Agent, or Both.
- § 1:09. Incorporators.
- § 1:10. Organizational Meeting.
- § 1:11. Bylaws.
- § 1:12. —Form for Bylaws.
- § 1:13. Corporate Minutes.
- § 1:14. —Form for Corporate Minutes.
- § 1:15. Powers of a Nonprofit Corporation.
- § 1:16. Defense of Ultra Vires.
- § 1:17. Procedures To Amend Articles of Incorporation.
- § 1:18. —Articles of Amendment.
- § 1:19. —Form for Articles of Amendment.
- § 1:20. Authorization To Do Business in Another State.
- § 1:21. —Certificate of Authority.
- § 1:22. —Form for Application for Certificate of Authority.
- § 1:23. Books and Records.
- § 1:24. Benefits to Members.
- § 1:25. Licenses and Permits.
- § 1:26. —Permits for Charitable Solicitations.
- § 1:27. Obtaining Tax Exempt Status.
- § 1:28. Checklist of Points To Remember.

CHAPTER 2 *Members and Directors of a Nonprofit Corporation*
- § 2:01. Members.
- § 2:02. —Meetings.

*The material in this book was previously published in *Nonprofit Enterprises: Law and Taxation* (1987) by Marilyn E. Phelan

Table of Contents

§ 2:03. —Notice of Members' Meetings.
§ 2:04. ——Form of Notice of Meeting of Members.
§ 2:05. ——Form of Notice of Special Meeting.
§ 2:06. —Right To Vote.
§ 2:07. —Voting by Proxy.
§ 2:08. ——Form of Proxy.
§ 2:09. —Right of Members To Inspect Books and Records.
§ 2:10. —Derivative Actions of Members.
§ 2:11. —Removal of Members.
§ 2:12. Directors.
§ 2:13. —Election of Directors.
§ 2:14. —Meetings of Directors.
§ 2:15. —Management of Affairs of a Nonprofit Corporation.
§ 2:16. —Action of the Board of Directors.
§ 2:17. —Removal of Director.
§ 2:18. Checklist of Points To Remember.

CHAPTER 3 *Officers and Employees*

§ 3:01. Selection of Officers.
§ 3:02. Duties of Officers.
§ 3:03. Authority of Officers.
§ 3:04. Officers as Employees.
§ 3:05. Liability of Officers.
§ 3:06. Removal of Officers.
§ 3:07. Employees.
§ 3:08. Discrimination in Employment—Title VII.
§ 3:09. —Equal Pay Act.
§ 3:10. Age Discrimination in Employment Act.
§ 3:11. Vocational Rehabilitation Act.
§ 3:12. —Vietnam Era Veterans' Readjustment Assistance Act.
§ 3:13. Retirement Plans for Employees of Nonprofit Enterprises.
§ 3:14. —Qualified Plans.
§ 3:15. ——Participation and Vesting Requirements.
§ 3:16. ——Funding of Qualified Plans.
§ 3:17. —Limitations on Contributions.
§ 3:18. —Integration with Social Security.
§ 3:19. ——Reporting Requirements for Qualified Plans.
§ 3:20. ——Plan Termination.
§ 3:21. ——Taxation of Benefits.
§ 3:22. —Individual Retirement Accounts.
§ 3:23. —Simplified Employee Pension.

TABLE OF CONTENTS   vii

§ 3:24.   —Tax-Sheltered Annuities for Employees of §501(c)(3) Organizations.
§ 3:25.   Checklist of Points to Remember.

CHAPTER 4   *Legal Problems of Nonprofit Enterprises*

§ 4:01.   Legal Action Involving Nonprofit Enterprises.
§ 4:02.   Right of Association.
§ 4:03.   —Discriminatory Practices of Private Associations.
§ 4:04.   —Judicial Intervention in Religious Associations.
§ 4:05.   —Standing of Association To Seek Judicial Relief.
§ 4:06.   Tort Liability of Nonprofit Enterprises.
§ 4:07.   —Charitable Immunity.
§ 4:08.   Application of the Copyright Act to Nonprofit Enterprises.
§ 4:09.   —Sources of Copyright Ownership.
§ 4:10.   —Copyright Protection.
§ 4:11.   —Public Performances of Copyrighted Music by Nonprofit Enterprises.
§ 4:12.   —Fair Use of Copyrighted Works.
§ 4:13.   Securities Laws.
§ 4:14.   —Exemptions for Securities Issued by Nonprofit Enterprises.
§ 4:15.   —Sale of Securities Donated to a Nonprofit Organization.
§ 4:16.   —Compliance with State Securities Laws.
§ 4:17.   Application of Antitrust Laws to Nonprofit Enterprises.
§ 4:18.   Unfair Competition.
§ 4:19.   Labor Laws.
§ 4:20.   —Selection of Labor Representative.
§ 4:21.   —Duty To Bargain in Good Faith.
§ 4:22.   —Subject Matter of Bargaining.
§ 4:23.   —Unfair Labor Practices.
§ 4:24.   —Strikes.
§ 4:25.   —Right To Work Laws.
§ 4:26.   Checklist of Points To Remember.

CHAPTER 5   *Merger, Consolidation, and Dissolution*

§ 5:01.   Procedure for Merger or Consolidation.
§ 5:02.   Effect of Merger or Consolidation.
§ 5:03.   Articles of Merger or Consolidation.
§ 5:04.   —Form of Articles of Merger.
§ 5:05.   —Form of Articles of Consolidation.
§ 5:06.   —Form of Articles of Merger or Consolidation of Domestic and Foreign Corporation.

Table of Contents

§ 5:07. Withdrawal of a Foreign Corporation.
§ 5:08. Sale of Assets.
§ 5:09. Voluntary Dissolution of a Nonprofit Corporation.
§ 5:10. Distribution of Assets.
§ 5:11. —Cy Pres Doctrine.
§ 5:12. —Articles of Dissolution.
§ 5:13. —Form for Articles of Dissolution.
§ 5:14. Involuntary Dissolution.
§ 5:15. Procedures After Dissolution.
§ 5:16. Bankruptcy.
§ 5:17. Checklist of Points To Remember.
Appendix—Model of Nonprofit Corporation Act

*Representing
the
Nonprofit
Organization*

CHAPTER 1

CREATION OF A NONPROFIT CORPORATION

§ 1:01. Organization of a Nonprofit Corporation.
§ 1:02. Articles of Incorporation.
§ 1:03. —Form for Articles of Incorporation.
§ 1:04. —Purpose Clause.
§ 1:05. Corporate Name.
§ 1:06. —Form for Application for Reservation of Corporate Name.
§ 1:07. Registered Office and Agent.
§ 1:08. —Form for Statement of Change of Registered Office or Registered Agent, or Both.
§ 1:09. Incorporators.
§ 1:10. Organizational Meeting.
§ 1:11. Bylaws.
§ 1:12. Form for Bylaws.
§ 1:13. Corporate Minutes.
§ 1:14. —Form for Corporate Minutes.
§ 1:15. Powers of a Nonprofit Corporation.
§ 1:16. Defense of Ultra Vires.
§ 1:17. Procedures To Amend Articles of Incorporation.
§ 1:18. —Articles of Amendment.
§ 1:19. —Form for Articles of Amendment.
§ 1:20. Authorization To Do Business in Another State.
§ 1:21. —Certificate of Authority.
§ 1:22. —Form for Application for Certificate of Authority.
§ 1:23. Books and Records.
§ 1:24. Benefits to Members.
§ 1:25. Licenses and Permits.
§ 1:26. —Permits for Charitable Solicitations.
§ 1:27. Obtaining Tax Exempt Status.
§ 1:28. Checklist of Points To Remember.

§1:01. *Organization of a Nonprofit Corporation.*

A corporation has been defined as "an artificial being, invisible, intangible, and existing only in contemplation of law."[1] Being a creature of law, a corporation possesses only those powers granted it by law.[2] In addition, because it is a creature of law, it cannot be created by agreement of interested parties or members; it requires authority from a sovereign power, either express or implied.[3] This means that a corporation can be created and corporate powers granted only by constitutional provisions or by or under authority of an act of the legislature.[4] Thus, the legislature of the state, as the state sovereignty, has inherent power to create corporations, to determine the procedure for incorporation, the purposes for which a corporation can be created, and the powers to be conferred upon a corporation.[5]

Corporations can be private, public, quasi-public, profit and nonprofit. Public corporations are those corporations, connected with the administration of the government, that are created for public purposes only. Incorporated municipalities and school districts are examples of public corporations; their authority to act comes from the government.[6] Private corporations are created for private purposes; the fact that a private corporation serves a public interest does not make it a public corporation.[7] Thus, a nonprofit corporation created by individuals is a private corporation even though it was created to administer a public charity.[8] In addition, a corporation organized by individuals does not become a public corporation because it is subject to state regulations or to inspection by public officers.[9] A quasi-public corporation is a private corporation that has been given powers of a public nature, such as the power of eminent domain, in order that it may fulfill duties of a public nature.[10]

Corporations are further classified as profit or nonprofit. Profit corporations are business corporations organized to benefit their shareholders; nonprofit corporations are devoted to charitable or other purposes whereby profits may not be distributed to the members.[11]

Because a corporation cannot exist without consent from the sovereignty, a corporation cannot exist until a charter, or general law, grants it such authority.[12] State statutes prescribe the procedures by which persons may form corporations. These statutes generally provide that a charter or a certificate or incorporation authorizing a corporation to do business will issue upon compliance with the provisions of the statutes.[13] In most states, the first step is the filing of articles of incorporation with the secretary of state.[14] While the initial requirements for organizing a corporation are substantially the same whether the corporation is for profit or not-for-profit, the statutes of each individual state must be consulted to ascertain whether any special provisions may be applicable.

FOOTNOTES

[1] **United States.** Dartmouth College v. Woodward, 4 Wheat 518, 636, 17 US 518, 4 LEd 629 (1819).

[2] **United States.** See Bank of United States v. Deneaux, 5 Cranch 61, 9 US 194 3 L Ed 38 (1810).

[3] **United States.** In re Lloyds of Texas, 43 F2d 383 (1930).

[4] **United States.** United States v. State Tax Commission of State of Mississippi, 505 F2d 633 (CA 5 1974).

[5] **Arizona.** See Board of Regents of University of Arizona v. Sullivan, 405 Ariz 245, 42 P2d 619, 623 (1935).

[6] **United States.** Dartmouth College v. Woodward, 4 Wheat 518, 17 US 518, 4 L Ed 629 (1819).

[7] **South Carolina.** York County Fair Association v. South Carolina Tax Commission, 249 SC 337, 154 SE2d 361 (1967).

6 Representing the Nonprofit Organization

Texas. Miller v. Davis, 136 Tex 299, 150 SW2d 973 (1941).
[8] **United States.** Dartmouth College v. Woodward, 4 Wheat 518, 17 US 518, 4 L Ed 629 (1819).
Texas. Miller v. Davis, 136 Tex 299, 150 SW2d 973 (1941).
[9] **Massachusetts.** Cemetery v. Boston, 158 Mass 509, 33 NE 695 (1893).
Wisconsin. Wisconsin Keely Institute Co. v. Milwaukee County, 95 Wis 153, 70 NW 68 (1897).
[10] **Massachusetts.** Attorney General v. Haverhill Gaslight Co., 215 Mass 394, 101 NE 1061 (1913).
[11] See § 1:01 for a discussion of nonprofit corporations.
[12] **Georgia.** Rogers v. Toccoa Power Co., 161 Ga 524, 131 SE 517 (1926).
[13] **Delaware.** Clendaniel v. Conrad, 3 Del 549, 83 A 1036, error dismd, 235 US 712, 59 L Ed 437, 35 S Ct 203 (1914).
Minnesota. Finnegan v. Knights of Labor, 52 Minn 239, 52 NW 1150 (1893).
[14] The New York Not-for-Profit Corporation Law (§ 404) requires that most nonprofit corporations obtain various approvals or consents prior to incorporation. For example, type B and C corporations must obtain approval of a justice of the supreme court of the judicial district in which the office of the corporation is to be located prior to incorporation. Corporations organized for the care of destitute, delinquent, abandoned, neglected or dependent children, or for combating juvenile delinquency, or for reducing or relieving unemployment among youth, must obtain approval of both a justice of the supreme court of the judicial district in which the office of the corporation is to be located and the commissioner of social services. Every nonprofit corporation which has a purpose for which a corporation could be chartered by the regents of the university must have the approval of the commissioner of education. Cemetery corporations must be endorsed by the cemetery board. A fire corporation must be approved by the authorities of each city, village, town or fire district in which the corporation proposes to act. Every corporation which has a purpose or power that includes the establishment or maintenance of a hospital or facility providing health related services or the solicitation of contributions for any such purpose must have the approval of the public health council as well as a justice of the supreme court of the judicial district in which the office of the corporation will be located. Any corporation which has as a purpose the betterment, protection, or advancement of wage earners must have approval of the industrial board of appeals. (See NY Not-for-Profit Corp Law § 404 for these and other consents required of other nonprofit organizations prior to incorporation.)

§ 1:02. *Articles of Incorporation.*

The contents of the articles of incorporation are determined by the statutes of the state of incorporation. The Model Nonprofit Corporation Act[1] provides that the articles of incorporation shall include the following information:

(1) The name of the corporation.
(2) The period of duration, which may be perpetual.
(3) The purpose or purposes for which the corporation is organized.
(4) Any provisions, not inconsistent with law, which the incorporators elect to set forth in the articles for the regulation of the internal affairs of the corporation, including any provision for distribution of the assets on dissolution or final liquidation.
(5) The address of the initial registered office of the corporation and the name of its initial registered agent at such address.
(6) The number of directors constituting the initial board of directors, and the names and addresses of the persons who are to serve as the initial directors.
(7) The name and address of each incorporator.

If a nonprofit corporation seeks federal tax exempt status under §501(c)(3) of the Internal Revenue Code, its articles of incorporation must limit the purposes of the corporation to one or more of the exempt purposes set out in §501(c)(3) of the Code. In addition, the articles must dedicate the corporate assets to an exempt purpose. The articles must provide that upon dissolution, all assets of the corporation will be distributed for one or more exempt purposes, or to the federal government, or to a state or local government, for a public purpose. The articles, or the law of the state in which the organization is created, may not provide that the assets may, upon dissolution, be distributed to its members or shareholders. The articles of incorporation for a charitable corporation that is a private foundation must include provisions that require it to act or to refrain from acting in a manner that would cause it to become liable for penalty taxes imposed by §§4941-45 of the Internal Revenue Code.

Generally, duplicate originals of the articles of incorporation are filed with the Secretary of State of the state in which the corporation is organized.[2] Under the Model Act, if the Secretary finds that the articles comply with the law, the Secretary shall, upon receipt of the proper incorporation fees, file one of the duplicate originals in the office of the secretary and attach the other to a certificate of incorporation which is returned to the incorporators.[3] Upon issuance of the certificate of incorporation, the corporate existence begins.[4] The certificate of incorporation is conclusive that the incorporators have complied with all required conditions precedent.[5]

FOOTNOTES

[1] Model Nonprofit Corporation Act §29 (1964). The "Certificate of Incorporation" for nonprofit corporations organized in the State of New York must contain several additional clauses. The certificate of incorporation must state the type of corporation, and in the case of a type C corporation the lawful public or quasi-public objective which each business will achieve. See NY Not-for-Profit Corp Law §402. The Certificate of Incorporation must also contain a statement that all required approvals or consents have been obtained as endorsed upon or annexed to the certificate. See §1:01. The certificate must also contain certain statements relating to those special nonprofit corporations set out in Article 14 of the New York Act. See New York Not-for-Profit Corp Law §1401-1411.

[2] See Model Nonprofit Corporation Act §30 (1964).

[3] Model Nonprofit Corporation Act §30 (1964).

[4] Model Nonprofit Corporation Act §31 (1964).

[5] Model Nonprofit Corporation Act §31 (1964).

§1:03. —Form for Articles of Incorporation.

ARTICLES OF INCORPORATION[1]
OF
_____

The undersigned, acting as incorporator—of a corporation under the _____ Nonprofit Corporation Act, adopt—the following Articles of Incorporation for such corporation:

FIRST: The name of the corporation is _____.

SECOND: The period of its duration is _____.

THIRD: The purpose or purposes for which the corporation is organized are: _____.

FOURTH: Provisions for the regulation of the internal affairs of the corporation, including provisions for the distribution of assets on dissolution or final liquidation, are:[2] _____.

FIFTH: The address of the initial registered office of the corporation is _____, and the name of its initial registered agent at such address is _____.

SIXTH: The number of directors constituting the initial Board of Directors of the corporation is _____, and the names and addresses of the persons who are to serve as the initial directors are:

NAME	ADDRESS
_____	_____
_____	_____
_____	_____

SEVENTH: The name and address of each incorporator is:

NAME	ADDRESS
_____	_____
_____	_____
_____	_____

Dated _____, 19___.

_____   Incorporators

FOOTNOTES

[1] Taken from the Model Nonprofit Corporation Act, Official Forms, No. 4.

[2] If no provisions for the regulation of the internal affairs of the corporation or for the distribution of assets on dissolution or final liquidations are to be set forth, insert "none."

§1:04. —Purpose Clause.

Corporate statutes generally require a statement in the articles of incorporation of the purpose or purposes for which the corporation is to be formed. The Model Nonprofit Corporation Act[1] provides that nonprofit corporations may be formed for any lawful purpose or purposes, including, though not limited to, the following: charitable, benevolent, eleemosynary, educational, civic, patriotic, political, religious, social, fraternal, literary, cultural, athletic, scientific, agricultural, horticultural, animal husbandry, and professional, commercial, industrial or trade association. It further provides that labor unions, cooperative organizations, and organizations subject to any provisions of the insurance laws of the state may be organized under the Act.[2]

New York has the most innovative provisions relating to the purposes for which a nonprofit corporation may be formed.[3] Provided the proper consents have been obtained, nonprofit corporations may be formed for four types of purposes. A corporation is then classified according to which of the four types of purposes it is formed. A type A corporation may be formed for any lawful nonbusiness purpose or purposes including, but not limited to, any one or more of the following nonpecuniary purposes: civic, patriotic, political, social, fraternal, athletic, agricultural, horticultural, animal husbandry, and as a professional, commercial, industrial, trade or service association.[4] A type B corporation may be formed for any one or more of the following nonbusiness purposes: charitable, educational, religious, scientific, literary, cultural, or for the prevention of cruelty to children or animals.[5] A type C corporation is one formed for any lawful business purpose to achieve a lawful public or quasi-public objective. Type D corporations may be formed for any business or nonbusiness, pecuniary or nonpecuniary purpose or purposes specified by any other law.[6]

Those corporations seeking federal tax exempt status under §501(c)(3) of the Internal Revenue Code (whereby contributions to such corporations will be tax deductible as a charitable contribution), must satisfy the provisions of §501(c)(3) of the Internal Revenue Code as to the purpose clause. The purpose clause of these organizations must limit the organization to one or more of the "exempt" purposes set out in §501(c)(3) of the Code. A corporation that is organized for both exempt and nonexempt purposes will not qualify as a charitable organization for federal income tax purposes. These types of nonprofit corporations correspond to the Type B corporation under New York law.

FOOTNOTES

[1] Model Nonprofit Corporation Act §4 (1964).
[2] Model Nonprofit Corporation Act §4 (1964).
An alternative purpose clause provides that a nonprofit corporation "may be organized for any lawful purpose except the following. . . ." See Model Nonprofit Corporation Act, alt § 4.
[3] NY Not-for-Profit Corp Law §201 (1964).
[4] NY Not-for-Profit Corp Law §201(b) (1964).
[5] NY Not-for-Profit Corp Law §201(b) (1964).
[6] NY Not-for-Profit Corp Law §201(b) (1964).

§1:05. Corporate Name.

The Model Nonprofit Corporation Act provides that a corporate name may not contain any word or phrase which indicates or implies that the corporation was organized for any purpose other than one or more of the purposes contained in its articles of incorporation.[1] It also provides that the name cannot be the same as, or deceptively similar to, the name of any corporation, whether for profit or not for profit, existing under the laws of the state or incorporation, or any foreign corporation, whether for profit or not for profit, authorized to transact business or conduct affairs in the state, or a corporate name reserved or registered as permitted by the laws of the state.[2] Some states statutes have additional requirements, such as, that the corporate name must contain the word "corporation" or "incorporated," or an abbreviation of one of the words.[3]

Most states permit incorporators to reserve the exclusive right to use a corporate name prior to the filing of articles of incorporation.[4]

It has been recognized at common law that a party may be enjoined from using a name under which it is incorporated if the name creates confusion and deceives the public.[5] Thus, injunctive relief is available against the use of a corporate name in instances where the public might be deceived into believing there was some connection between two corporations with similar names.[6]

FOOTNOTES

[1] Model Nonprofit Corporation Act §7 (1964).

[2] Model Nonprofit Corporation Act §7 (1964).

[3] See NY Not-for-Profit Corp Law §301 which has this requirement. However, it is not a requirement in New York for charitable or religious corporations or for those for which approval of the commissioner of social services or the public health council is required, or for bar associations.

[4] See Model Nonprofit Corporation Act §7A.

[5] **Illinois.** Northwest Suburban Congregation Beth Judea v. Rosen, 49 Ill App 3d 1147, 432 NE2d 335 (1982).

[6] **Florida.** Children's Bootery v. Sutker, 91 Fla 60, 107 So 345 (1926).

§1:06. —Form for Application for Reservation of Corporate Name.

APPLICATION FOR RESERVATION OF NAME[1]

_____

To the Secretary of State of the State of _____:

The undersigned, pursuant to Section — of the Nonprofit Corporation Act, hereby requests that the following name (or names) be reserved for the exclusive use of the applicant for a period of 120 days:

_____
Signature of Applicant

_____
If a corporation, by its President or Vice-President

Attest:

_____

Its Secretary or Assistant Secretary

_____

FOOTNOTES

[1] Taken from Model Nonprofit Corporation Act, Official Forms, No. 1.

§1:07. Registered Office and Agent.

Each corporation must have, and must continuously maintain, a registered office and agent within the state of incorporation.[1] Under the Model Nonprofit Corporation Act, the secretary of state must be notified of any change in the registered office or registered agent.[2] The registered agent is the person designated by the corporation upon whom process against the corporation may be served.[3] If a corporation should fail to appoint or maintain a registered agent within the state, or whenever the registered agent cannot be found, most states provide that the secretary of the state is an agent for service of process for the corporation.[4]

FOOTNOTES

[1] See Model Nonprofit Corporation Act §8 (1964).
[2] Model Nonprofit Corporation Act §9 (1964).
[3] See Model Nonprofit Corporation Act §10 (1964).
[4] See Model Nonprofit Corporation Act §10 (1964).

§1:08. —Form for Statement of Change of Registered Office or Registered Agent, or Both.

STATEMENT OF CHANGE OF REGISTERED OFFICE AND AGENT[1]
OF
_____

To the Secretary of State of the State of _____:
Pursuant to the provisions of Section ___ of the Nonprofit Corporation Act, the undersigned corporation, organized under the laws of the State of _____, submits the following statement for the purpose of changing its registered office or its registered agent, or both, in the State of _____:

FIRST: The name of the corporation is _____.
SECOND: The address of its present registered office is _____.

THIRD: The address to which its registered office is to be changed is _____.

FOURTH: The name of its present registered agent is _____.

FIFTH: The name of its successor registered agent is _____.

SIXTH: The address of its registered office and the address of the business office of its registereed agent as changed, will be identical.

SEVENTH: Such change was authorized by resolution duly adopted by its Board of Directors. P Dated _____, 19__.

By: _____
Its: _____

FOOTNOTES

[1] Taken from Model Nonprofit Corporation Act. Official Forms. No. 2.

§1:09. Incorporators.

The number and qualification of the incorporators depend on the state statute. Generally one or more persons may incorporate a corporation; no specific qualifications are specified. The Model Nonprofit Corporation Act simply provides that one or more persons may incorporate a corporation by signing and delivering the articles in duplicate to the Secretary of State.[1]

Some states permit other corporations to be incorporators; others require that "natural" persons be incorporators.[2] Some states require that a portion of the incorporators be residents of the state; others require that the incorporators be adult persons.[3] The tendency, however, is to permit any "person" to be an incorporator.

FOOTNOTES

[1] Model Nonprofit Corporation Act §28 (1964.)

[2] The Model Business Corporation Act provides that corporations may be incorporators. See Model Business Corporation Act §53 (1964).

[3] The Uniform Business Corporation Act §2 provided that some incorporators had to be citizens of the United States and that all incorporators had to be adults. The Uniform Business Corporation Act has been withdrawn.

§ 1:10. Organizational Meeting.

After the certificate of incorporation is issued, an organizational meeting of the board of directors named in the articles of incorporation must be held, either within or without the state of incorporation, at the call of a majority of the incorporators.[1] The purpose of the organizational meeting is to adopt bylaws, elect officers and transact any other business.[2] The Model Nonprofit Corporation Act provides that the incorporators calling such a meeting should give at least three days' notice stating the time and place of the meeting.[3]

A first meeting of the members may be held at the call of a majority of the directors. The Model Nonprofit Corporation Act provides that at least three days' notice should be given to members.[4] Generally notice need not be given to any director or incorporator who submits a signed waiver of notice before or after the meeting, or who attends the meeting without protesting as to a lack of notice.[5]

FOOTNOTES

[1] Model Nonprofit Corporation Act §32 (1964).

[2] Model Nonprofit Corporation Act §32 (1964).

[3] Model Nonprofit Corporation Act §32 (1964).

[4] Model Nonprofit Corporation Act §32 (1964).

[5] See NY Not-for-Profit Corp Law §405.

§1:11. Bylaws.

The bylaws of a corporation determine the rights and duties of the members with reference to the internal governance of the corporation and the management of its affairs.[1] A bylaw is an agreement or contract between the corporation and its members to conduct the corporation affairs.[2] It includes all regulations of the corporation; until repealed, bylaws are continuing rules for the governance of the corporation and its officers.[3]

The Model Nonprofit Corporation Act provides that the initial bylaws of a corporation shall be adopted by the board of directors.[4] The power to alter, amend or repeal the bylaws or to adopt new bylaws is vested in the board of directors unless otherwise provided in the articles of incorporation or in the bylaws.[5] The bylaws may contain any provisions for the regulation and management of the affairs of the corporation that are not inconsistent with the law or with the articles of incorporation.[6]

The power to make bylaws resides in the corporate body, either the corporate members or the corporate shareholders.[7]

FOOTNOTES

[1] **Oklahoma.** Colcord v. Granzow, 137 Okla 194, 278 P 654 (1928).
[2] **California.** Cheney v. Canfield, 158 Cal 342, 111 P 92 (1910).
[3] **Pennsylvania.** Elliott v. Lindquist, 356 Pa 385, 52 A2d 180 (1947).
[4] Model Nonprofit Corporation Act §12 (1964).
[5] Model Nonprofit Corporation Act §12 (1964).
[6] Model Nonprofit Corporation Act §12 (1964).
[7] **New Jersey.** See, Moorestown Management, Inc. v. Moorestown Bookshop, Inc., 104 NJ Super 250, 249 A2d 623 (1969).

§1:12. Form for Bylaws.

BYLAWS[1]
OF
_____

Article I. Offices

The principal office of the corporation in the State of _____ will be located in the City of _____, County of _____. The corporation may have such other offices, either within or without the State of _____, as the Board of Directors may determine or as the affairs of the corporation may require from time to time.

The corporation will have and continuously maintain a registered office, and a registered agent whose office is identical with the registered office. The registered office may be, but need not be, identical with the principal office, and the address of the registered office may be changed from time to time by the Board of Directors.

Article II. Members

Section 1. Classes of Members. The corporation will have _____ class (or classes) of members. The designation of such class (or classes) and the qualifications and rights of the members of such class (or classes) are as follows: _____ [list]

Section 2. Election of Members. Members will be elected by the Board of Directors. An affirmative vote of two-thirds of the Directors is required for election.

Section 3. Voting Rights. Each member is entitled to one vote on each matter submitted to a vote of the members.

Section 4. Termination of Membership. The Board of Directors, by affirmative vote of two-thirds of all of the members of the Board, may suspend or expel a member for cause after an appropriate hearing, and may, by a majority vote of those present at any regularly constituted meeting, terminate the membership of any member who becomes ineligible for membership, or suspend or expel any member who is in default in the payment of dues for the period fixed in Article XI of these bylaws.

Section 5. Resignation. Any member may resign by filing a written resignation with the Secretary, but such resignation will not relieve the member so resigning of the obligation to pay any dues, assessments, or other charges theretofore accrued and unpaid.

Section 6. Reinstatement. Upon written request signed by a former member and filed with the Secretary, the Board of Directors may, by the affirmative vote of two-thirds of the members of the Board, reinstate the former members to membership upon such terms as the Board of Directors may deem appropriate.

Section 7. Transfer of Membership. Membership in this corporation is not transferable or assignable.

Article III. Meeting of Members

Section 1. Annual Meeting. An annual meeting of the members will be held on the _____ day in the month of _____ in each year, at the hour of _____ o'clock, —M., for the purpose of electing Directors and for the transaction of such other business as may come before the meeting. If the day fixed for the annual meeting is a legal holiday, the meeting will be held on the next succeeding business day. If the election of Directors is not held on the day designated for any annual meeting, or at any adjournment thereof, the Board of Directors will cause the election to be held at a special meeting of the members as soon thereafter as convenient.

Section 2. Special Meetings. Special meetings of the members may be called by the President, the Board of Directors, or by not less than one-tenth of the members having voting rights.

Section 3. Place of Meeting. The Board of Directors may designate any place, either within or without the State of _____, as the place of meeting for any annual meeting or for any special meeting called by the Board of Directors. If no designation is made, or if a special meeting is otherwise called, the place of meeting will be the registered office of the corporation; but if all of the members meet at any time and place, either within or without the State of _____, and consent to the holding of a meeting, such meeting will be valid without call or notice, and at such meeting any corporate action may be taken.

Section 4. Notice of Meetings. Written notices stating the place, day and hour of any meeting of members will be delivered, either personally or by mail, to each member entitled to vote at such meeting, not less than ten nor more than fifty days before the date of the meeting, by or at the direction of the President, or the Secretary, or the officers or persons calling the meeting. In case of a special meeting, or when required by statute or by these bylaws, the purpose or purposes for which the meeting is called will be stated in the notice. If mailed, the notice of a meeting will be deemed to be delivered when deposited in the United States mail addressed to the member at his address as it appears on the records of the corporation, with postage thereon prepaid.

Section 5. Informal Action by Members. Any action required by law to be taken at a meeting of the members, or any action which may be taken at a meeting of the members, may be taken without a meeting if a consent in writing, setting forth the action so taken, will be signed by all of the members entitled to vote with respect to the subject matter thereof.

Section 6. Quorum. The members holding one- _____ of the votes which may be cast at any meeting will constitute a quorum at such meeting. If a quorum is not present at any meeting of members, a majority of the members present may adjourn the meeting from time to time without further notice.

Section 7. Proxies. At any meeting of members, a member entitled to vote may vote by proxy executed in writing by the member or by his duly authorized attorney-in-fact. No proxy will be valid after eleven months from the date of its execution, unless otherwise provided in the proxy.

Section 8. Manner of Acting. A majority of the votes entitled to be cast on a matter to be voted upon by the members present or represented by proxy at a meeting at which a quorum is present will be necessary for the adoption thereof unless a greater proportion is required by law or by these bylaws.

Section 9. Voting by Mail. Where directors or officers are to be elected by members or any class or classes of members, such election may be conducted by mail in such manner as the Board of Directors determines.

Article IV. Board of Directors

Section 1. General Powers. The affairs of the corporation will be managed by its Board of Directors. Directors need not be residents of the State of _____ or members of the corporation.

Section 2. Number, Tenure and Qualifications. The number of Directors will be _____. Each Director will hold office until the next annual meeting of members and until his successor will have been elected and qualified.

Section 3. Regular Meetings. A regular annual meeting of the Board of Directors will be held without other notice than this bylaw, immediately after, and at the same place as, the annual meeting of members. The Board of Directors may provide by resolution the time and place, either within or without the State of _____, for the holding of additional regular meetings of the board without other notice than such resolution.

Section 4. Special Meetings. Special meetings of the Board of Directors may be called by or at the request of the President or any two Directors. The person or persons authorized to call special meetings of the Board may fix any place, either within or without the State of _____, as the place for holding any special meeting of the Board called by them.

Section 5. Notice. Notice of any special meeting of the Board of Directors will be given at least two days previously thereto by written notice delivered personally or sent by mail or telegram to each Director at his address as shown by the records of the corporation. If mailed, such notice will be deemed to be delivered when deposited in the United States mail in a sealed envelope so addressed, with postage thereon prepaid. If notice is given by telegram, such notice will be deemed to be delivered when the telegram is delivered to the telegraph company. Any Director may waive notice of any meeting. The attendance of a Director at any meeting will constitute a waiver of notice of such meeting, except where a Director attends a meeting for the express purpose of objecting to the transaction of any business because the meeting is not lawfully called or convened. Neither the business to be transacted at, nor the purpose of, any regular or special meeting of the Board need be specified in the notice or waiver of notice of such meeting, unless specifically required by law or by these bylaws.

Section 6. Quorum. A majority of the Board of Directors will constitute a quorum for the transaction of business at any meeting of the Board; but if less than a majority of the Directors are present at said meeting, a majority of the Directors present may adjourn the meeting from time to time without further notice.

Section 7. Manner of Acting. The act of a majority of the Directors present at meeting at which a quorum is present will be the act of the Board of Directors, unless the act of a greater number is required by law or by these bylaws.

Section 8. Vacancies. Any vacancy occurring in the Board of Directors and any directorship to be filled by reason of an increase in the number of directors may be filled by the affirmative vote of a majority of the remaining directors, though less than a quorum of the Board of Directors. A Director elected to fill a vacancy will be elected for the unexpired term of his predecessor in office.

Section 9. Compensation. Directors as such will not receive any stated salaries for their services, but by resolution of the Board of Directors a fixed sum and expenses of attendance, if any, may be allowed for attendance at each regular or special meeting of the Board; but nothing herein contained will be construed to preclude any Director from serving the corporation in any other capacity and receiving compensation therefor.

Section 10. Informal Action by Directors. Any action required by law to be taken at a meeting of directors, or any action which may be taken at a meeting of directors, may be taken without a meeting if a consent in writing, setting forth the action so taken, is signed by all the Directors.

Article V. Officers

Section 1. Officers. The officers of the corporation will be a President, one or more Vice Presidents (the number to be determined by the Board of Directors), a Secretary, a Treasurer and such other officers as may be elected in accordance with the provisions of this Article. The Board of Directors may elect or appoint such other officers, including one or more Assistant Secretaries and one or more Assistant Treasurers, as it deems desirable, such officers to have the authority, and to perform the duties prescribed, from time to time, by the Board of Directors. Any two or more offices may be held by the same person, except the offices of President and Secretary.

Section 2. Election and Term of Office. The officers of the corporation will be elected annually by the Board of Directors at the regular annual meeting of the Board of Directors. If the election of officers will not be held at such meeting, such election will be held as soon thereafter as is convenient. New offices may be created and filled at any meeting of the Board of Directors. Each officer will hold office until his successor will have been duly elected and will have qualified.

Section 3. Removal. Any officer elected or appointed by the Board of Directors may be removed by the Board of Directors whenever in its judgment the best interests of the corporation would be served thereby, but such removal will be without prejudice to the contract rights, if any, of the officer so removed.

Section 4. Vacancies. A vacancy in any office because of

death, resignation, removal, disqualification or otherwise, may be filled by the Board of Directors for the unexpired portion of the term.

Section 5. President. The President will be the principal executive officer of the corporation and will in general supervise and control all of the business and affairs of the corporation. He will preside at all meetings of the members and of the Board of Directors. He may sign, with the Secretary or any other proper officer of the corporation authorized by the Board of Directors, any deeds, mortgages, bonds, contracts, or other instruments which the Board of Directors has authorized to be executed, except in cases where the signing and execution thereof is expressly delegated by the Board of Directors or by these bylaws or by statute to some other officer or agent of the corporation; and in general he will perform all duties incident to the office of President and such other duties as may be prescribed by the Board of Directors from time to time.

Section 6. Vice President. In the absence of the President or in event of his inability or refusal to act, the Vice President (or in the event there be more than one Vice President, the Vice Presidents in the order of their election) will perform the duties of the President, and when so acting, will have all the powers of and be subject to all the restrictions upon the President. Any Vice President will perform such other duties as from time to time may be assigned to him by the President or by the Board of Directors.

Section 7. Treasurer. If required by the Board of Directors, the Treasurer will give a bond for the faithful discharge of his duties in such sum and with such surety or sureties as the Board of Directors determines. He will have charge and custody of and be responsible for all funds and securities of the corporation; receive and give receipts for moneys due and payable to the corporation from any source whatsoever, and deposit all such moneys in the name of the corporation in such banks, trust companies or other depositaries as are selected in accordance with the provisions of Article VII of these bylaws; and in general perform all the duties incident to the office of Treasurer and such other duties as from time to time may be assigned to him by the President or by the Board of Directors.

Section 8. Secretary. The Secretary will keep the minutes of the meetings of the members and of the Board of Directors in one or more books provided for that purpose; see that all notices are duly given in accordance with the provisions of these bylaws or as required by law; be custodian of the corporate records and of the seal of the corporation and see that the seal of the corporation is affixed to all documents, the execution of which on behalf of the corporation under its seal is duly authorized in accordance with the provisions of these bylaws; keep a register of the post-office address of each member which shall be furnished to the Secretary by such member; and in general perform all duties incident to the office of Secretary and such other duties as from time to time may be assigned to him by the President or by the Board of Directors.

Section 9. Assistant Treasurers and Assistant Secretaries. If required by the Board of Directors, the Assistant Treasurers shall give bonds for the faithful discharge of their duties in such sums and with such sureties as the Board of Directors shall determine. The Assistant Treasurers and Assistant Secretaries, in general, shall perform such duties as shall be assigned to them by the Treasurer or the Secretary or by the President or the Board of Directors.

Article VI. Committees

Section 1. Committees of Directors. The Board of Directors, by resolution adopted by a majority of the Directors in office, may designate and appoint one or more committees, each of which shall consist of two or more Directors, which committees, to the extent provided in said resolution, shall have and exercise the authority of the Board of Directors in the management of the corporation, except that no such committee shall have the authority of the Board of Directors in reference to amending, altering or repealing the bylaws; electing, appointing or removing any member of any such committee or any Director or officer of the corporation; amending the articles of incorporation; restating articles of incorporation; adopting a plan of merger or adopting a plan of consolidation with another corporation; authorizing the sale, lease, exchange or mortgage of all or substantially all of the property and assets of the corporation; authorizing the voluntary dissolution of the corporation or revoking proceedings therefor; adopting a plan for the distribution of the assets of the corporation; or amending, altering or repealing any resolution of the Board of Directors which by its terms provides that it shall not be amended, altered or repealed by the committee. The designation and appointment of any such committee and the delegation thereto of authority shall not operate to relieve the Board of Directors, or any individual Director, of any responsibility imposed upon it or him by law.

Section 2. Other Committees. Other committees not having and exercising the authority of the Board of Directors in the management of the corporation may be appointed in such manner as may be designated by a resolution adopted by a majority of the Directors present at a meeting at which a quorum is present. Except as otherwise provided in such resolution, members of each such committee shall be members of the corporation, and the President of the corporation shall appoint the members thereof. Any members thereof may be removed by the person or persons authorized to appoint such member whenever in their judgment the best interests of the corporation shall be served by such removal.

Section 3. Term of Office. Each member of a committee shall continue as such until the next annual meeting of the members of the corporation and until his successor is appointed, unless the committee shall be sooner terminated, or unless such member be removed from such committee, or unless such member shall cease to qualify as a member thereof.

Section 4. Chairman. One member of each committee shall

be appointed chairman by the person or persons authorized to appoint the members thereof.

Section 5. Vacancies. Vacancies in the membership of any committee may be filled by appointments made in the same manner as provided in the case of the original appointments.

Section 6. Quorum. Unless otherwise provided in the resolution of the Board of Directors designating a committee, a majority of the whole committee shall constitute a quorum and the act of a majority of the members present at a meeting at which a quorum is present shall be the act of the committee.

Section 7. Rules. Each committee may adopt rules for its own government not inconsistent with these bylaws or with rules adopted by the Board of Directors.

Article VII. Contracts, Checks, Deposits and Funds

Section 1. Contracts. The Board of Directors may authorize any officer or officers, agent or agents of the corporation, in addition to the officers so authorized by these bylaws, to enter into any contract or execute and deliver any instrument in the name of and on behalf of the corporation, and such authority may be general or confined to specific instances.

Section 2. Checks, Drafts, etc. All checks, drafts, or orders for the payment of money, notes or other evidences of indebtedness issued in the name of the corporation, shall be signed by such officer or officers, agent or agents of the corporation and in such manner as shall from time to time be determined by resolution of the Board of Directors. In the absence of such determination by the Board of Directors, such instruments shall be signed by the Treasurer or an Assistant Treasurer and countersigned by the President or a Vice President of the corporation.

Section 3. Deposits. All funds of the corporation shall be deposited from time to time to the credit of the corporation in such banks, trust companies or other depositaries as the Board of Directors may select.

Section 4. Gifts. The Board of Directors may accept on behalf of the corporation any contribution, gift, bequest or devise for the general purpose or for any special purpose of the corporation.

Article VIII. Certificates of Membership

Section 1. Certificates of Membership. The Board of Directors may provide for the issuance of certificates evidencing membership in the corporation, which shall be in such form as may be determined by the Board. Such certificates shall be signed by the President or a Vice President and by the Secretary or an Assistant Secretary and shall be sealed with the seal of the corporation. All certificates evidencing membership of any class shall be consecutively numbered. The name and address of each member and the date of issuance of the certificate shall be entered on the records of the corporation. If any certificate shall become lost, mutilated or destroyed, a new certificate may be issued therefor upon such terms and conditions as the Board of Directors may determine.

Section 2. Issuance of Certificates. When a member has been elected to membership and has paid any initiation fee and dues that may then be required, a certificate of membership shall be issued in his name and delivered to him by the Secretary, if the Board of Directors shall have provided for the issuance of certificates of membership under the provisions of Section 1 of this Article VIII.

Article IX. Books and Records

The corporation shall keep correct and complete books and records of account and shall also keep minutes of the proceedings of its members, Board of Directors and committees having any of the authority of the Board of Directors, and shall keep at its registered or principal office a record giving the names and addresses of the members entitled to vote. All books and records of the corporation may be inspected by any member, or his agent or attorney, for any property purpose at any reasonable time.

Article X. Fiscal Year

The fiscal year of the corporation shall begin on the first day of January and end on the last day of December in each year.

Article XI. Dues

Section 1. Annual Dues. The Board of Directors may determine from time to time the amount of initiation fee, if any, and annual dues payable to the corporation by members of each class.

Section 2. Payment of Dues. Dues shall be payable in advance on the first day of _____ in each fiscal year. Dues of a new member shall be prorated from the first day of the month in which such new member is elected to membership, for the remainder of the fiscal year of the corporation.

Section 3. Default and Termination of Membership. When any member of any class shall be in default in the payment of dues for a period of _____ months from the beginning of the fiscal year or period for which such dues became payable, his membership may thereupon be terminated by the Board of Directors in the manner provided in Article III of these bylaws.

Article XII. Seal

The Board of Directors shall provide a corporate seal, which shall be in the form of a circle and shall have inscribed thereon the name of the corporation and the words "Corporate Seal _____."

Article XIII. Waiver of Notice

Whenever any notice is required to be given under the provisions of the _____ Nonprofit Corporation Act or under the provisions of the articles of incorporation or the bylaws of the corporation, a waiver thereof in writing signed by the person or persons entitled to such notice, whether before or after the time stated therein, shall be deemed equivalent to the giving of such notice.

Article XIV. Amendments to Bylaws

These bylaws may be altered, amended or repealed and new bylaws may be adopted by a majority of the Directors present at any regular meeting or at any special meeting, if at least two days' written notice is given of intention to alter, amend or repeal or to adopt new bylaws at such meeting.

FOOTNOTES

[1] Taken from Model Nonprofit Corporation Act, Official Forms, No. 27.

§ 1:13. Corporate Minutes.

The minutes of each meeting of the members or directors of a corporation are the official records of corporate transactions. These minutes are retained in a minute book.[1] The corporation secretary has the responsibility for preparing and maintaining the corporate minutes.[2] Minutes should be signed by the secretary and any corrections should be initialed in the margin by the secretary and the presiding officer at the next meeting. The presiding officer should then indicate that the minutes are correct by adding his/her signature.

Minutes of a corporate meeting are prima facie evidence of what happened at the meeting.[3] Many states require that nonprofit corporations keep and maintain minutes of their meetings.[4] In instances where the sale or mortgage of corporate property requires the consent of a majority of the members or directors, evidence of such consent is recorded in the minutes.

Express authority to examine the corporate minutes is generally given members of a nonprofit corporation.[5] Some states give this right to the general public.[6]

FOOTNOTES

[1] **Michigan.** See, Chapin v. Cullis, 299 Mich 101, 299 NW 824 (1941).
[2] **Georgia.** See, Hornaday v. Goodman, 167 Ga 55, 146 SE 173 (1928).
Texas. Mauritz v. Schwind, 101 SW2d 1085, 1090 (Tex Civ App, 1937).
[3] **Oregon.** Stipe v. First National Bank of Portland, 301 P2d 175 (1956).

CREATION OF A NONPROFIT CORPORATION 31

[4] See Ohio Rev Code Ann §1701.94. See also Model Nonprofit Corporation Act §25 (1964).

[5] See Cal Corp Code §§6330, 8330.

[6] See Texas Nonprofit Corporation Act §1396-2.23A.

§1:14. —Form for Corporate Minutes.

MINUTES OF THE FIRST MEETING OF THE BOARD OF DIRECTORS OF _____

The following are the minutes of the first meeting of the Board of Directors of _____, a corporation in the State of _____, held at _____ on _____, 19_____, said meeting having been held on the call of the incorporators named in the Articles of Incorporation.

Present at the meeting were _____ who are the persons named as the initial Directors of the corporation in its Articles of Incorporation.

These Directors have filed their written waivers of notice and consents to the holding of this meeting which waivers and consents have been filed with the corporate records and are made a part of the minutes of this meeting.

On motion duly made, _____ was elected Chairman of the meeting and _____ was elected to act as Secretary.

A document consisting of _____ pages entitled "By-Laws of _____ Corporation" was then presented to and considered by the Directors. After a review of such bylaws and a discussion of particular parts, on motion duly made and seconded, it was unanimously:

RESOLVED, that the bylaws presented to and considered at this meeting are adopted as the bylaws of this corporation.

A corporate seal was then presented to the meeting and on motion duly made and seconded, it was unanimously:

RESOLVED, that a corporate seal, consisting of _____, containing the words "_____ Corporation," is adopted as the corporate seal of the corporation, and the Secretary is instructed to impress such seal on the minutes of this meeting.

The Chairman stated that nominations were in order for the election of officers of the corporation, which would be a President, a Vice President, a Secretary, and a Treasurer. Thereafter, the following slate of officers was nominated:

——————————— ——————————— ———————————

There being no other nominations, on motion made, seconded, and unanimously carried, the slate of officers nominated was duly elected to hold office until their respective successors are duly elected. Each officer so elected, being present, accepted his or her office.

The following motions were adopted:

RESOLVED, that this corporation establish in its name a deposit account with _____ Bank and that the following named officers of this corporation be and they hereby are, authorized to establish such accounts; and

RESOLVED, that the following officers be, and they hereby are, authorized to withdraw funds of this corporation from said account signed as provided herein, and said bank is hereby authorized to honor and pay any and all checks so signed, and

RESOLVED, that the treasurer of this corporation be, and (s)he is hereby authorized to pay the expenses of incorporation and organization of this corporation.

There being no further business to come before the meeting, on motion duly made, seconded, and unanimously carried, the meeting was adjourned.

———————————
Secretary

Approved:

———————————
Chairman

§1:15. Powers of a Nonprofit Corporation.

The Model Nonprofit Corporation Act[1] lists the following powers of a nonprofit corporation:

(a) to have perpetual succession by its corporate name unless a limited period of duration is stated in the articles of incorporation,

(b) to sue and be sued, complain and defend, in its corporate name,

(c) to have a corporate seal which may be altered at pleasure and to use the seal by causing it, or a facsimile, to be impressed or affixed, or in any other manner reproduced,

(d) to produce, take, receive, lease, take by gift, devise or bequest, or otherwise acquire, own, hold, improve, use and otherwise deal in and with real or personal property, or any interest therein,

(e) to sell, convey, mortgage, pledge, lease, exchange, transfer and otherwise dispose of all or any part of its property and assets,

(f) to lend money to its employees other than its officers and directors and otherwise assist its employees, officers, and directors,

(g) to purchase, take, receive, subscribe for, or otherwise acquire, own, hold, vote, use, employ, sell, mortgage, lend, pledge, or otherwise dispose of, and otherwise use and deal in and with, shares or other interests in, or obligations of, other domestic or foreign corporations, whether for profit or not for profit, associations, partnerships or individuals, or direct or indirect obligations of the United States, or of any other government, state, territory, governmental district or municipality or of any instrumentality thereof,

(h) to make contracts and incur liabilities, borrow money at such rates of interest as the corporation may determine, issue its notes, bonds, and other obligations, and secure any of its obligations by mortgage or pledge of all or any of its property, franchises and income,

(i) to lend money for its corporate purposes, invest and reinvest its funds, and take and hold real and personal property as security for the payment of funds so loaned or invested,

(j) to conduct its affairs, carry on its operations, and have offices and exercise the powers granted by the act in any state, territory, district, or possession of the United States, or in any foreign country,

(k) to elect or appoint officers and agents of the corporation who may be directors or members, and define their duties, and fix their compensation,

(l) to make and alter bylaws, not inconsistent with its articles of incorporation or with the laws of the State, for the administration and regulation of the affairs of the corporation,

(m) unless otherwise provided in the articles of incorporation, to make donations for the public welfare or for charitable, scientific or educational purposes; and in time of war to make donations in aid of war activities,

(n) to indemnify any director or officer or former director or officer of the corporation, or any person who may have served at its request as a director or officer of another corporation in which it owns shares of capital stock or of which it is a creditor, against expenses actually and reasonably incurred by the director or officer in connection with the defense of any action, suit or proceeding, civil or criminal, in which he/she is made a party by reason of being or having been such director or officer, except in relation to matters as to which he/she is adjudged in such action, suit or

proceeding to be liable for negligence or misconduct in the performance of duty to the corporation; and to make any other indemnification authorized by the articles or bylaws, or resolution adopted after notice by the members entitled to vote,
(o) to pay pensions and establish pension plans or pension trusts for any or all of its directors, officers and employees,
(p) to cease its corporate activities and surrender its corporate franchise,
(q) to have and exercise all powers necessary or convenient to effect any or all of the purposes for which the corporation was organized.

FOOTNOTES

[1] Model Nonprofit Corporation Act §5. The New York statutes provide that corporations formed to provide parks, playgrounds, or cemeteries, or buildings and grounds for camp or grove meetings, temperance, missionary, educational, scientific, musical and other meetings, may (subject to the ordinances and police regulations of the county, city, town or village in which such parks, playgrounds, cemeteries, buildings and grounds are situated) appoint one or more special policemen, to preserve order in the parks, or other grounds. See NY Not-for-Profit Corp Law §202(d). A policeman appointed under the New York statute must, while on duty, wear conspicuously a metallic shield with the name of the corporation which appointed him inscribed thereon. Compensation for such policemen must be paid by the corporation by which they are appointed.

Pennsylvania has a similar provision. See Pa Stat Ann tit 15 § 7310.

California statutes provide that nonprofit corporations have "all of the powers of a natural person, including, without limitation . . . ." See Cal Corp Code §§5140, 7140. Thus, nonprofit corporations are given unlimited powers. One power specifically granted is the power to carry on a business at a profit and to apply any profit that results from the business activity to any activity in which the corporation may lawfully engage. See Cal Corp Code §§5140(a), 7140(1).

§1:16. Defense of Ultra Vires.

The Model Nonprofit Corporation Act specifies that no act of a corporation and no conveyance or transfer of real or personal property to or by a corporation will be invalid because the corporation was without power to perform the act to convey or transfer the power.[1] However, the lack of capacity or power may be asserted in a proceeding by a member or a director against the corporation to enjoin the performing of unauthorized acts or transfer of property to or by the corporation.[2] In addition, the corporation itself may assert lack of capacity or power as against officers or directors of the corporation who have exceeded their authority.[3] The Model Act also provides that the Attorney General may bring a proceeding to enjoin a nonprofit corporation from performing unauthorized acts or to dissolve the corporation.[4]

FOOTNOTES

[1] Model Nonprofit Corporation Act §6 (1964).

The New York Statute (NY Not-for-Profit Corp Law §203) provides that no act and no transfer of property will be invalid by reason of the fact that the corporation was without capacity or power to perform the act or transfer the property, "if duly approved or authorized by a judge, court or administrative department or agency as required."

The California Code provides that any contract or conveyance made in the name of a corporation which is authorized or ratified by the board or is done within the scope of authority, actual or apparent, will bind the corporation. See Cal Corp Code §§5141, 7141. However, the California Code does permit actions to enjoin, correct, or obtain damages for, or to otherwise remedy, a breach of a charitable trust. Such actions may be initiated by persons with a reversionary, contractual, or property interest in the assets subject to the charitable trust, as well as by officers and directors of the corporation and by the Attorney General. See Cal Corp §§5142, 7142.

[2] Model Nonprofit Corporation Act §6(a) (1964).

[3] Model Nonprofit Corporation Act §6(b) (1964).

[4] Model Nonprofit Corporation Act §6(c) (1964).

§1:17. Procedures To Amend Articles of Incorporation.

A nonprofit corporation may amend its articles of incorporation in as many respects as may be needed so long as the amendments contain provisions that would have been lawful in the original articles of incorporation.[1] State statutes prescribe the manner in which the articles of incorporation may be amended and must, of course, be followed. Generally, the Board of Directors adopts a resolution setting forth the proposed amendment or amendments and directs that the amendments be submitted to a vote either at a special meeting or at the annual meeting of members of the corporation.[2] Written notice of the proposed changes must be given to each member entitled to vote within the prescribed time and manner.[3] The Model Nonprofit Corporation Act provides for a two-thirds vote of all members present or represented by proxy in order to adopt an amendment to the articles of incorporation.[4]

If the corporation does not have members, an amendment may be adopted upon a majority vote of the directors.[5]

Any number of amendments may be submitted and voted upon at any one meeting.[6]

FOOTNOTES

[1] Model Nonprofit Corporation Act §33 (1964).
[2] Model Nonprofit Corporation Act §34(a) (1964).
[3] Model Nonprofit Corporation Act §34(a) (1964).
[4] Model Nonprofit Corporation Act §34(a) (1964).
The New York Not-for-Profit Corporation Law provides that amendments may be authorized by a majority vote of the members. See NY Not-for-Profit Corp Law §802.
[5] Model Nonprofit Corporation Act §34(b) (1964).
[6] Model Nonprofit Corporation Act §34(b) (1964).

§1:18. —Articles of Amendment.

The articles of amendment must be executed by the president or a vice president of the corporation and by the secretary or an assistant secretary.[1] The articles must specify the name of the corporation, the amendment so adopted, the date of the meeting of members at which the amendment was adopted, that a quorum was present, and that the amendment received the required number of votes.[2] If the corporation has no members, a statement to that fact, as well as the date of the meeting of the board of directors at which the amendment was adopted and that the amendment received a majority vote of the directors, must be included.[3]

Duplicate originals of the articles of amendment are filed with the Secretary of State.[4] If the articles are in proper form, the Secretary of State will issue a certificate of amendment to which will be attached one of the original articles of amendment.[5] The articles of incorporation will be deemed to have been amended upon the issuance of the certificate of amendment.[6]

An amendment to the articles of incorporation will not affect any existing proceeding by or against the corporation, nor will it affect the rights of any persons other than members.[7]

FOOTNOTES

[1] Model Nonprofit Corporation Act §35 (1964).

[2] Model Nonprofit Corporation Act §35(c) (1964).

[3] Model Nonprofit Corporation Act §35(d) (1964).

[4] Model Nonprofit Corporation Act §36 (1964).

[5] Model Nonprofit Corporation Act §36 (1964). A certificate of amendment may not be filed in New York if the amendment adds, changes or eliminates a purpose, power or provision the inclusion of which in the certificate of incorporation required the consent or approval of a justice of the supreme court, a governmental body or officer, or any other person or body, or the

giving of notice to the attorney general, or if the amendment changes the name of a corporation whose certificate of incorporation had such consent or approval endorsed thereon, unless the required consent or approval is endorsed or annexed to the certificate of amendment and proper notice has been given to the attorney general. See NY Not-for-Profit Corp Law §804(a).

[6] Model Nonprofit Corporation Act §36 (1964).

[7] Model Nonprofit Corporation Act §36 (1964).

§1:19. —Form for Articles of Amendment.

ARTICLES OF AMENDMENT TO THE ARTICLES OF INCORPORATION[1] OF

_____

Pursuant to the provisions of section _____ of the _____ Nonprofit Corporation Act, the undersigned corporation adopts the following Articles of Amendment to its Articles of Incorporation.

FIRST: The name of the corporation is _____.

SECOND: The following amendment of the Articles of Incorporation was adopted by the corporation: _____.

THIRD: The amendment was adopted in the following manner:[2] _____.

Dated _____, 19_____.

By:_____
Its President

and _____
Its secretary

FOOTNOTES

[1] Taken from Model Nonprofit Corporation Act, Official Forms, No. 6.
[2] One of the following statements should be added:
(1) The amendment was adopted at a meeting of members held on _____, at which a quorum was present, and the amendment received at least two-thirds of the votes, which members present or represented by proxy at such meeting, were entitled to cast.
(2) The amendment was adopted by a consent in writing signed under date of _____ by all members entitled to vote with respect thereto.

§1:20. Authorization To Do Business in Another State.

Incorporation in one state does not permit that corporation to perform activities in another state. A corporation must obtain a certificate of authority to conduct any affairs in other states.[1] However, such an authorization merely permits the corporation to operate in the other state; it does not give the second state the right to regulate the internal affairs of the corporation.[2] Once a certificate of authority is obtained from another state, the corporation has the same rights as corporations incorporated within that state.[3]

A certificate of authority will not be issued if the corporation seeking such authorization has a name that is the same as, or deceptively similar to, the name of any corporation incorporated, or authorized to do business, within that state.[4] The corporation would be required to change its name to one that would be available within that state.

The following activities are generally permitted within a state even though the corporation does not have authorization to do business within the state:[5]

(a) maintaining or defending any actions or lawsuits or any other administrative or arbitration proceedings,
(b) holding meetings of the directors or members or carrying on other activities concerning the internal affairs of the corporation,
(c) maintaining bank accounts,
(d) creating debts, mortgages or liens on real or personal property,
(e) securing or collecting debts due it or enforcing any rights it may have in property,
(f) conducting its affairs in interstate commerce,
(g) granting funds,
(h) distributing information to its members, and
(i) conducting an isolated transaction completed within a period of thirty days and not in the course of a number of repeated transactions of like nature.

FOOTNOTES

[1] See Model Nonprofit Corporation Act §63 (1964).

The California Code requires foreign nonprofit corporations to seek a "certificate of qualification" to transact intrastate business within the State of California. See Cal Corp Code §§6910, 2101.

The New York Not-for-Profit Corporation Law provides that a foreign nonprofit corporation may conduct any activities within the State of New York which it could conduct lawfully in the State of New York as a domestic corporation to the extent that it is authorized to conduct such activities in the state in which it is incorporated. See NY Not-for-Profit Corp Law §1301.

[2] Model Nonprofit Corporation Act §63 (1964).

[3] Model Nonprofit Corporation Act §64 (1964).

[4] Model Nonprofit Corporation Act §65 (1964).

[5] Model Nonprofit Corporation Act §63 (1964). Always check the statutes of the state to determine if these limited activities are permitted without a certificate of authority.

§ 1:21. —Certificate of Authority.

A corporation makes application for authorization to do business in another state by filing with the Secretary of State duplicate originals of Application for a Certificate of Authority.[1] The application should state the name of the corporation, the state in which it is incorporated, the date of incorporation, the period of duration, the address of the principal office of the corporation in the state in which it is incorporated, the address of the proposed registered office and name of the proposed registered agent in the state in which it is seeking authorization, the purpose or purposes of the corporation which it proposes to pursue in the state in which it is seeking authorization, and the names and addresses of the directors and officers of the corporation.[2] If the Secretary of State approves the application, one original will be attached to a certificate of authority to conduct affairs within that state and the other will be filed in the office of the Secretary of State.[3]

Upon issuance of a certificate of authority by the Secretary of State, the corporation will be authorized to conduct affairs within that state.[4]

Should the corporation amend its article of incorporation, the amendments must be filed with the Secretary of State in which the corporation is authorized to do business.[5]

FOOTNOTES

[1] Model Nonprofit Corporation Act §67 (1964).

[2] Model Nonprofit Corporation Act §67 (1964).

[3] Model Nonprofit Corporation Act §68 (1964).

[4] Model Nonprofit Corporation Act §69 (1964). See Chapter 5 for procedures to withdraw certificate of authority.

[5] Model Nonprofit Corporation Act §73 (1964). The Model Act provides that the amendments be filed within thirty days after they become effective.

§1:22. —Form for Application for Certificate of Authority.

APPLICATION FOR CERTIFICATE OF AUTHORITY[1]
of
_____

To the Secretary of State of the State of _____:

Pursuant to the provisions of section _____ of the _____ Nonprofit Corporation Act, the undersigned corporation applies for a Certificate of Authority to conduct affairs in your State, and for that purpose submits the following statement:

FIRST: The name of the corporation is _____.

SECOND: It is incorporated under the laws of _____.

THIRD: The date of its incorporation is _____ and the period of its duration is _____.

FOURTH: The address of its principal office in the state or country under the laws of which it is incorporated is _____.

FIFTH: The address of its proposed registered office in your State is _____, and the name of its proposed registered agent in your State at that address is _____.

SIXTH: The purpose or purposes which it proposes to pursue in conducting its affairs in your State are _____.

SEVENTH: The names and respective addresses of its directors and officers are:

Name	Office	Address
_____	Director	_____
_____	Director	_____
_____	Director	_____
_____	President	_____

_____ Vice President _____
_____ Secretary _____
_____ Treasurer _____

EIGHTH: This Application is accompanied by a copy of its articles of incorporation and all amendments thereto, duly certified by the proper officer of the state or country under the laws of which it is incorporated.

Date _____, 19____.

By _____
Its President

and _____
Its Secretary

FOOTNOTES

[1] Taken from Model Nonprofit Corporation Act, Official Forms, No. 19.

§1:23. Books and Records.

A nonprofit corporation must keep correct and complete books and records of account and must keep minutes of the proceedings of its members, board of directors and committees.[1] It must keep at its registered office or principal office a record of the names and addresses of its members entitled to vote.[2] All books and records may be inspected by any member, or the member's agent or attorney for any proper purpose at any reasonable time.[3]

The records of a corporation include the charter and bylaws, the minutes of its meetings, its account books, and written evidence of its contracts and transactions.[4] The books are the property of the corporation and not of the officers or employees. In most states annual reports of the activities of the nonprofit corporation must be filed with the Attorney General.[5] Those charitable corporations that are tax exempt under § 501(c)(3) of the Internal Revenue Code but that are classified as private foundations, must file copies of their federal income tax returns with the Attorney General of the State.

FOOTNOTES

[1] See Model Nonprofit Corporation Act §25 (1964).
[2] Model Nonprofit Corporation Act §25 (1964).
[3] Model Nonprofit Corporation Act §25 (1964).

The Cal Corp Code §§6330, 8330 provides that a member may inspect and copy the record of all the members' names, addresses and voting rights, at reasonable times, upon five business days' prior written demand upon the corporation stating the purpose for which the inspection rights are requested, or may obtain from the secretary of the corporation, upon written demand and tender of a reasonable charge, a list of the names, addresses and voting rights of the members. The corporation may, within 10 business days after receiving such a demand, deliver to the person making the demand an alternative method of achieving the purposes stated in the demand without providing access to or a copy of the membership list. The Cal Corp Code also provides that a membership list is a corporate asset. See Cal Corp Code §§6338, 8338. A membership list may not be used by any person for any purpose not reasonably related to a member's interest as a member without consent of the board.

The New York Not-for-Profit Corporation Law provides that any member of record of a corporation for at least six months immediately preceding the demand, or any member having at least five percent of any outstanding capital certificates, may examine the minutes of the proceedings of members of the corporation and the membership list, upon giving five days' written demand. A person demanding to see the membership list may be required to furnish an affidavit that the inspection will not be used for a purpose not in the interest of the corporation and that the person has not sold or offered to sell any membership list within a five year period. See NY Not-for-Profit Corp Law §621(b), (c).

Texas Nonprofit Corporation Act provides that the board of directors of a nonprofit corporation must annually prepare or approve a report of the financial activity of the corporation for the preceding year. The report must conform to accounting standards as promulgated by the American Institute of Certified Public Accountants and must include a statement of support, revenue, expenses and changes in fund balances, a statement of functional expenses, and balance sheets for all funds. See Tex Rev Civ Stat art 1396-2.23A. All records, books, and annual reports of the financial activities of nonprofit corporations in Texas must be kept at the registered office or principal office of the corporation for at least three years after the close of the fiscal year and must be available to the public for inspection and copying during normal business hours. Failure to maintain financial records, prepare reports, or make the financial record or annual report available to the public is a Class B misdemeanor. See Tex Rev Civ Stat art 1396-2.23A. There are exceptions for corporations that solicit funds only from the members; for religious institutions; for schools and institutions of higher education; for trade association or professional societies whose income is principally derived from membership dues and assessments, sales or services; for organizations whose charitable activities relate to public concern in the conservation and protection of wildlife, fisheries, and natural resources; and for alumni associations of institutions of higher education, provided the association is recognized and acknowledged by the institution as its official alumni association. See Tex Civ Stat art 1396-2.23A.

[4] **United States.** United States v. Louisville & N.R. Co., 236 US 318, 59 L Ed 598, 35 S Ct 363 (1914).

[5] Most states now permit use of the Form 990, the official reporting form for IRS purposes, as the annual statement to be filed with the state. Those states that have adopted the Uniform Supervision of Trustees for Charitable Purposes Act require that the existence and administration of any property held for charitable purposes must be reported to the Attorney General of the state. See discussion at §1:25.

§1:24. Benefits to Members.

Most states prohibit nonprofit corporations from issuing shares of stock.[1] For those few that do permit the issuance of shares of stock, the payment of dividends is nonetheless prohibited.[2] While a nonprofit corporation may pay compensation in a reasonable amount to its members, directors, or officers for services rendered, it may not distribute any profits to its members, directors or officers.[3] Most states do permit nonprofit corporations to confer benefits upon their members in conformity with the corporate purposes and do permit a distribution of assets to the members upon dissolution or final liquidation.[4] However, conferring benefits upon members or permitting a distribution of assets to members upon dissolution or final liquidation may cause the organization to lose its federal tax exempt status or to lose its classification as a §501(c)(3) organization so that contributions by its donors will no longer be tax deductible to the donors.

Most states prohibit nonprofit corporations from making loans to their directors or officers.[5] Any director or officer who assents to or participates in the making of such a loan is liable in most states to the corporation for the amount of the loan until it is repaid.[6]

FOOTNOTES

[1] See Model Nonprofit Corporation Act §26 (1964). The New York Not-for-Profit Corporation Law §501 prohibits the issuance of stock or share certificates but does permit the issuance of nontransferable membership certificates or cards to evidence membership, whether or not connected with any financial contribution to the corporation. The New York statutes require that the fact that the corporation is not-for-profit and that the membership certificate or card is nontransferable be noted conspicuously on the face or back of each such certificate or card. For those members making capital contributions, the corporation may not repay or redeem the contribution except upon dissolution of the corporation or upon redemption as provided for in the certificate of incorporation. See NY Not-for-Profit Corp Law §502(e).

[2] For example, the Pennsylvania Nonprofit Corporation Law (Pa Stat Ann tit 15, §7304), provides that a nonprofit corporation may issue share certificates; however, no dividends may be directly or indirectly paid on any such shares. Shareholders, under the Pennsylvania statutes, are not entitled to any portion of the earnings of the corporation. However, the shareholders are entitled to a pro rata distribution of the assets, after the payment of all debts, as represented by the shares outstanding, at the time of dissolution. The share certificates may not be transferred.

[3] See Model Nonprofit Corporation Act §26. See Texas Non-Profit Corporation Act, Tex Civ Stat art 1396-2.24 and New York Not-for-Profit Corporation Act §515.

[4] See Model Nonprofit Corporation Act §26 (1964). The New York Not-for-Profit Corporation Act §515 provides that a corporation may confer benefits upon members and nonmembers in conformity with its purposes, may redeem its capital certificates, and may make other distributions of cash or property to its members or former members, directors, or officers prior to dissolution or final liquidation except when the corporation is currently insolvent or would thereby become insolvent.

[5] See Model Nonprofit Corporation Act §27. The New York Not-for-Profit Corporation Law §716 provides that no loans may be made to officers other than through the purchase of bonds, debentures, or similar obligations of the types customarily sold in public offerings or through ordinary deposit of funds in a bank.

[6] See Model Nonprofit Corporation Act §27.

§1:25. Licenses and Permits.

A nonprofit organization must obtain whatever licenses or permits are required by a particular state, county, or city in order to conduct activities within that state. Generally, a nonprofit organization is subjected to the same licensing requirements as are profit organizations, but often to additional, special requirements.

While the charter or certificate of incorporation grants the nonprofit corporation a license to do business within the state, some states also require that a special license tax be paid.[1] In some states, nonprofit organizations must obtain other special licenses or permits either prior to incorporation or prior to conducting activities.[2] For example, states generally require separate licenses for nonprofit organizations operating day care centers, old-age homes, health care centers, and schools.

Most states require that a corporation or any other business obtain a sales tax permit or license prior to conducting activities. While some states exempt certain types of nonprofit organizations from this requirement, others do not.[3] Some states impose an admission tax on entertainment or amusement areas or on dues to social, athletic or sporting events.[4]

State and local governmental control over private philanthropy is a growing trend. A number of states have enacted laws to control the solicitation of funds from the public. Some of these are in the form of a requirement to report to the Attorney General of the state the existence and administration of property held for charitable purposes.[5] Others require that some form of permit or license be obtained before any solicitation can take place within the state.[6] Generally any required permits are handled at the municipal level through local regulations or ordinances.

The constitutionality of ordinances requiring registration prior to solicitation is often an issue in the courts.[7] The regulation of religious organizations is particularly a problem; such regulation may involve an encroachment by the state into constitutionally protected areas under the religion clause of the First Amendment to the U.S. Constitution. Thus, a state may not examine a church in the same manner it does other public charities.[8]

For other charities, courts have generally upheld ordinances that are not arbitrary or discriminatory, on the theory that a municipality may reasonably regulate solicitation to protect its citizens from fraudulent appeals.[9] However, the Supreme Court recently ruled unconstitutional a Maryland statute prohibiting a charitable organization from paying expenses of more than 25% of the amount raised for fund raising activities.[10] The Court was of the opinion that there is no connection between fraud and high solicitation and administrative costs.[11]

In addition, a district court held a portion of the Minnesota statute relating to the regulation of fund raising to be unconstitutional.[12] Chapter 309 of the Minnesota statutes requires that all charitable organizations soliciting funds within Minnesota must file a registration statement with the Commissioner and must be licensed. Heritage, a professional fund raiser, sued on its behalf and on behalf of its client, American Christian Voice Foundation, challenging the provisions on the basis of the First Amendment. The court cited Secretary of State of

Maryland v. Joseph Munson Co., 467 US 947, 81 L Ed 2d 786, 104 S Ct 2839 (1984), as authority for its determination that that portion of the Minnesota statutes placing limitations on the amount of expenditures a charity can make with respect to charitable fund raising, was unconstitutional. The court noted, however, that a majority of the Minnesota statute was narrowly drawn to meet strong, subordinating interests of the state without unnecessarily interfering with free speech.

FOOTNOTES

[1] See Ala Code §40-12-40; Alaska Stat §43.70.030; Fla Stat §§205.032, 205.042; La Rev Stat Ann §47.341; Miss Code Ann §27-15-11; NC Gen Stat §105-33; Tenn Code Ann §§67-4005, 67-4006. Even though such a license tax is imposed, some states exempt certain types of nonprofit organizations. See, for example, Fla Stat §205.022 (which exempts religious, charitable, or educational activities of nonprofit organizations); Md Ann Code §406; and SC Code Ann §12-21-2420.

[2] For example, the New York Not-for-Profit Corporation Law requires approval for most nonprofit corporations from a justice of the supreme court of the judicial district in which the office of the nonprofit will be located prior to incorporation. See NY Not-for-Profit Corp Law §404. Approvals are also required from various other boards and departments depending upon the type of nonprofit.

[3] For example, Arizona exempts sales by any nonprofit organizations organized and operated exclusively for charitable purposes. See Ariz Rev Stat art 42-1231. Arkansas exempts sales by churches and charitable organizations. See Ark Stat Ann §84-1904. It also exempts sales to nonprofit orphans' or children's homes, sales to humane societies, and sales to charitable hospitals and sanitaria. See Ark Stat Ann §§84-1904, 84-1904, 84-1905. Colorado exempts sales to nonprofit religious, charitable, scientific, or educational organizations. See Colo Rev Stat §§36-26-102, 39-26-114. Illinois exempts sales to charitable, religious, and educational organizations, or nonprofit corporations organized for the recreation of persons age 55 or older. See Ill Rev Stat ch 120, par 440.

[4] See Conn Gen Stat §§12-541 to 12-543; Ind Code §6-9-13-1; and SC Code Ann §12-21-2420.

[5] See Uniform Supervision of Trustees for Charitable Purposes Act, 7A

CREATION OF A NONPROFIT CORPORATION 51

Unif Laws 748, which has been adopted in California, Illinois, Michigan, and Oregon. See Cal Gov't Code §§12580-12597; Ill Rev Stat ch 14, pars 51-64; MSA §§26.1200(1) et seq.; MCL §14.251 et seq.; Or Rev Stat §§128.610-128.990. See discussion of the Uniform Supervision of Trustees for Charitable Purposes Act at §1:04.

[6] See Ohio Rev Code Ann, tit 17, §1716.02. The Ohio statute applies only to solicitations of funds that may exceed $500 in one year. It also exempts certain types of organizations, such as churches and colleges.

See also Mass Gen Laws Ann ch 68, §§18-32. Massachusetts' solicitations statute has 11 exemption classifications.

See further discussion at §1:26.

[7] See, e.g.:
United States. Largent v. Texas, 318 US 418, 87 L Ed 873, 63 S Ct 667 (1943); Cantwell v. Connecticut, 310 US 296, 84 L Ed 1378, 60 S Ct 900 (1940); Hornsby v. Allen, 326 F2d 605 (CA5, 1964).
California. In re Dart, 172 Cal 47, 155 P 63 (1916).
Ohio. American Cancer Society, Inc. v. City of Dayton, 160 Ohio State 114, 114 NE2d 219 (1953).

[8] **United States.** See Wisconsin v. Yoder, 406 US 205, 220, 32 L Ed 2d 15, 92 S Ct 1526 (1971). The Supreme Court has recognized that regulation neutral on its face may nonetheless offend the constitutional requirement for governmental neutrality if it unduly burdens the free exercise of religion.

See also Cantwell v. Connecticut, 310 US 296, 84 L Ed 1378, 63 S Ct 667 (1943). In Cantwell, the Supreme Court overturned the conviction of a Jehovah's Witness for soliciting religious contributions without a state license.

California statutes have provisions that provide for the creation of nonprofit religious corporations. See Cal Corp Code §§9230-9246. Section 9230 authorizes the Attorney General to examine a religious corporation to determine whether wrongful activity has occurred and to institute action in the name of the state to correct wrongful activity. Section 9230 also permits the Attorney General to determine whether church expenditures are fraudulent or are made for personal benefit. The Attorney General can investigate whether a church is engaged primarily in carrying out a religious purpose. However, the role prescribed for the Attorney General in the enforcement of religious corporations is much narrower than that authorized in the case of public benefit and mutual benefit corporations. The more the secular activities performed by a church, the greater the state's interest in securing a proper allocation of the funds, and hence, the greater the role in policing the organization.

[9] **United States.** Streich v. Pennsylvania Commission on Charitable Organizations, 579 F Supp 172 (MD Pa, 1984), involved a constitutional challenge

52   Representing the Nonprofit Organization

to the Pennsylvania Solicitation of Charitable Funds Act. The court determined that the fee charged for registration was reasonably related to the cost of supervising and policing charities and that the requirement that a charity file a financial statement with the state was not an unconstitutional intrusion into a charity's internal financing operations. The court upheld the provision of the act limiting administration expenses to 35% of funds raised and its provision for a waiver on a showing of a reasonable basis for exceeding that limit. Thomas v. Collins, 323 US 516, 89 L Ed 430, 63 S Ct 667 (1943); National Foundation v. City of Fort Worth, 415 F2d 41 (CA5, 1969), cert den, 396 US 1040 (1969).

[10] **United States.** Secretary of State of Maryland v. Joseph Munson Co., 467 US 386, 81 L Ed 2d 786, 104 S Ct 2839 (1984). As a result of the Joseph Munson case, Maryland, North Dakota, and West Virginia repealed their percentage limitations in 1985. See Md Ann Code §41-103D, ND Cent Code §50-22-04.1, and W Va Code §29-19-7.

[11] **United States.** Secretary of State of Maryland v. Joseph Munson Co., 467 US 386, 81 L Ed 2d 786, 104 S Ct 2839 (1984). As a result of the Joseph Munson case, Maryland, North Dakota, and West Virginia repealed their percentage limitations in 1985. See Md Ann Code §41-103D, ND Cent Code §50-22-04.1, and W Va Code §29-19-7.

[12] See Heritage Pub. Co. v. Fishman, 634 F Supp 1489 (D Minn, 1986).

§1:26.   —Permits for Charitable Solicitations.

Many states require those nonprofit organizations engaged in solicitations within the state, to register, generally with the Secretary of State, and often to pay a solicitation fee.[1] Many of the states having such a requirement have exemptions for certain charitable groups, such as churches, educational institutions, and hospitals.[2] In addition, those organizations receiving a small amount of contributions, as well as those whose fund raising is carried on by volunteers, are often exempt from registration.[3] Most states require that charitable organizations file annual financial reports with the Attorney General, or some other official, of the state.[4]

Some states require that a certain percentage of the total

CREATION OF A NONPROFIT CORPORATION 53

contributions received must be used for the charitable purposes for which the funds were collected.[5] Some require that any contracts with professional fund raising groups be reported.[6] In addition, some states require professional fund raising consultants and professional solicitors to register annually and pay a fee to the state.[7]

FOOTNOTES

[1] See, as examples, Ark Stat Ann §64-1602; Conn Gen Stat §19-322m; DC Code Ann §2-2103; Fla Stat Ann §496.03; Hawaii Rev Stat §467B-2; Ill Rev Stat ch 23, par 5102; Kan Stat Ann §17-1740; Md Ann Code §41-103B; Minn Stat Ann §309.52; Okla Stat Ann tit 18, §552.3; Tenn Code Ann §48-2204; Va Code §57-49; W Va Code §29-19-5; Wis Stat Ann §440.41(2).

[2] See, as examples, Ark Stat Ann §64-1604; Fla Stat Ann §§496.02, 496.04; Hawaii Rev Stat §467B-11; Minn Stat Ann §309.515-1(b).

The Arkansas statute on solicitations exempts organizations that solicit solely for church, missionary, or religious purposes as well as other charitable organizations that receive less than $1,000 annually if their fund raising is performed by volunteers.

California exempts religious organizations, educational institutions, and hospitals.

Florida exempts religious organizations entirely and exempts groups receiving contributions from ten persons or fewer and using only volunteers, groups receiving less than $4,000 annually, and groups soliciting only from and by members. The exemption is lost, however, if the organization hires a professional solicitor.

Hawaii has broad exemptions; however, each organization must submit a statement to the Director of the Department of Regulatory Agencies citing the reason for the claim for exemption.

The Minnesota statute provided that only those religious organizations that received more than half of their total contributions from members or from affiliated organizations were exempt from the registration and reporting requirements of the act. See Minn Stat Ann § 309.515-1(b). But see Larson v. Valente, 456 US 228, 72 L Ed 2d 33, 102 S Ct 1673 (1982). The Supreme Court held in the Larsen case that the Minnesota statute granted denominational preferences, and, thus, was unconstitutional. The Court stated that the principal effect of the 50% rule was to impose the registration and reporting requirements of the Act on some religious organizations but not on others.

[3] See, as examples, Conn Gen Stat § 19-323n; D C Code Ann §2-2103; Ga Code Ann §35-1003; Okla Stat Ann, tit 18 §552.4.

Connecticut exempts, among others, those organizations that do not receive more than $5,000 annually or do not receive contributions from more than ten persons so long as only volunteers are used.

The District of Columbia exempts those groups, among others, that make solicitations exclusively among the membership and others, by regulation, that receive $1,500 or less during the year.

Georgia exempts, among others, those organizations receiving less than $15,000 annually.

Oklahoma exempts any organization that collects less than $10,000 annually.

[4] See, as examples, Md Ann Code §41-103B; Okla Stat Ann, tit 18, §552.5; Or Rev Stat §128.670. The Uniform Supervision of Trustees for Charitable Purposes Act, 7A Uniform Laws Ann 748, which has been adopted in California, Illinois, Michigan, and Oregon, requires that charitable trusts, including both charitable corporations and charitable trusts, file periodic reports with the attorney general of the state. See Cal Gov't Code §§12580-12597; Ill Rev Stat ch 14, pars 51-64; MSA §26.1200(1) et seq.; MCL §14.251 et seq.; Or Rev Stat §§128.610-128.990.

[5] See, as examples, Ga Code §35-1008; Kan Stat Ann §17-1747. Statutes that prohibit a charitable organization from paying more than a certain percentage of its receipts for fund raising expenses have been held to be unconstitutional. See Md Laws ch 787, § 103D as an example.

United States. See Secretary of State of Maryland v. Joseph Munson Company, 467 US—, 81 L Ed 2d 786, 104 S Ct 2839 (1984); Village of Schaumburg v. Citizens for Better Environment, 444 US 610, 63 L Ed 2d 73, 100 S Ct 826 (1980). In the Village of Schaumburg case the Supreme Court concluded that a municipal ordinance prohibiting the solicitation of contributions by a charitable organization that did not use 75% of its receipts for "charitable purposes" was unconstitutionally broad. In the Maryland case, the Supreme Court concluded that a waiver provision that permits a charity to demonstrate that its solicitation costs, though high, are nevertheless reasonable, does not save such an ordinance. The Court stated that such a waiver does not help the charity whose solicitation costs are high because the charity chooses to disseminate information as a part of its fund raising. The Court stated that the flaw in such statutes is the mistaken premise that high solicitation costs are an accurate measure of fraud. The Court concluded that the Maryland statute imposed a direct restriction on protected First Amendment activity.

[6] See Ark Stat Ann §64-1610; Hawaii Rev Stat § 467B-6; Ill Rev Stat ch 23, par 5107; Kan Stat Ann § 17-1745; Va Code §57-54.

[7] See, as examples, Kan Stat Ann § 17-1744; Ohio Rev Code Ann, tit 17, § 1716-02; SD Codified Laws Ann § 47-27-21; Wis Stat Ann § 440-41(5).

§1:27. Obtaining Tax Exempt Status.

Nonprofit organizations may be exempt from federal taxation and from some state and local taxation. However, incorporation as a nonprofit organization does not, of itself, assure tax exempt status. Satisfying the state nonprofit incorporation law may assure exemption from state franchise taxes in some states; however, others exempt only charitable nonprofit organizations while some do not exempt any nonprofit organizations.[1] Exemption from federal income taxes requires that application for exempt status be made with the Internal Revenue Service as certain provisions of the Internal Revenue Code must be satisfied before exemption is granted.

Exemption from the many and varied state and local taxes depends on the statutes of the different states. To obtain possible exemption from these taxes, state and local laws should be consulted.

FOOTNOTES

[1] For example, Texas exempts most nonprofit corporations from payment of franchise taxes. See Tex Civ Stat Ann §§54.010, 54.013, 171.057-171.080.

West Virginia exempts educational, literary, agricultural, scientific, religious or charitable corporations, cemeteries, lodges or Masons, Odd Fellows and the like. W Va Code §§11-12-76, 11-12-78, 11-12-80, 11-12-89.

Alabama exempts benevolent, educational and religious corporations. Ala Code §§40-14-40 to 40-14-41.

Kansas, Iowa, and Washington subject both profit and nonprofit organizations to the franchise tax. See Kan Stat Ann §§17-7503, 17-7504; Iowa Code §§496A.12, 496A.127; Wash Rev Code §§23A.40.060, 23A.44.110).

Kentucky exempts those corporations exempt from federal income tax

under §501 of the Internal Revenue Code from the Kentucky state license tax. See Ky Rev Stat §126.070.
New Mexico exempts all nonprofit corporations. See NM Stat Ann §53-3-12.

§1:28. Checklist of Points To Remember.

__ 1. The initial requirements for organizing a nonprofit corporation are substantially the same as for a profit corporation.[1]

__ 2. A corporation must first obtain a charter or certificate of incorporation authorizing the corporation to do business within the state.[2] In most states the first step is the filing of articles of incorporation with the secretary of state.[3] New York requires that most nonprofit corporations obtain various approvals or consents prior to incorporation.[4]

__ 3. The purpose clause in the articles of incorporation must indicate a nonprofit purpose.[5] Those corporations seeking tax exempt status as a charitable corporation for which charitable contributions will be tax deductible must limit the nonprofit purposes of the corporation to those set out in § 501(c)(3) of the Internal Revenue Code.[6]

__ 4. The corporate name must not be the same, or deceptively similar to, the name of another corporation existing within the state.[7]

__ 5. A registered agent and a registered office must be designated and maintained.[8]

__ 6. While the number and qualifications of the incorporators depend upon state law, generally one or more persons may incorporate an organization; no specific qualifications are specified.[9]

__ 7. After a certificate of incorporation is received from the state, the board of directors named in the articles of incorporation must hold an organizational meeting to adopt bylaws, elect officers, and transact any necessary business.[10]

___ 8. The bylaws determine the rights and duties of the members and the management of the corporation.[11] Times and places of meetings of the directors and of the members should be stated in the bylaws. The bylaws should also contain provisions relating to the number, qualifications, compensation, and duties of directors and officers.[12] Provisions relating to classes of members, voting rights, quorums, proxies, termination, and reinstatement of members should be included in the bylaws.[13] A procedure for amending the bylaws should be added. Bylaws can be amended by the organization; any amendments to the articles of incorporation must follow requirements of state law and must be sent to the secretary of state.[14]

___ 9. Incorporation in one state does not permit a corporation to do business in another state. If the corporation intends to conduct any affairs in other states, a certificate of authority must be obtained from each such state.[15]

___ 10. State statutes and city and county ordinances must be consulted to determine if any licenses or permits must be obtained before doing business within the state and the city or county.[16]

___ 11. Many states require nonprofit organizations engaged in solicitations within the state to register with the state.[17] Some states require payment of a solicitation fee. State statutes must be consulted before undertaking a solicitation program.[18]

___ 12. Necessary procedures to obtain federal and state tax exempt status must be followed.[19]

___ 13. Articles of incorporation generally may be amended by a two-thirds vote of members of the corporation.[20]

Nonprofit corporations having no members may amend the articles by a majority vote of the directors.[21]

— 14. A nonprofit corporation must keep correct and complete books and records of account and must keep minutes of the proceedings of its members, board of directors, and committees.[22]

— 15. Most states prohibit nonprofit corporations from issuing shares of stock.[23] No states permit the payment of dividends to members or shareholders.[24] Profits may not be distributed to members, directors, or officers. However, a nonprofit corporation generally may confer benefits upon its members in conformity with its corporate purposes and generally may distribute its assets to its members upon dissolution or final liquidation.[25] Nonetheless, to do so may cause the organization to lose its federal tax exempt status or cause it to lose its §501(c)(3) status so that contributions to it will no longer be tax deductible to its donors.[26]

FOOTNOTES

[1] See §1:01.
[2] See §1:01.
[3] See §1:01.
[4] See §1:01.
[5] See §1:04.
[6] See §1:04.
[7] See §1:05.
[8] See §1:07.
[9] See §1:09.
[10] See §1:10.
[11] See §1:11.
[12] See §1:12.
[13] See §1:12.

[14] See §1:12.
[15] See §1:20.
[16] See §1:25.
[17] See §1:25.
[18] See §1:26.
[19] See §1:27.
[20] See §1:17.
[21] See §1:17.
[22] See §1:23.
[23] See §1:24.
[24] See §1:24.
[25] See §1:24.
[26] See §1:24.

CHAPTER 2

MEMBERS AND DIRECTORS OF A NONPROFIT CORPORATION

§ 2:01.   Members.
§ 2:02.   —Meetings.
§ 2:03.   —Notice of Members' Meetings.
§ 2:04.   ——Form of Notice of Meeting of Members.
§ 2:05.   ——Form of Notice of Special Meeting.
§ 2:06.   —Right to Vote.
§ 2:07.   —Voting by Proxy.
§ 2:08.   ——Form of Proxy.
§ 2:09.   —Right of Members To Inspect Books and Records.
§ 2:10.   —Derivative Actions of Members.
§ 2:11.   —Removal of Members.
§ 2:12.   Directors.
§ 2:13.   —Election of Directors.
§ 2:14.   —Meetings of Directors.
§ 2:15.   —Management of Affairs of a Nonprofit Corporation.
§ 2:16.   —Action of the Board of Directors.
§ 2:17.   —Removal of Director.
§ 2:18.   Checklist of Points To Remember.

§2:01. Members.

A nonprofit corporation may have one or more classes of members or it may have no members.[1] If the corporation has members, the designation of the class of membership, the manner of election or appointment and the qualifications and rights of the members of each class must be set out in the articles of incorporation or in the bylaws.[2] If the corporation has no members, that fact must also be stated in the articles or in the bylaws.[3]

Courts have held that, although a nonprofit membership corporation is a corporate entity, nonetheless members in such nonprofit corporations are treated much the same as members in unincorporated associations. As a general rule, the same rules concerning members apply to both.[4] Consequently, a member of a nonprofit corporation does not acquire a severable right to any of the property or funds of the corporation, but rather merely a right to the joint use and enjoyment of the corporate property so long as he or she continues to be a member.[5] If a member withdraws from or abandons the nonprofit corporation, his membership can generally be terminated and his right to share in the corporation's property upon dissolution will be lost. Those remaining who succeed him become entitled to his interest.[6] The 1986 Revised Model Nonprofit Corporation Act,[7] however, provides that a mutual benefit corporation[8] may purchase the membership of a member who resigns or whose membership is terminated for the amount and pursuant to conditions set forth in or authorized by its articles or bylaws.[9]

Termination of a member's interest must generally be by voluntary act of the member or by act of the organization pursuant to authority granted it by the bylaws. However, waiver or abandonment also terminates a member's interest.[10]

Some states permit corporations to become members of nonprofit corporations;[11] consequently, control through holding companies can occur.

While issuance of shares of stock is forbidden in most states, some states do permit nonprofit corporations to issue shares of stock.[12]

FOOTNOTES

[1] Model Nonprofit Corporation Act §11 (1964). See Cal Corp Code §§5310, 7310. Nonprofit corporations in California have no members unless the articles of incorporation or the bylaws provide otherwise. If the corporation has no members, approval of the board is required of transactions otherwise requiring approval of the members. Cal Corp Code §§5310, 7310. If corporations have members, no person may hold more than one membership. Cal Corp Code §§5312, 7312.

New York statutes provide that members of nonprofit corporations have no preemptive right. NY Not-for-Profit Corp Law §620.

[2] Model Nonprofit Corporation Act §11 (1964).

[3] Model Nonprofit Corporation Act §11 (1964).

[4] See e.g.:

United States. Order of St. Benedict v. Steinhauser, 234 US 640, 58 L Ed 1512, 34 S Ct 932 (1914).

Arizona. Arizona Rangers Inc. v. Bisbee Company, 11 Ariz App 252, 463 P2d 836 (1970).

California. Perata v. Oakland Scavenger Company, 111 Cal App2d 378, 244 P2d 940 (1952).

Florida. Wall v. Bureau of Lathing & Plaster of Dade County, 117 So 2d 767 (Fla 1960).

Minnesota. Liggett v. Loivunen, 299 Minn 114, 34 NW2d 345 (1948).

New Mexico. Flanagan v. Benvie, 58 NM 525, 273 P2d 381 (1954).

Texas. Raulston v. Everett, 561 SW2d 635 (Tex Civ App, 1978).

See discussion of members of unincorporated nonprofit organizations at §§4:01 and 4:06. The unincorporated association is not a legal entity; thus, the rights and obligations of the association are the cumulative rights and obligations of its members. Associations may enact provisions governing admission of members and may prescribe the necessary qualifications of its members. Martin v. Curran, 303 NY 276, 101 NE2d 683 (1951); Evans v. Southside Place Park Association, 154 SW2d 914 (Tex Civ App, 1941).

Members of an association may be held personally liable for contracts of the association and may be held personally liable for torts committed by an individual acting in his or her capacity as an association member.

Trusts do not have members. The nature of a trust precludes members. A trust is established to benefit its beneficiaries which for a charitable trust would be specifically named charities or the general public.

[5] **Minnesota.** See Liggett v. Loivunen, 299 Minn 114, 34 NW2d 345 (1948).

[6] **New Mexico.** See Flanagan v. Benvie, 58 NM 525, 273 P2d 381 (1954).
Texas. Raulston v. Everett, 561 SW2d 635 (Tex Civ App 1978).

However, North Carolina statute protects members from denial of property rights to which they are entitled should they be expelled from membership. See NC Gen Stat §55A–29.

Arizona statutes also provide protection for members' property rights. See Ariz Rev Stat Ann §10–707 which provides that the property rights and interest of each member must be set forth in the bylaws as the general rule applicable to all members to determine and fix the property rights and interests of each member. The Arizona statute also provides that new members share in property of the nonprofit organization with the old members in accordance with the general rules. It provides that the bylaws that define property rights of the members cannot be altered, amended, or repealed except by written consent of three-fourths of the qualified voting members.

California statutes provide that all rights of membership cease upon a member's death or dissolution unless the articles or bylaws provide otherwise. See Cal Corp Code §§5320, 7320.

New York statute provides for termination of membership upon death, resignation, expulsion, expiration of a term of membership or dissolution or liquidation. See NY Not-for-Profit Corp Law §601(e).

[7] 1986 Revised Model Nonprofit Corporation Act §6.22.

[8] See §§1:01, 1:16.

[9] The 1986 Act is subject to change. Final adoption of the Act by the American Bar Association is scheduled for sometime in 1987.

[10] **Texas.** Raulston v. Everett, 561 SW2d 635 (Tex Civ App, 1978).
Washington. Schroeder v. Meridian Improvement Club, 36 Wash2d 925, 221 P2d 544 (1950).

See discussion of removal of members at §2:11.

[11] See NY Not-for-Profit Corp Law §601; Mont Code Ann §35–2–501.

See NJ Stat Ann §15A:5–13 which provides that if memberships are controlled by a corporate member, any memberships held by that corporation cannot be voted at any meeting.

[12] See Pa Stat Ann tit 15, §7752.

§2:02. —Meetings.

Meetings of members are generally held at the place designated in the bylaws. However, if the bylaws have no provision as to place of meetings of members, such meetings should be held at the registered office of the corporation.[1] The annual meeting of the members must be held at the time provided for in the bylaws.[2] However, failure to hold an annual meeting does not cause a forfeiture or dissolution of the corporation.[3]

Special meetings may be called by the president or by the board of directors. Special meetings may also be called by the corporate officers or by the number or proportion of members as provided in the articles of incorporation or in the bylaws.[4]

Should the board of directors fail to call the annual meeting at the designated time, some state statutes provide that any member may make demand that such a meeting be held within a reasonable time.[5] If the annual meeting is not called after such a demand is made, a member may compel the holding of the annual meeting by legal action directed against the board.[6]

At least one general meeting of members should be held annually to elect directors and to approve the annual reports. Meetings are required when the approval of members is necessary to enter into a particular transaction or to adopt, or to amend the bylaws.[7]

A quorum is the number of members required to be present at a meeting to make any business undertaken at the meeting binding upon the corporation. Generally this is a majority of the members; however, it may be a majority of the voting members present at a particular meeting.[8] The bylaws should specify the number of members constituting a quorum. Some state statutes specify the number of members required to enter into a particular transaction. If this is the case, a quorum cannot be set at a lesser number.[9]

FOOTNOTES

[1] Model Nonprofit Corporation Act §13 (1964).
[2] Model Nonprofit Corporation Act §13 (1964).
[3] Model Nonprofit Corporation Act §13 (1964).
[4] Model Nonprofit Corporation Act §13 (1964).
[5] See Tex Civ Stat §1396–2.10(2).
[6] Tex Civ Stat § 1396–2.10(2).

[7] Meetings generally must be held to elect directors, to adopt or amend bylaws, to amend the articles of incorporation, to sell, lease, or mortgage property, to merge with another corporation, or to dissolve the corporation.

However, Indiana statutes provide that the power to make, alter, amend, or repeal the bylaws of a corporation is vested in the board of directors unless the articles of incorporation provide otherwise. See Ind Stat Ann tit 23 §23-1-1.1-8.

Pennsylvania statutes provide that the members have the right to make, alter, amend, and repeal the bylaws but such authority may be vested in the board of directors if the articles or the bylaws so provide. However, the power is always subject to change by the members. See Pa Stat Ann tit 15, §7504.

California statutes provide that any action required or permitted to be taken by the members may be taken without a meeting if all members individually or collectively consent in writing to the action. The written consent must be filed with the minutes and has the same force and effect as the unanimous vote of the members. See Cal Corp Code §§5516 and 7516.

[8] See Ohio Rev Code Ann, tit 17, §1702.22.
[9] See Model Nonprofit Corporation Act § 16 (1964).

§2:03. —Notice of Members' Meetings.

Written notice stating the place, day and hour of a meeting of the members must be delivered to the members within a certain period of time before the date of the meeting. The Model Nonprofit Corporation Act specifies that notice should be delivered to the members not less than 10 nor more than 50 days before the date of the meeting.[1] If the meeting is a special meeting, the purpose or purposes for which the meeting is called should be a part of the notice.[2]

The notice of meeting may be delivered personally or by mail and should be delivered at the direction of the president, the secretary, or the officers or persons calling the meeting.[3] If the notice is delivered by mail, it is deemed delivered when it is deposited in the United States mail addressed to the member at the address on the corporate records.[4]

Notice of a meeting need not be given to a member who submits a signed waiver of notice, in person or by proxy, either before or after the meeting. The attendance of a member at a meeting, in person or proxy, without protesting prior to the conclusion of the meeting of a lack of notice of the meeting, constitutes a waiver of notice by that member.[5]

FOOTNOTES

[1] Model Nonprofit Corporation Act §14 (1964).
[2] Model Nonprofit Corporation Act §14 (1964). See NY Not-for-Profit Corp Law §605.
[3] Model Nonprofit Corporation Act §14 (1964).
[4] Model Nonprofit Corporation Act §14 (1964).
[5] See NY Not-for-Profit Corp Law §606.

§2:04. ——*Form of Notice of Meeting of Members.*

TO THE MEMBERS OF _____ CORPORATION:

Notice is hereby given that the annual meeting of the members of _____ Corporation will be held at the Corporation's office at _____ in the City of _____, State of _____, on the _____ day of _____ at _____ o'clock.

Dated _____, 19_____.

_____
President

§2:05.   ——Form of Notice of Special Meeting.

TO THE MEMBERS OF _____ CORPORATION:

Notice is hereby given that a special meeting of the members of _____ Corporation will be held at the corporate office at _____, in the city of _____, State of _____, on _____, the _____ day of _____, 19___, at _____ o'clock for the following purposes:

1. _____
2. _____

This meeting is called by the undersigned members*

_____
_____

Dated: _____, 19___.

*An alternative method of calling a special meeting would close as follows:

By order of the Board of Directors

_____
Secretary

Dated _____, 19_____.

§ 2:06.   —Right To Vote.

The right of members to vote may be limited, enlarged or denied to the extent provided for in the articles of incorporation or in the bylaws.[1] However, unless limited, each member, regardless of class, is entitled to one vote on each matter submitted to a vote of the members.[2] If the corporation provides that no members may vote, the directors have the sole voting power.[3]

The statutes of some states provide that the articles of incorporation or the bylaws may provide that in all elections of directors the members may cumulate their votes and, thus, give one candidate the number of votes equal to that member's vote multiplied by the number of directors to be elected.[4] If cumulative voting is permitted, it may also be used to distribute a member's votes among any number of candidates.[5] Some states have rejected cumulative voting for nonprofit corporations.[6]

While the right to vote has been considered a property right for a shareholder of a business corporation,[7] it is generally not a vested right for a member of a nonprofit corporation.[8] Courts have stated that the right of a member of a nonprofit corporation to vote is not constitutionally protected because a member of a nonprofit corporation does not have an interest in the property of the corporation.[9]

FOOTNOTES

[1] Model Nonprofit Corporation Act §15 (1964).

[2] Model Nonprofit Corporation Act §15 (1964). See Cal Corp Code §§5610, 7610.

[3] Model Nonprofit Corporation Act §15 (1964).

[4] Model Nonprofit Corporation Act §15 provides for cumulative voting. However, some states that have adopted the Model Act have rejected this provision. California, Indiana, and New York are states that have adopted the provision. See Cal Corp Code §§5616, 7615; Ind Stat Ann §25–515(e); and NY Not-for-Profit Corp Law §617.

[5] Model Nonprofit Corporation Act §15 (1964). See also NJ Stat Ann §15A:5–20.

[6] See, for example, Ohio Rev Code Ann, tit 17, § 1702.20.

Pennsylvania statute provides for cumulative voting but only if and to the extent a bylaw adopted by the members so provides. See Pa Stat Ann tit 15, §7758(c).

[7] See, e.g.:

Delaware. McLain v. Lanova Corp, 28 Del Ch 176, 39 A2d 209 (1944); Drob v. National Memorial Park, Inc., 28 Del Ch 254, 41 A2d 589 (1945).

Florida. Reimer v. Smith, 105 Fla 671, 142 So 603 (1932).

New York. Lord v. Equitable Life Assurance Society, 194 NY 212, 87 NE 443 (1909).

[8] See, e.g.:
Alabama. Mackey v. Moss, 278 Ala 713, 175 So 2d 749 (1965).
Illinois. American Aberdeen-Angus Breeders' Association v. Fullerton, 325 Ill 323, 329, 156 NE 314 (1927).
New York. In re Mt Sinai Hospital, 250 NY 103, 164 NE 871 (1928). See also NY Not-for-Profit Corp Law §612.

[9] *llinois.* Westlake Hospital Association v. Blix, 13 Ill 2d 183, 148 NE2d 471 (1958); Harris v. Board of Directors of Community Hospital of Evanston, 55 Ill App3d 392, 370 NE2d 1121 (1977).
New York. Petition of Sousa, 26 Misc 2d 474, 203 NYS2d 3, 5.

§2:07. —Voting by Proxy.

Members entitled to vote generally have the right to authorize one or more persons to vote for the member.[1] To do so, a member must execute a proxy statement authorizing the other person or persons to act in the member's behalf.[2] Such proxies are valid for a prescribed period of time from the date of the proxy. The Model Nonprofit Corporation Act provides that a proxy is not valid after 11 months from the date of its execution unless otherwise provided in the proxy.[3]

Normally, a proxy may not be irrevocable. However, New York statutes provide for an irrevocable proxy if the proxy is entitled "irrevocable proxy" and is held by a pledgee, by a person who has purchased, or agreed to purchase, the capital certificate of the member, by a creditor who extends or continues credit to the corporation in consideration of the proxy (the proxy must provide that it was given in consideration of an extension or continuation of credit, the amount of the credit, and the name of the person extending or continuing credit), or by a person who has contracted to perform services as an officer of the corporation when a proxy is required by the contract of employment (the proxy must state that it was given in consideration of the contract of employment, must state the name of the employee and the period of employment).[4]

Some states provide that the authority of a proxy statement continues even though the member granting the proxy is incompetent or has died. It does not become ineffective until the corporation receives written notice of an adjudication of incompetence of the member or of the death of the member.[5]

FOOTNOTES

[1] See Model Nonprofit Corporation Act §15 (1964). The Model Act provides that a member may vote by proxy unless the articles of incorporation or the bylaws provide otherwise.
See also Cal Corp Code §§5613, 7613. NJ Stat Ann §15A:5–18; NY Not-for-Profit Corp Law §609.
Pennsylvania statutes, on the other hand, provide that voting must be in person unless the bylaws specifically provide for voting by proxy. See Pa Stat Ann tit 15, §7759.

[2] Model Nonprofit Corporation Act §15 (1964).

[3] Model Nonprofit Corporation Act §15 (1964). The California and New York nonprofit corporation statutes also provide for the eleven-month period. See Cal Corp Code §§5613, 7613; NY Not-for-Profit Corp Law §609(a)(2).

[4] See NY Not-for-Profit Corp Law §609(a)(6). Nonetheless the proxy becomes revocable after the pledge is redeemed, the debt is paid, or the period of employment has terminated. See NY Not-for-Profit Corp Law §609(a)(7).

[5] See Cal Corp Code §§5613(c), 7613(c); NY Not-for-Profit Corp Law §609(A)(3).

§2:08. ——Form of Proxy.

I, the undersigned, member of _____ Corporation, do hereby appoint _____ of _____, State of _____, as my proxy to attend all meetings of the members of _____ Corporation, with full power to vote and act for me in the same manner and extent that I would be entitled should I be personally present at meetings of _____ Corporation.

Dated _____, 19_____.

---

§2:09. —Right of Members To Inspect Books and Records.

Members of a nonprofit corporation have the right to inspect the books and records of the corporation.[1] The Model Nonprofit Corporation Act provides that all books and records of a corporation may be inspected by any member, or his agent or attorney, for any proper purpose at any reasonable time.[2] New York statutes provide that a person who has been a member of record for at least 6 months immediately preceding his demand, or any person holding at least 5% of any class of outstanding capital certificates, may examine in person or by agent or attorney the minutes of the proceedings of the members during usual business hours but upon at least 5 days' written notice.[3]

California statutes provide that the right of a member to inspect the books and records of the corporation may not be limited by contract or by the articles of incorporation or the bylaws.[4] In addition, records must be made available in written form at the expense of the corporation.[5]

FOOTNOTES

[1] See Model Nonprofit Corporation Act §25 (1964); Cal Corp Code §§6333, 8333; NY Not-for-Profit Corp Law §621.

[2] Model Nonprofit Corporation Act §25 (1964).

[3] NY Not-for-Profit Corp Law §621(b).
[4] Cal Corp Code §§6313, 8313.
[5] Cal Corp Code §§6310, 8310.

§2:10. —Derivative Actions of Members.

New York, California, and the 1986 Revised Model Nonprofit Corporation Act provide members of a nonprofit corporation with an additional right—the right to bring a member's derivative action.[1] A member's derivative suit permits a member of a nonprofit corporation to institute a lawsuit for the corporation to secure a judgment in favor of the corporation for restoration of corporate property or for compensation to the corporation for losses suffered.[2]

In California, a member must demonstrate that he had informed the corporation or the board in writing of the ultimate facts of each cause of action, or had delivered a copy of the complaint to the corporation, and must allege the member's efforts to cause the board to bring the action.[3] The member must have been a member of the corporation at the time the particular transaction of which that member is complaining occurred.[4] A member's derivative action may be brought to secure damages for an improper distribution of property of the corporation,[5] for a self-dealing transaction between the corporation and one or more of its directors,[6] and for breach of a charitable trust.[7]

New York statutes provide that a member's derivative action may be brought by 5% or more of any class of members, capital certificate holders, or owners of a beneficial interest in the capital certificates of the corporation.[8] If the action is successful, the court may award the complaining members reasonable expenses, including reasonable attorneys' fees.[9]

FOOTNOTES

[1] Section 6.30 of the Revised Act provides for such a right in any member having 5% or more of the voting power or by 50 members, whichever is less, or by any director. The 1986 Act should be adopted, with some changes, by the American Bar Association sometime in 1987. See NY Not-for-Profit Corp Law §623; Cal Corp Code §§5710, 7710.

Pennsylvania statutes assume members have such a right by providing for indemnification for a person who is party to an action to procure a judgment in favor of the corporation. See Pa Stat Ann tit 15, §7742.

[2] **New York.** Fontheim v. Walker, 282 App Div 373, 122 NYS2d 642 (1953).

[3] Cal Corp Code §§5710(b)(2), 7710(b)(2).

[4] Cal Corp Code §§5710(b)(1), 7710(b)(1). An officer of the corporation or a member of the board may file a motion for a hearing to require the complaining member to file a bond for reasonable expenses including attorneys' fees that may be incurred by the member and the corporation in connection with the action. See Cal Corp Code §§5710(c), 7710(c).

[5] See Cal Corp Code §5420.

[6] Cal Corp Code §§5233, 7236.

[7] Cal Corp Code §§5142, 7142.

[8] NY Not-for-Profit Corp Law §623.

[9] NY Not-for-Profit Corp Law §623(e).

§2:11. —Removal of Members.

Most state statutes do not have provisions relating to the removal of members of a nonprofit corporation.[1] The power to expel is limited; one's membership in a nonprofit membership corporation may generally be terminated only by voluntary act of the member or by an act of the organization pursuant to authority granted it by the charter or the bylaws.[2] While the right of expulsion of a member as a penalty for an infraction or disobedience of the laws of the organization is well settled, there is nonetheless a presumption against the power to expel because it is in the nature of a forfeiture.[3] Where grounds and procedures for expulsion are prescribed in the bylaws, expulsion procedures must conform to the provisions of the bylaws.[4]

Courts are reluctant to interfere with the internal affairs of a membership corporation in regard to its disciplinary proceedings; thus, a court will generally look to the record to see whether the member's proceeding has been in accordance with the charter and bylaws of the organization, whether the charges were substantial, and whether the member had fair notice and opportunity to be heard.[5] If this be the case, a court will not ordinarily substitute its judgment for that of the organization.[6]

California statutes do have a provision for termination of memberships in nonprofit corporations.[7] A member may resign from membership at any time; however, the resigning member is still liable for all charges incurred, services or benefits actually rendered, and dues and assessments until that date.[8] A member may not be expelled or suspended unless the procedure set forth in the articles of bylaws is followed, and members must receive annual copies of these provisions.[9] In addition, 15 days' prior notice of expulsion, suspension or termination, along with the reasons, must be given the member.[10] The member must be given an opportunity to be heard, either orally or in writing, not less than 5 days before the effective date of the expulsion, suspension or termination by a person or body authorized to decide the issue.[11] An action challenging the expulsion must be brought within one year from the date of the expulsion. A member may be reinstated if the court finds that a wrongful expulsion was in bad faith.[12]

In Pennsylvania, by statute, a member of a nonprofit corporation may not be expelled without notice, trial and conviction, the form of which must be prescribed by the articles or bylaws.[13]

The 1986 Revised Model Nonprofit Corporation Act provides that no member of a nonprofit corporation may be expelled or suspended, and no membership may be terminated or suspended except pursuant to a procedure that is fair and reasonable and that is carried out in good faith.[14] A procedure is deemed to be fair and reasonable if it is set out in the articles or bylaws and provides not less than 15 days' prior written notice of the expulsion, suspension or termination and the reasons therefor. The member must have an opportunity to be heard, orally or in writing, not less than 5 days prior to the effective date of the termination.

The 1986 Act is subject to change and is scheduled for final adoption by the American Bar Association sometime in 1987.

FOOTNOTES

[1] The Model Nonprofit Corporation Act does not have a provision relating to the removal of a member. California and Pennsylvania do have prescribed procedures for removal of members of nonprofit corporations. See Cal Corp Code §§5341, 7341; Pa Stat Ann tit 15, §7767.

[2] **Texas.** See, Raulston v. Everett, 561 SW2d 635 (Tex Civ App, 1978); Mangum v. Swearingen, 565 SW2d 957 (Tex Civ App, 1978); David v. Carter, 222 SW2d 900 (Tex Civ App 1949). In the Mangum case, the court stated that a church had the right to decide for itself whom it would admit into fellowship and whom it would expel or exclude from its fold. A court could not question its actions if no civil or property rights were involved. However, in the David case, the court held that it would grant church members relief from disciplinary action shown to be a radical departure from a church's accepted customs and rules.

[3] **Georgia.** See Bartley v. Augusta Country Club, Inc., 254 Ga 144, 326 SE2d 442 (1985), in which the court held that disciplinary actions against members of a private club are not matters of constitutional law. Members' rights, if any, are governed by the bylaws of the club.

New York. See Collins v. Beinecke, 495 NE2d 335 (NY, 1986) in which a court refused to remove members of a charitable foundation, the former officers and directors of a corporation that was the creator of the foundation, even though stock in the creator corporation had been sold and new officers and directors were currently in control of the creator corporation. Because a substantial portion of the foundation's grants benefited company employees and many of its charitable programs were continuations of programs established and conducted by the creator corporation, it had been the practice that only officers and directors of the creator corporation served as members of the foundation. However, the court held that customs and practices of the past are not enough to impose a duty upon the members to resign or to install current officers of the creator corporation as members of the foundation. See, National League of Commission Merchants v. Hornung, 148 App Div 355, 132 NYS 871 (1911); Van Campen v. Olean Gen. Hospital, 210 App Div 204, 205 NYS 554 (1924); aff'd, 239 NY 615, 147 NE 219; Matter of Reed, 95 Misc 695, 160 NYS 907 (1916).

[4] **New York.** See, Pepe v. Missanellses Society of Mutual Aid, 141 Misc 7, 252 NYS 60 (1930).

Pennsylvania. In Petition of Board of Directors of State Police Civic Ass'n, 80 Pa Commw 405, 472 A2d 731 (1984), the court held that where an application for membership in a beneficial association incorporates by reference the constitution and bylaws of the association, the constitution and bylaws become terms of a contract between the prospective member and the association upon approval of the membership application by the association. Further, if specific rights of a member become fixed pursuant to a contract between himself and the association, subsequent amendments to the bylaws or constitution will not affect those rights. The court held this to be the law as to substantial rights even though the membership application contained an agreement to abide by the provisions of the constitution and bylaws currently in force or that may be subsequently amended. However, if a member's rights are not fixed, then the members are bound by amendments to the constitution and bylaws.

Indiana. See Lozanoski v. Sarafin, 485 NE2d 669 (Ind App, 1985), in which the court stated that the articles of incorporation and the bylaws are a contract between the members and the nonprofit organization. Courts in Indiana will not interfere with the internal affairs of a private organization unless a personal liberty or property right is jeopardized.

[5] **New York.** People v. Independent Dock Builders' Benev. Union, 164 App Div 267, 149 NYS 771 (1914); Van Campen v. Olean Gen. Hospital, 210 App Div 204, 205 NYS 554 (1924), affd, 239 NY 615, 147 NE 219; Williamson v. Randolph, 48 Misc 96, 96 NYS 664 (1905); National League v. Hornung, 148 App Div 355, 132 NYS 871 (1911).

[6] **New York.** See, People v. Independent Dock Builders' Benev. Union, 164 App Div 267, 149 NYS 711 (1914).

See further discussion of expulsion of members at §4:03.

[7] See Cal Corp Code §§5341, 7341. However, the provision governs only the procedures for expulsion. An expulsion which would violate contractual or other rights is not made valid by compliance with the statute. See Cal Corp Code §§5341(f), 7341(f).

[8] Cal Corp Code §§5340, 7340.

[9] Cal Corp Code §§5341(c)(1), 7341(c)(1).
[10] Cal Corp Code §§5341(c)(2), 7341(c)(2).
[11] Cal Corp Code §§5341(c)(3), 7341(c)(3).
[12] Cal Corp Code §§5341(e), 7341(e).
[13] Pa Stat Ann tit 15, §7767.
[14] 1986 Revised Model Nonprofit Corporation Act §6.21.

§2:12. Directors.

The affairs of a nonprofit corporation are managed by a board of directors.[1] The Model Nonprofit Corporation Act provides that directors need not be residents of the state of incorporation unless the articles of incorporation or the bylaws provide otherwise.[2]

The Model Act provides that there should be at least 3 directors of a nonprofit corporation.[3] The number of directors is fixed by the bylaws (with the exception of the first board of directors where the number is fixed by the articles of incorporation).[4] A change in the number of directors may be made by amending the bylaws (unless the articles of incorporation provide that a change in the number can only be made by amending the articles).[5]

Generally the term of office of a director is one year.[6] The first board of directors, named in the articles of incorporation, holds office until the first annual election of directors or for such time as prescribed in the articles of incorporation or in the bylaws.[7] Thereafter, directors are elected or appointed in the manner stated in the articles or in the bylaws.[8] Terms of office of directors need not be uniform.[9] Each director holds office until his or her successor is elected or appointed.[10]

A majority of the number of directors fixed by the bylaws or by the articles of incorporation generally constitutes a quorum for the transaction of business.[11] The Model Nonprofit Corporation Act provides that the articles of incorporation or the

MEMBERS AND DIRECTORS OF A NONPROFIT CORPORATION 79

bylaws can provide otherwise but in no event shall a quorum be less than one-third of the number of directors.[12] An act of the majority of the directors present at a meeting at which a quorum is present constitutes an act of the board of directors unless the articles or bylaws provide for a greater number.[13]

FOOTNOTES

[1] Model Nonprofit Corporation Act §17 (1964).
The Texas Nonprofit Corporation Act has a provision authorizing a church to vest management of its affairs in its members. See Tex Civ Stat art §1396–2.14(C).

[2] Model Nonprofit Corporation Act §17 (1964). See also Tex Civ Stat art 1396-2.15; Ill Ann Stat ch 32 § 136a16; NY Not-for-Profit Corp Law §702(a), Ind Stat Ann §23–7.1–10. California statutes provide that the bylaws will establish the number of directors. See Cal Corp Code §§5151, 7151.

[3] Model Nonprofit Corporation Act §18 (1964).

[4] Model Nonprofit Corporation Act §18 (1964).

[5] Model Nonprofit Corporation Act §18 (1964).

[6] Model Nonprofit Corporation Act §18 (1964). See also NY Not-for-Profit Corp Law §703(b); Ill Ann Stat ch 32 § 136a17.

[7] Model Nonprofit Corporation Act §18 (1964).

[8] Model Nonprofit Corporation Act §18 (1964).

[9] Model Nonprofit Corporation Act §18 (1964).

[10] Model Nonprofit Corporation Act §18 (1964).

[11] Model Nonprofit Corporation Act §20 (1964).

[12] Model Nonprofit Corporation Act §20 (1964).

[13] Model Nonprofit Corporation Act §20 (1964).

§2:13. —Election of Directors.

Directors are elected or appointed in the manner and for the terms provided in the articles of incorporation or in the bylaws.[1] A vacancy occurring in the board of directors is generally filled by vote of a majority of the remaining directors (unless the articles or bylaws provide for some other method).[2] A director elected or appointed to fill a vacancy is elected or appointed for the unexpired term of his or her predecessor.[3]

The Model Nonprofit Corporation Act provides that any directorship to be filled by reason of an increase in the number of directors may be filled by vote of a majority of the remaining directors.[4] Some states that have adopted the Model Act have not followed this provision. They have provided instead, that any such directorship must be filled by election at either an annual meeting or a special meeting of members of the corporation.[5] If the corporation has no members, or no members having a right to vote, such directorship should be filled as provided for in the articles of incorporation or in the bylaws.[6]

FOOTNOTES

[1] Model Nonprofit Corporation Act §18 (1964).
[2] Model Nonprofit Corporation Act §19 (1964).
[3] Model Nonprofit Corporation Act §19 (1964).
[4] Model Nonprofit Corporation Act §19 (1964). See also NY Not-for-Profit Corp Law §705(a); Ariz Rev Stat §10–71(D).
[5] See Tex Civ Stat art 1396–2.16. California statutes provide that once members have been admitted, a bylaw changing a fixed number of directors or changing from a fixed to a variable board (or vice versa) may only be adopted by approval of the members. See Cal Corp Code §§5151, 7151.
[6] Tex Civ Stat art 1396–2.16.

§2:14. Meetings of Directors.

Meetings of the board of directors, whether regular or special meetings, may be held within or without the state of incorporation.[1] Attendance of a director at any meeting constitutes a waiver of notice of the meeting except when a director attends a meeting for the express purpose of objecting to the transaction of any business because the meeting was not lawfully called or convened.[2]

Some states provide that regular meetings of the board of directors may be held without notice.[3] Special meetings are held upon such notice as is prescribed in the bylaws.[4]

FOOTNOTES

[1] Model Nonprofit Corporation Act §22. See also Tex Civ Stat art 1396–2.19(A); Cal Corp Code §§5211(a)(5), 7211(a)(5); NY Not-for-Profit Corp Law §710.

[2] Model Nonprofit Corporation Act §22 (1964).

[3] See Tex Civ Stat art 1396–2.19(B); Cal Corp Code §§5211(a)(2), 7211(a)(2); NY Not-for-Profit Corp Law §711(a).

[4] Tex Civ Stat art 1396–2.19(B).

§2:15. —Management of Affairs of a Nonprofit Corporation.

Except for actions required by the articles of incorporation or the bylaws to be approved by members of the corporation, as well as certain inherent powers in the members, the activities and affairs of a nonprofit corporation are conducted, and all corporate powers are exercised, under direction of the board of directors.[1] Courts have stated that bylaw provisions vesting in the board of directors of a nonprofit corporation the right to manage the corporation affairs and even to control the election of successors to the board do not infringe upon any property or other enforceable right of the members.[2] It is not unlawful, arbitrary or unreasonable for the board of directors of a nonprofit corporation to be granted such powers.[3]

82 Representing the Nonprofit Organization

As a general rule, the board of directors may delegate the management of activities of the corporation to committees, but all activities and affairs of the corporation must be managed, and all corporate power exercised, under the ultimate direction of the board.[4] The Model Nonprofit Corporation Act provides that committees may be designated and appointed by the board if the articles or the bylaws so provide and if the board appoints such committees by resolution adopted by a majority of the directors.[5] The Model Act also provides that such committees may not exercise extraordinary powers, such as appointing or removing members, altering bylaws, amending or restating the articles of incorporation, selling, purchasing, leasing or mortgaging property, or adopting a plan of merger, consolidation or of corporate dissolution.[6]

For those states that have not adopted the Model Act and its provisions authorizing the board of directors to delegate its management powers, or for those that do not have a similar provision providing for delegation of board authority, there is some question about the authority of a board for a nonprofit organization to delegate its duties.[7] If a board of directors is subject to the more restrictive delegation rules applicable to trusts, delegation of its duties by the board is limited.[8]

FOOTNOTES

[1] See Model Nonprofit Corporation Act §17 (1964). See also Cal Corp Code §§5210, 7210; NY Not-for-Profit Corp Law §701; Tex Civ Stat art 1396–1.14.

[2] **New York.** Bailey v. American Society for Prevention of Cruelty to Animals, 282 App Div 502, 125 NYS 2d 18 (1953).
Texas. Brown v. Giuffre, 548 SW2d 102 (Tex Civ App, 1977).

[3] **New York.** In re Mt. Sinai Hospital, 250 NY 103, 164 NE 871 (1928).
Texas. Brown v. Giuffre, 548 SW2d 102 (Tex Civ App, 1977).

[4] See Cal Corp Code §§5210, 7210; Ind Code Ann §23–7–1.1–10.

[5] Model Nonprofit Corporation Act §21 (1964).

Model Nonprofit Corporation Act §21 (1964).

[7] See Cary & Bright, The Delegation of Investment Responsibility for Endowment Funds, 74 Colo L Rev 207 (1974).

[8] The Uniform Management of Institutional Funds Act, which has been adopted by a number of states, specifically authorizes boards of nonprofit organizations to delegate to committees, officers or employees, or to outside agents, including investment counsel, the authority to act in place of the board in investment and reinvestment of institutional funds.

§2:16. —Action of the Board of Directors.

All corporate action to be taken by the board of directors generally requires action at a meeting of the board.[1] The vote of a majority of the directors present at the time of the vote, if a quorum is present at such time, is the act of the board.[2] Directors acting separately and not collectively as a board cannot bind the corporation.[3]

State statutes, or the articles or bylaws, may provide that any action required or permitted to be taken by the board of directors may be taken without a meeting if all members of the board consent in writing to the adoption of a resolution authorizing the action.[4] Such a resolution and the written consents by members of the board must be filed with the minutes of the proceedings of the board.[5] The articles or bylaws may provide that participation in a meeting of the board may be by means of a conference telephone, or similar communications equipment allowing all persons participating in the meeting to hear each other at the same time. If so, participation by such means constitutes presence in person at a meeting.[6]

FOOTNOTES

[1] See NY Not-for-Profit Corp Law §708; Cal Corp Code §§5211(a)(8), 7211(a)(8); Tex Civ Stat art 1396–2.17(c).

[2] NY Not-for-Profit Corp Law §708; Cal Corp Code §§5211(a)(8), 7211(a)(8); Tex Civ Stat art 1396–2.17(c).

[3] *New York.* See Bayer v. Beran, 49 NYS2d 2 (Misc 1944).

[4] See NY Not-for-Profit Corp Law §708(b).

[5] NY Not-for-Profit Corp Law §708(b).

[6] See Cal Corp Code §§5211(a)(6), 7211(a)(6); NY Not-for-Profit Law Corp §708(c).

§2:17. Removal of Director.

The Model Nonprofit Corporation Act provides that a director may be removed from office pursuant to any procedure provided for in the articles of incorporation.[1] The 1986 Revised Model Nonprofit Corporation Act, however,[2] provides that members of a nonprofit corporation may remove without cause a director elected by them.[3] A director may be removed only if the number of votes cast to remove the director would be sufficient to elect the director. An entire board of directors may be removed without cause if sufficient votes to elect such board are cast. A special meeting must be called for such purposes, and notice of the meeting must state the purpose. Under the 1986 Act, the board of directors may remove a director without cause if the director was elected by a ⅔ vote of the directors then in office.[4] A director may be removed by a court in a proceeding commenced either by the corporation, its members holding at least 10% of the voting power, or the attorney general in the case of a public benefit corporation if the court finds that the director engaged in fraudulent conduct or grossly abused his or her authority or discretion.[5] New York statutes provide that any or all of the directors may be removed for cause by vote of the members, or by vote of the directors provided there is a quorum of not less than a majority present at the meeting of directors at which the action was taken.[6] Further, if the certificate of incorporation or the bylaws provide, a director may be removed without cause by vote of the members.[7]

Pennsylvania statutes provide that, unless the articles or bylaws provide otherwise, the entire board of directors or any individual director may be removed from office, without assigning any cause, by a majority vote of the qualified voting members.[8] New directors may be elected at the same meeting.[9]

California statutes provide that directors may be removed without cause if such action is approved by the members or, in a corporation without members, if it is approved by a majority of the directors then in office.[10]

Arizona statutes provide that a member may bring charges against a director by filing them in writing with the secretary together with a petition for removal signed by 10% of the members.[11] Removal must be voted upon at the next regular meeting or at a special meeting; the association may remove the director at the meeting by a majority vote of the members. The director must be informed in writing of the charges prior to the meeting and the director may be heard in person or by counsel and may call witnesses.[12]

Case law has provided that a corporation possesses the inherent power to remove a director for cause, regardless of the presence of such a provision in the charter or bylaws.[13] However, in the absence of some provision in the charter or in the state statutes, a director generally cannot be removed or suspended from office without cause until the end of his or her term.[14]

FOOTNOTES

[1] Model Nonprofit Corporation Act §18 (1964).
See also Ind Code Ann §23-7-1.1-11. The Indiana statute provides, in addition, for removal, with or without cause, at a special meeting of the members called for that purpose.

86 Representing the Nonprofit Organization

[2] The 1986 Act is subject to change. A final version is scheduled for adoption by the American Bar Association in 1987.

[3] 1986 Revised Model Nonprofit Corporation Act §8.08.

[4] 1986 Revised Model Nonprofit Corporation Act §8.08(h).

[5] 1986 Revised Model Nonprofit Corporation Act §8.10.

[6] NY Not-for-Profit Corp Law §706. Section 706 provides that an action to procure a judgment removing a director for cause may be brought by the attorney general or by 10% of the members whether or not entitled to vote. The court may bar from reelection any director so removed for a period fixed by the court.

[7] NY Not-for-Profit Corp Law §706(b).

[8] Pa Stat Ann tit 15, §7726. Unless provided otherwise in the bylaws, the board of directors may declare vacant an office of a director if the director is declared of unsound mind by an order of the court or is convicted of felony, or for any other proper cause specified in the bylaws, or if, within 60 days after notice of selection, the director does not accept the office either in writing or by attending a meeting of the directors. See Pa Stat Ann tit 15, §7726(b). The court may remove a director in case of fraudulent or dishonest acts, or gross abuse of authority or discretion with reference to the corporation, or for any other proper cause upon petition of any member or director. The corporation is made a party to such an action. See Pa Stat Ann tit 15, §7726(c).

[9] Pa Stat Ann tit 15, §7726(a).

[10] Cal Corp Code §§5222, 7222.

[11] Ariz Rev Stat Ann §10–713.

[12] Ariz Rev Stat Ann §10–713.

[13] **New York.** See Grace v. Grace Institute, 19 NY2d 307, 226 NE2d 531 (1967); Tremsky v. Green, 106 NYS2d 572 (Misc 1951).

[14] **New York.** See People v. Powell, 201 NY 194, 94 NE 634 (1911); Tremsky v. Green, 106 NYS2d 572 (Misc 1951).

In Collins v. Beinecke, 67 NY2d 479, 495 NE2d 335 (1986), the officers of a foundation were the officers and directors of the foundation's creator corporation from which the foundation received its sole financial support. A substantial portion of the foundation's grants benefited the corporation's employees and many of its charitable programs were continuations of programs established and conducted by the corporation. In 1986, another corporation purchased all the stock of the creator corporation, including all the stock of the defendants in the Collins case. However, the defendants refused to resign as directors of the foundation. The court held that though it had been the practice that officers and directors of the creator corporation would serve as directors of the foundation, customs and practices of the past are not enough to impose a fiduciary duty upon the defendants to resign. In the absence of evidence that the defendants had misused foundation assets or a showing that their acts were "unfair, oppressive or manifestly detrimental to the foundation's interests," there was no basis for an invocation of the court's equitable power to annul the defendants' acts nor to interfere in the legal relationship that the parties had structured for themselves.

§ 2:18. Checklist of Points To Remember.

— 1. A nonprofit corporation may have one or more classes of members or it may have no members.[1]
— 2. Annual meetings of members are generally held at the place designated in the bylaws.[2] Should the board of directors fail to call the annual meeting, any member may make demand that such a meeting be held within a reasonable time.[3]
— 3. The bylaws should specify the number of members constituting a quorum at a members' meeting.[4]
— 4. Written notice stating the place, the day and the hour of a meeting of the members must be delivered to the members within a certain period of time before the date of the meeting.[5]
— 5. Notice of a special meeting should state the purpose of the meeting.[6]
— 6. The right of members to vote may be limited, enlarged or denied to the extent provided for in the articles of incorporation or in the bylaws.[7] The right to vote is not a vested right. However, unless limited, each member, regardless of class, is entitled to one vote.[8]
— 7. In some states members may cumulate their votes.[9]
— 8. Members entitled to vote generally have the right to vote by proxy.[10]
— 9. Members of a nonprofit corporation have the right to inspect the books and records of the corporation.[11]

___ 10. A few states provide members of a nonprofit corporation with the right to bring a member's derivative action. A member's derivative suit permits a member to institute action for the corporation to secure a judgment in favor of the corporation for restoration of corporate property or for compensation to the corporation for losses suffered by the corporation.[12]

___ 11. The power to expel a member is limited.[13] Membership in a nonprofit corporation generally may be terminated only by voluntary act of the member or by an act of the organization pursuant to authority granted it by the charter or by the bylaws. Where grounds and procedures for expulsion are prescribed in the bylaws, expulsion procedures must conform to those provisions.[14]

___ 12. The affairs of a nonprofit corporation are managed by a board of directors.[15]

___ 13. Generally there should be at least 3 directors.[16] Most state statutes provide that the directors need not be residents of the state of incorporation.[17]

___ 14. The term of office of a director is generally one year.[18]

___ 15. The first board of directors, named in the articles of incorporation, holds office until the first annual election of directors. Thereafter, directors are elected or appointed in the manner stated in the articles or in the bylaws.[19]

___ 16. A majority of the directors generally constitutes a quorum for the transaction of business.[20]

___ 17. A vacancy on the board of directors is filled either by a vote of the majority of the remaining directors or by election at a meeting of members of the corporation.[21]

___ 18. All corporate action to be taken by the board of directors generally requires action at a meeting of the board by a vote of a majority of the directors present if a quorum is present. Directors acting separately and

not collectively as a board cannot bind the corporation.[22]
— 19. A director generally may be removed from office pursuant to any procedure provided in the articles of incorporation or the bylaws.[23]

FOOTNOTES

[1] See §2:01.
[2] See §2:02.
[3] See §2:02.
[4] See §2:02.
[5] See §2:03.
[6] See §2:03.
[7] See §2:06.
[8] See §2:06.
[9] See §2:06.
[10] See §2:07.
[11] See §2:09.
[12] See §2:10.
[13] See §2:11.
[14] See §2:11.
[15] See §2:12.
[16] See §2:12.
[17] See §2:12.
[18] See §2:12.
[19] See §2:12.
[20] See §2:12.
[21] See §2:13.
[22] See §2:16.
[23] See §2:17.

CHAPTER 3

OFFICERS AND EMPLOYEES

§ 3:01. Selection of Officers.
§ 3:02. Duties of Officers.
§ 3:03. Authority of Officers.
§ 3:04. Officers as Employees.
§ 3:05. Liability of Officers.
§ 3:06. Removal of Officers.
§ 3:07. Employees.
§ 3:08. Discrimination in Employment—Title VII.
§ 3:09. —Equal Pay Act.
§ 3:10. Age Discrimination in Employment Act.
§ 3:11. Vocational Rehabilitation Act.
§ 3:12. —Vietnam Era Veterans' Readjustment Assistance Act.
§ 3.13. —Retirement Plans for Employees of Nonprofit Enterprises.
§ 3:14. —Qualified Plans.
§ 3:15. ——Participation and Vesting Requirements.
§ 3:16. ——Funding of Qualified Plans.
§ 3:17. ——Limitations on Contributions.
§ 3:18. ——Integration with Social Security.
§ 3:19. ——Reporting Requirements for Qualified Plans.
§ 3:20. ——Plan Termination.
§ 3:21. ——Taxation of Benefits.
§ 3:22. —Individual Retirement Accounts.
§ 3:23. —Simplified Employee Pension.
§ 3:24. —Tax-Sheltered Annuities for Employees of §501(c)(3) Organizations.
§ 3:25. Checklist of Points To Remember.

§3:01. Selection of Officers.

The Model Nonprofit Corporation Act states that the officers of a nonprofit corporation should be a president, one or more vice-presidents, a secretary, a treasurer and such other officers and assistant officers as may be deemed necessary.[1] Each officer is elected or appointed at the time and in the manner prescribed in the articles of incorporation or in the bylaws.[2] The term of office should be set out in the articles of incorporation or in the bylaws but should not exceed three years.[3] If the articles of incorporation or bylaws do not provide for the election or appointment of officers, the officers must be elected or appointed annually by the board of directors.[4]

Any two offices, except the offices of president and secretary, may be held by the same person.[5] Officers may be designated by any additional titles as provided for in the articles of incorporation or in the bylaws.[6]

The articles of incorporation or bylaws may provide that any one or more officers of the nonprofit corporation will be ex officio members of the board of directors.[7]

For an unincorporated association, officers are elected informally by members of the association.[8] If the association has articles of association and bylaws, these should specify the manner in which officers are elected.[9]

A nonprofit organization in the form of a charitable trust would not have officers. Trustees of a trust, over whom the beneficiaries have no control, are not employees.[10] Further, a trust is under a duty not to delegate the performance of acts which the trustee can reasonably be required personally to perform.[11]

FOOTNOTES

[1] Model Nonprofit Corporation Act §23 (1964).
The California Nonprofit Corporation Law provides that a nonprofit cor-

poration will have a chairman of the board or a president or both, a secretary, a financial officer and such other officers with such titles and duties as are stated in the bylaws or determined by the board and as may be necessary to enable it to sign instruments. See Cal Corp Code §§5213, 7213.

[2] Model Nonprofit Corporation Act §23 (1964).

[3] Model Nonprofit Corporation Act §23 (1964).

[4] Model Nonprofit Corporation Act §23 (1964).

The California Nonprofit Corporation Law provides that unless otherwise provided in the articles or bylaws, officers of a nonprofit corporation are chosen by the board and serve at the pleasure of the board, subject to any rights of an officer under any contract of employment. See Cal Corp Code §§5213, 7213.

The New Jersey Nonprofit Corporation Act also provides that officers are elected or appointed by the board of directors unless otherwise provided in the bylaws. See NJ Stat Ann §15A:6-15.

[5] Model Nonprofit Corporation Act §23 (1964).

[6] Model Nonprofit Corporation Act §23 (1964).

[7] Model Nonprofit Corporation Act §23 (1964).

[8] See discussion of unincorporated nonprofit associations in Henn & Pfeifer, Nonprofit Groups: Factors Influencing Choice of Form, 11 Wake Forest L Rev 181, 188 (1975).

[9] **Oregon.** Marvin v. Manash, 175 Ore 311, 153 P2d 251 (1944).

[10] See Scott, Law of Trusts, §8 (3d ed).

[11] Scott, Law of Trusts, §224.2 (3d ed).

§3:02. Duties of Officers.

The duties of the officers of nonprofit corporations parallel the duties of corporate officers generally. Officers are agents of the corporation and have whatever authority is delegated to them by the board of directors to execute and administer policies determined by the board.[1] As delegates of the board of directors, officers are fiduciaries of the corporation and, within the scope of their delegated management functions, are subject to the same fiduciary duties as are directors.[2]

The president of a corporation is normally recognized to be

the general manager of the corporation.[3] The board of directors may grant the president authority to act as the chief executive officer of the corporation. Often, in a nonprofit corporation the person designated as the general manager of the corporation is called a director, rather than president. In this case, the "director" should be distinguished from a director who is a member of the board of directors.

A vice-president has no authority by virtue of the office.[4] However, in the event of the disability or absence of the president, a vice-president may exercise whatever authority the president has.[5]

The secretary and treasurer also have no authority by virtue of their office to bind the corporation.[6] The secretary is a ministerial officer who keeps the minutes of meetings of members and of the board of directors. The secretary gives notices, prepares certified copies of corporate records, and keeps and attests the corporate seal.[7]

FOOTNOTES

[1] See Henn & Alexander, Laws of Corporations, §217 (3d Ed).

[2] The 1986 Revised Model Nonprofit Corporation Act §8.42, provides standards of conduct for officers. An employee must discharge his or her duties in good faith and with the care that an ordinarily prudent person in a like position would exercise under similar circumstances and in a manner that the officer reasonably believes to be in the best interests of the corporation. In discharging his or her duties as an officer, an individual may rely on information, opinions, reports, or other statements, including financial statements, prepared by one or more officers or employees of the corporation whom the corporation reasonably believes to be reliable and competent in the matters presented, or on legal counsel or public accountants. The Act provides that an officer will not be liable for any action taken as an officer, or any failure to take action, if the officer performed the duties of office in compliance with §8.42.

Fletcher Cyc Corp §838.

See also Kempin, The Corporate Officer and the Law of Agency, 44 Va L Rev 1273 (1958).

[3] Fletcher Cyc Corp §553.
[4] Fletcher Cyc Corp §627.
[5] Fletcher Cyc Corp §627.
[6] Fletcher Cyc Corp §§637, 645.
[7] Henn & Alexander, Laws of Corporations, §225 (3d Ed).

The California Code provides that the original or a copy of the following: bylaws; minutes of any meeting of the incorporators, the members, the directors or a committee; or any resolution adopted by the board, a committee of the board, or by the members, which has been certified to be a true copy by a person purporting to be the secretary or an assistant secretary of the corporation, is prima facie evidence of the adoption of the resolution or of the due holding of the meeting and of the matters stated therein. See Cal Corp Code §§5215, 7215.

§3:03. Authority of Officers.

The authority of the officers of nonprofit corporations is essentially the same as that of corporate officers generally. While the vice-president, secretary, and treasurer of a corporation normally have no authority by virtue of their offices to bind the corporation, the president, as general manager of the corporation, may bind the corporation through contracts that are necessary, proper, or usual to be made in the ordinary course of business.[1] Though traditionally the president of a corporation presided at meetings and played no active part in management,[2] most courts have adopted what has been deemed to be a more modern rule that a president is head of the corporation, subject to the control of the board of directors, but with power to bind the corporation in regard to contracts involved in the everyday business of the corporation.[3]

As one court stated, a corporation is a fictitious person and can only act through human instrumentality; its corporate power must be exercised and its business conducted by individuals.[4] While management powers may be exercised by the board of directors, the everyday affairs of the corporation cannot wait upon the periodical meetings of the board, but must be handled by officers and agents of the corporation. The officer on whom such responsibility naturally falls is the president.[5]

Officers of a corporation are agents of the corporation. The authority of an officer or agent of a corporation need not necessarily be express. It may be implied from the circumstances.[6] The law of agency provides that the general manager of a business has implied authority to make contracts and to perform other acts necessary to operate the business.[7] Even though state statute may provide that the affairs of a corporation are managed by the board of directors, should the corporation indicate to third persons that an officer of the corporation may act for the corporation, the officer may have "apparent authority" to act.[8] If a third person relies on the apparent authority of the officer, the corporation will be bound by any action on the part of the officer, assuming the reliance was reasonable and there would otherwise be detriment to the third party.[9] Consequently, the fact that a corporate president is considered to be the general manager of the corporation can cause the president to have authority to bind the corporation as to its ordinary business transactions by virtue of the office.[10]

FOOTNOTES

[1] Henn & Alexander, Laws of Corporations §225 (3d Ed); Fletcher Cyc Corp §593.

Montana. Trent v. Sherlock 24 Mont 255, 61 P 650 (1900).

New Jersey. Snyder Realty Company v. National Newark & Essex Banking Company of Newark, 101 A2d 544, 548 (1953).

[2] **Texas.** See Ennis Business Forms v. Todd, 523 SW2d 83 (Tex Civ App, 1975).

See also Henn & Alexander, Laws of Corporations §225 (3d Ed).

[3] **Montana.** Mayger v. St. Louis Mining & Milling Company of Montana, 68 Mont 492, 219 P 1102 (1923).

[4] **United States.** Northern Mining Corporation v. Trunz, 124 F2d 14 (CA9, 1941).
[5] **United States.** Northern Mining Corporation v. Trunz, 124 F2d 14 (CA9, 1941).
[6] **Oklahoma.** See Barnett v. Kennedy, 185 Okl 409, 92 P2d 963 (1939).
[7] Restatement (Second) of Agency §73.
[8] See Henn & Alexander, Laws of Corporations §226 (3d Ed); Fletcher Cyc Corp §§442, 742.
[9] See Troyer, Agency-Apparent Authority-Liability of Corporation on Unauthorized Note of General Manager, 55 Mich L Rev 447 (1957).
[10] **United States.** See Victory Investment Corporation v. Muskogee Electric Traction Company, 150 F2d 889, 893 (CA 10, 1945).

§3:04. Officers as Employees.

There are distinctions between corporate officers and the regular employees of a corporation, including a nonprofit corporation. The duties of corporate officers are created by the charter or by the bylaws. In addition, officers are either elected by the board of directors or by members of the corporation.[1] An employee, on the other hand, is employed by the managing officer of the corporation and normally occupies no office.[2] While officers are in a quasi-fiduciary relationship to members of the corporation, employees are not.[3] Employees are under the control of the corporate officers while the officers exercise management powers under the policies or direction of the board.[4] An officer is not generally required to work under any specific schedule of hours because an officer devotes whatever time and effort is necessary to accomplish the business of the corporation. Consequently, officers are not paid overtime as are employees.[5]

Even though an officer occupies a management position in a corporation, an officer is nonetheless considered an employee by the Internal Revenue Service.[6] A corporate officer is subject to withholding for income tax and social security purposes just as are regular employees.[7] On the other hand, a corporate director is not considered to be an employee by the IRS.[8] The IRS treats directors' fees as self-employment income.[9]

FOOTNOTES

[1] **Florida.** See Flight Equipment & Engineering Corporation v. Shelton, 103 So 2d 615 (1958).
[2] **Florida.** Flight Equipment & Engineering Corporation v. Shelton, 103 So 2d 615 (1958).
[3] **Florida.** Flight Equipment & Engineering Corporation v. Shelton, 103 So 2d 615, 623 (1958).
[4] **Florida.** Flight Equipment & Engineering Corporation v. Shelton, 103 So 2d 615, 623 (1958).
[5] **Florida.** Flight Equipment & Engineering Corporation v. Shelton, 103 So 2d 615, 623 (1958).
[6] Rev Rul 57–246, 1957 CB 338.
[7] Rev Rul 57–246, 1957 CB 338.
[8] Rev Rul 57–246, 1957 CB 338.
[9] Rev Rul 57–246, 1957 CB 338.

§3:05. *Liability of Officers.*

Because an officer of a corporation, including a nonprofit corporation, is in a quasi-fiduciary position, the officer is bound to be loyal to the corporation and to give the corporate enterprise the benefit of the officer's best care and judgment.[1] The officer must exercise the powers of the office solely in the interest of the corporation and its members.[2] In a like manner with corporate directors, officers of a corporation are liable for damages resulting from a breach of trust.[3] Liability rests both upon the officers' fiduciary status and upon agency principles.[4]

Officers may also be liable to third persons on contracts executed without authority from the corporation, for torts personally committed, for corporate debts, and for taxes.[5] Thus, any indemnification provided for corporate directors should include corporate officers.

FOOTNOTES

[1] **Florida.** See Flight Equipment & Engineering Corporation v. Shelton, 103 So 2d 615, 626 (1958).

[2] **Florida.** Flight Equipment & Engineering Corporation v. Shelton, 103 So 2d 615, 616 (1958).

[3] **Florida.** Flight Equipment & Engineering Corporation v. Shelton, 103 So 2d 615, 616 (1958).

[4] **Florida.** Flight Equipment & Engineering Corporation v. Shelton, 103 So 2d 615, 617 (1958).
See also Fletcher Cyc Corp §838.

[5] Henn & Alexander, Laws of Corporations §230 (3d Ed).

§3:06. *Removal of Officers.*

The Model Nonprofit Corporation Act provides that any officer may be removed by the persons authorized to elect or appoint the officer whenever, in their judgment, it is in the best interests of the corporation.[1] However, the removal of an officer must not be contrary to any contract rights of the officer.[2] The election or appointment of an officer does not of itself create a contract right.[3]

New York statutes provide that any officer elected or appointed by the board may be removed by the board with or without cause; however, an officer elected by the members may be removed only by the vote of the members (with or without cause).[4] Removal without cause may not be contrary to any contract rights of the officer.[5] The attorney general, any director, and 10% of the members may bring an action to remove an officer.[6]

California statutes provide that officers serve at the pleasure of the board, subject to the rights, if any, of an officer under any contract of employment.[7]

FOOTNOTES

[1] Model Nonprofit Corporation §24 (1964).
New York. See Weiss v. Opportunities for Cortland County, Inc., 40 App 2d 890, 337 NYS2d 409 (1972). The court stated in Weiss that unless a definite period of employment is specified by contract with a not-for-profit corporation, hiring is at will and the board of directors may appoint or remove employees with or without cause.
Ohio. Northeast Property Owners Civic Association v. Kennedy, 117 Ohio App 79, 181 NE2d 495 (1962).
Texas. Mangum v. Swearingen, 565 SW2d 957 (Tex Civ App, 1978). The court stated in the Mangum case that the power to remove a corporate officer is one necessarily incident to every corporation. The court held that the church membership in that case could remove the deacons.

[2] Model Nonprofit Corporation Act §24 (1964).
[3] Model Nonprofit Corporation Act §24 (1964).
[4] NY Not-for-Profit Corp Law §713.
[5] NY Not-for-Profit Corp Law §713.
[6] NY Not-for-Profit Corp Law §713.
[7] Cal Corp Code §§5213, 7213.

§ 3:07. Employees.

Employees of nonprofit organizations are employed by officers of the organization and are subject to control, regarding performance of work, by the organization.[1] The power to appoint and discharge for a nonprofit corporation is normally vested by the bylaws in a corporate officer or in the directors.

The law does not require that employment be rational, wise, or well-considered.[2] Generally, in the absence of a contract to the contrary, an employer has sole discretion in hiring and has the authority to discharge an employee with or without cause.[3] However, this general rule has been limited by nondiscrimination provisions of both state and federal statutes.[4] Because managers of a nonprofit organization must be aware of statutes prohibiting discrimination in employment, provisions of the major federal statutes are summarized in subsequent sections.[5]

FOOTNOTES

[1] **United States.** Aberdeen Aerie No. 24 of Fraternal Order of Eagles v. United States, 50 F Supp 734 (D Wash, 1943).

For a charitable trust, employees are employed by the trustee. However, the trustee is limited in the number of employees it can hire. A trustee cannot delegate duties which the trustee can personally perform. See Scott, Law of Trusts, §§8, 171, 188.3 (3d Ed). While a corporation can only act through its directors, officers, and employees, a trust cannot delegate the administration of the trust unless the trust agreement permits. See Scott, Law of Trusts, §§171, 171.4 (3d Ed). If a trustee employs someone to perform acts which involve an improper delegation of the trustee's duties, not only may the trustee incur a liability to the beneficiaries for so doing, but he is not allowed a credit in his accounts for the expense of employing that person. See Scott, Law of Trusts, §188.3 (3d ed).

[2] **United States.** Powell v. Syracuse University, 580 F2d 1150 (CA2, 1978).

[3] See e.g.:
United States. Phillips v. Goodyear Tire & Rubber Company, 651 F2d 1051 (CA5, 1981).

In Mayon v. Southern Pacific Transp. Co., 632 F Supp 944 (ED Tex, 1986), a federal district court interpreted the Texas law as set forth in Sabine Pilot Service, Inc. v. Hauck, 687 SW2d 733 (Tex, 1985), to provide only a limited exception to the at-will employment doctrine. The court held that an employee who was discharged for pursuing his or her legal rights under the Federal Employees Liability Act was not discharged for refusing to perform an illegal act; thus, there was no exception to the at-will employment doctrine. See also O'Louglin v. Procon, Inc., 627 F Supp 675 (ED Tex, 1986).

Arizona. See Wagner v. City of Globe, 722 P2d 250 (Ariz, 1986), in which the Supreme Court of Arizona listed three exceptions to the at-will employment doctrine. One is the implied contract exception wherein there is an implied promise of continued employment. Another is the public policy exception wherein an employer has undermined an important public policy. The third exception is the good faith and fair dealing exception which protects employees from termination for bad cause. As the court stated in the Wagner case, Arizona recognizes all three exceptions. The court noted that an at-will employment contract can be modified by personnel manuals, guides or rules by the employer. Whether the parties intended to modify their at-will contract by use of a personnel manual or otherwise is a question of fact. The court noted that the public policy exception protects an employee who refused to participate in illegal behavior. The court cited whistle-blowing activity as one that serves a public purpose and should be protected. Higdon v. Evergreen International Airlines, Inc., 138 Ariz 163, 673 P2d 907 (1983).

Maine. Maine Human Rights Commission v. Canadian Pacific Ltd., 458 A2d 1225 (Me, 1983).

Michigan. Allen v. Southeastern Michigan Transp. Authority, 132 Mich App 533, 349 NW2d 204 (1984).

Missouri. See Boyle v. Vista Eyewear, Inc., 700 SW2d 859 (Mo App, 1985), in which the court cited the history of a public policy exception to the employment at-will doctrine. The court noted that although employers generally are free to discharge employees at will with or without cause, they are not free to require employees, on penalty of losing their jobs, to commit unlawful acts or acts in violation of a clear mandate of public policy expressed in the constitution, statutes and regulations promulgated pursuant to statute. The employer is bound to know the public policies of the state. The court noted that the at-will employment doctrine seems to be falling most heavily and harshly upon professional and upper and middle level employees. These employees have the most to lose, frequently being the long-term employees who have greatest responsibility, substantial investment in, and highest expectations from their careers. Often they are at an age when replacement of their life and medical insurance programs and their retirement plans are difficult or impossible. At-will employment doctrine does not include nor contemplate a privilege in the employer to subject its employees to risks of civil and criminal liability. According to the court, a public policy exception is narrow enough in its scope and application to be no threat to employers who operate within the mandates of the law and clearly established public policy as set out in duly adopted laws. Such employers will never be troubled by public policy exception because their operations and practices will not violate public policy.

New York. Weiss v. Opportunities for Cortland County, Inc. 40 A2d 890, 337 NYS2d 409 (1972).

Ohio. Henkel v. Educational Research Council of America, 48 Ohio St 2d 249, 344 NE2d 118 (1976).

Officers and Employees 103

Tennessee. Savage v. Spur Distributing Company, 228 SW2d 122 (Tenn App, 1949).

Tennessee. Price v. Mercury Supply Co., 682 SW2d 924 (Tenn App, 1984).

Texas. Robertson v. Panhandle & S.F. Ry. Company, 77 SW2d 1078 (Tex Civ App, 1934); Scruggs v. George A. Hormel and Company, 464 SW2d 730 (Tex Civ App, 1971); United Service Auto Association v. Tull, 571 SW2d 551 (Tex Civ App, 1978); Cactus Feeders, Inc. v. Wittler, 509 SW2d 934 (Tex Civ App, 1974).

In Sabine Pilot Service, Inc. v. Hauck, 687 SW2d 733 (Tex, 1985), the Supreme Court of Texas carved out a narrow exception to the employment at-will doctrine. The exception covers the discharge of an employee for refusing to perform an illegal act, i.e., an act that carries a criminal penalty for performance. However, the Supreme Court noted that numerous commentators have advocated exceptions to the at-will doctrine based upon a public policy exception, and the concurring opinion in the case stated that the decision did not preclude the Court from broadening the exception when it may be warranted.

Texas. In Ramos v. Henry C. Beck Co., 711 SW2d 331 (Tex Civ App, 1986), the court held that an employee, who can prove his or her employment at will is subject to an oral or written agreement that the employee will not be terminated except for good cause can recover for wrongful discharge.

Virginia. See Bowman v. State Bank of Keysville, 331 SE2d 797 (Va, 1985) in which the court held that while Virginia has not deviated from the common-law doctrine of employment-at-will, the rule is not absolute. The court applied a narrow exception to the doctrine when shareholder-employees were discharged for exercising their protected rights as shareholders in questioning the manner in which proxies were obtained for a proposed merger.

Wisconsin. Samens v. Labor & Industry Review Commission, 117 Wis 2d 646, 345 NW2d 432 (1984).

[4] **United States.** See Powell v. Syracuse University, 580 F2d 1150, 1157 (CA2, 1978).

[5] See §§3:08-3:12.

State statutes on employment discrimination vary. Some states have established Civil Rights Commissions to receive, investigate, and conduct hearings regarding charges of discrimination in hiring and firing. See, e.g., Colo Rev Stat §24-34-304 and Ohio Rev Code Ann §4112.03. In Ohio, it is an unlawful discrimination practice for any employer to discharge without just cause or to refuse to hire or otherwise to discriminate because of race, color, religion, sex, national origin, handicap, age, or ancestry. See Ohio Rev Code Ann §4112.02. In Colorado, it is an unfair employment practice to refuse to hire, promote or demote, or discharge based on race, creed, color, sex, national origin, or ancestry. See Colo Rev Stat §24-34-304.

Until 1983, Texas statutes did not provide for a civil rights commission. However, officers and employees of the state, or a political subdivision of the state, could not refuse to employ or discharge a person because of race, religion, color, or national origin. See Tex Civ Stat art 6252-16. In 1983, the Commission on Human Rights was established to execute the policies embodied in Title VII of the federal Civil Rights Act 42 USC §2000e. The Texas statute provides that it is an unlawful employment practice for an employer, employment agency, or labor union, to refuse to hire or to otherwise discriminate against an individual because of race, color, handicap, religion, sex, national origin, or age. See Tex Civ Stat art 5221k. The Commission on Human Rights receives, investigates, and passes on complaints alleging violations of the statute.

§3:08. Discrimination in Employment—Title VII.

Nonprofit organizations that are engaged in activities affecting commerce and that have 15 or more employees on each working day in each of 20 or more calendar weeks in the current or preceding year are subject to the Civil Rights Act of 1964, which is referred to as Title VII.[1] Title VII makes it an unlawful employment practice for any employer to fail or refuse to hire or to discharge any individual, or otherwise to discriminate against any individual with respect to compensation, terms, conditions, or privileges of employment, because of an individual's race, color, religion, sex, or national origin.[2] The Act also prohibits an employer from limiting, segregating, or classifying employees or applicants for employment in any way that would deprive, or tend to deprive, any individual of employment opportunities or would otherwise affect his or her status as an employee, because of the individual's race, color, religion, sex, or national origin.[3] The Act is enforced by the Equal Employment Opportunity Commission.[4]

The appropriate starting point for evaluation of a personal claim of employment discrimination under Title VII is the case of McDonnell Douglas Corporation v. Green.[5] In that case the Supreme Court stated that a complainant in a Title VII trial must carry the initial burden of establishing a prima facie case of racial or sex discrimination. A complainant may establish a prima facie case of racial or sex discrimination by showing that he or she is a member of a minority, that he or she applied and was qualified for a position for which the institution was seeking applicants, that despite proper qualifications the applicant was rejected and that, after the rejection, the position remained open and the institution continued to seek applications from persons with the complainant's qualifications.[6] The burden then shifts to the institution to articulate some legitimate, nondiscriminatory reason for the applicant's rejection.[7] If the institution is able to sustain its burden, the burden shifts back to the complainant to demonstrate that the institution's stated reason for the complainant's rejection was in fact pretext.[8]

A prima facie case of employment discrimination may be proved under a theory of disparate impact or disparate treatment.[9] Discriminatory motive is critical in demonstrating disparate treatment.[10] However, such motive may be inferred from the mere fact of differences in treatment.[11] Disparate impact is used to attack employment practices that are facially neutral but that fall more harshly on a protected class of employees.[12] The disparate impact model requires proof of a causal connection between a challenged employment practice and the composition of the work force. Aptitude tests, height and weight requirements, and similar selection criteria all may be shown to affect one class of employees more harshly than another.[13] However, absent proof that the disparate impact is caused by one or more of the challenged employment practices, a court will not require an employer to justify the legitimacy of any (or all) of its employment practices.[14] In addition, while disproportionate impact might cause further inquiry, an inference of discrimination may nonetheless be negated by an employer's affirmative efforts to recruit minorities.[15]

To dispel an adverse inference from a prima facie showing of employment discrimination, the employer need only articulate some legitimate, nondiscriminatory reason for the applicant's rejection.[16] Statistical proof that the work force was racially or sexually imbalanced or contained a disproportionately higher percentage of minority employees could be considered in determining motivation; however, courts will not require different business practices for an employer until a violation of the Civil Rights Act has been proven.[17] If there is such a showing, the burden which shifts to the employer is proving that its employment decision was based on a legitimate consideration and not an illegitimate one such as race or sex.[18] There is no requirement that an employer hire a minority or female applicant whenever that person's objective qualifications are equal to those of a white male applicant.[19]

The purpose of Title VII is to achieve equality of employment opportunities and to remove barriers that have operated in the past to favor an identifiable group of white employees over other employees.[20] However, discriminatory preference for any group, minority or majority, is precisely and only what Congress has proscribed. Employers have faced loss of substantial federal contracts and liability to minorities for refusing to initiate affirmative action as a remedy for past discrimination; however, they have also faced liability to whites for any voluntary preferences accorded minorities.[21] Because of the dilemma facing employers, courts have been reluctant to discourage implementation of bona fide affirmative action plans.[22] Consequently, a plaintiff in a reverse discrimination case must present evidence that would show some reason other than a remedial reason motivated an employer in implementing an affirmative action plan or that the plan adopted unreasonably exceeded its remedial purpose.[23]

It is not an unlawful employment practice to apply different standards of compensation, or different terms, conditions, or privileges of employment pursuant to a bona fide seniority system, provided that such differences are not the result of an intention to discriminate because of race, color, religion, sex, or national origin.[24]

FOOTNOTES

[1] 42 USC §2000e(b). An organization is engaged in activities affecting commerce if the organization has employees engaged in commerce or in the production of goods for commerce. However, even if materials produced are consumed in the business, the organization may be subject to the act. If the materials used by employees previously moved in interstate commerce, the organization is engaged in activities affecting commerce.

42 USC §2000e-1 provides that the act does not apply to a religious corporation, association, educational institution, or society with respect to the employment of individuals of a particular religion.

United States. See Ohio Civil Rights Commission v. Dayton Christian Schools, US, 91 L Ed 2d 512, 106 S Ct 2718 (1986), in which the Supreme Court reversed the decision of the Sixth Circuit, 766 F2d 932 (CA6, 1985). The Supreme Court ruled that the state commission violated no constitutional rights by merely investigating the circumstances of the discharge if only to ascertain whether the ascribed religious-based reason was in fact the reason for the discharge.

See Amos v. Corporation of Presiding Bishop of Church of Jesus Christ of Latter-Day Saints, 618 F Supp 1013 (D Utah, 1985), in which the court held that a substantial fact issue existed as to whether a garment industry, operated as an unincorporated division of the Mormon church structure, that made garments worn by members of the church when they enter the temple, was religious in nature so as to be exempt from the employment discrimination law.

See Marshall v. Whitehead, 463 F Supp 1329 (MD Fla, 1978). In the Marshall case, the court held that the defendant who operated a wholly intrastate garbage removal service and whose only tie to interstate commerce was that it had four employees who used gasoline and oil—products that had moved in interstate commerce—in operating and maintaining the company's truck was engaged in activities affecting commerce. A 1974 amendment to the act extended coverage of the act to employers who conduct wholly intrastate businesses, but whose employees, in the course of that business, use and handle any products that have moved in interstate commerce, even though the products were purchased locally.

[2] 42 USC §2000e-2. It is a violation of Title VII for a job advertisement to

indicate preference, limitation, specification, or discrimination based on sex or race, though specification based on sex is permitted if sex is a bona fide occupational qualification for a particular job. A bona fide occupational qualification exception as to sex is interpreted narrowly. Refusal to hire a person because of sex cannot be based on stereotyped characterizations of the sexes, nor may the preferences of coworkers, the employer, clients, or customers be considered. Benefits provided employees must be the same for male and female. See 29 CFR Part 1604.

United States. See Local 28 of Sheet Metal Workers' International Ass'n v. EEOC, US, 92 L Ed 2d 344, 106 S Ct 3019 (1986), in which the Supreme Court held that the remedies provision of Title VII did not preclude a district court from ordering preferential relief benefiting individuals who were not actual victims of discrimination, ordering contempt fines, and issuing an order that such fines be placed in a special fund to increase the nonwhite membership of a union. The Court held that neither the imposition of nonwhite membership goal nor the fund order were violative of either Title VII or the equal protection clause of the Fourteenth Amendment.

[3] 42 USC §2000e-2. Employer toleration of a racially discriminatory work atmosphere violates Title VII.

United States. See Meritor Sav. Bank v. Vinson, US, 91 L Ed 2d 49, 106 S Ct 2399 (1986), in which the Supreme Court held that a claim of a hostile environment in the form of sexual harassment is sex discrimination that is actionable under Title VII. The Court stated that the language of Title VII is not limited to economic or tangible discrimination. A former employee of a bank brought action against the bank and her former supervisor claiming that during her employment at the bank she had been subjected to sexual harassment by her supervisor. The Supreme Court held that the Court of Appeals in that case had erred in concluding that employers are always automatically liable for sexual harassment by their supervisors. However, the Court stated that the absence of notice to the employer does not necessarily insulate the employer from liability. The bank's grievance procedure required an employee to complain first to her supervisor regarding such problems. The Supreme Court stated that since the supervisor was the guilty party, failure to invoke the procedure and report the grievance to him did not insulate the employer from liability.

In Scott v. Sears, Roebuck & Co., 798 F2d 210 (CA7, 1986), the court found no liability on the part of the plaintiff's employer when the plaintiff failed to show that the sexual harassment was sufficiently severe or pervasive to alter her conditions of employment and to create an abusive working environment. The court stated that the question of whether an employer is liable for sexual harassment by fellow employees becomes: did demeaning conduct and sexual stereotyping cause such anxiety and debilitation to the plaintiff that working conditions for her were poisoned.

In Bohen v. City of East Chicago, Indiana, 799 F2d 1180 (CA7, 1986), the court held the plaintiff's employer to be liable in damages for sexual harassment by fellow employees. The court presented an outline for a claim of sexual harassment under the equal protection clause. The court noted that the ultimate inquiry is whether the sexual harassment constitutes intentional discrimination. A plaintiff can make an ultimate showing of sex discrimination either by showing that sexual harassment amounted to intentional sex discrimination or by showing that the conscious failure of the employer to protect the plaintiff from abusive conditions created by fellow employees amounted to intentional discrimination. The court noted that a single act of a sufficiently high-ranking policymaker is sufficient to establish a policy or custom of harassment by the entity. Practices of state officials can be so permanent and well-settled as to constitute a custom or usage with the force of law.

See Taylor v. Jones, 653 F2d 1193 (CA8, 1981).

[4] 42 USC §2000e-5.

[5] 411 US 792, 36 L Ed 2d 668, 93 S Ct 1817 (1973).

[6] **United States.** McDonnell Douglas Corporation v. Green, 411 US 792, 36 L Ed 2d 668, 93 S Ct 1817 (1973).

[7] **United States.** McDonnell Douglas Corporation v. Green, 411 US 792, 36 L Ed 2d 668, 93 S Ct 1817 (1973).

[8] **United States.** McDonnell Douglas Corporation v. Green, 411 US 792, 36 L Ed 2d 668, 93 S Ct 1817 (1973).

[9] **United States.** See Lewis v. NLRB, 750 F2d 1266 (CA5, 1985), in which the court held that the plaintiff's challenge to an employer's promotion practices was subject to disparate treatment rather than disparate impact. Under such an analysis, the court held that the employer must have had a discriminatory intent. Nonetheless the court stated that racial discrimination may be inferred if gross statistical disparities are shown in an analysis of the relevant statistics. In determining intent, the court noted that the trial court may examine "history of the employer's practices, anecdotal evidence of class members, and the degree of opportunity to treat employees unfairly in the appraisal process."

See Bryant v. International Schools Services Inc., 675 F2d 562 (CA3, 1982).

[10] **United States.** Bryant v. International Schools Services Inc, 675 F2d 562 (CA3, 1982).

[11] **United States.** Bryant v. International Schools Services Inc, 675 F2d 562 (CA3, 1982).

110   Representing the Nonprofit Organization

[12] United States. Pouncy v. Prudential Insurance Company of America, 668 F2d 795 (CA 5, 1982).

[13] United States. Pouncy v. Prudential Insurance Company of America, 668 F2d 795 (CA 5, 1982); Griggs v. Duke Power Company, 401 US 424, 28 L Ed 2d 158, 91 S Ct 849 (1970).

[14] United States. Pouncy v. Prudential Insurance Company of America, 668 F2d 795 (CA5, 1982).

[15] United States. See Washington v. Davis, 426 US 229, 248, 48 L Ed 2d 597, 96 S Ct 2040 (1976).

[16] United States. See Furnco Construction Corporation v. Waters, 438 US 567, 57 L Ed 2d 957, 98 S Ct 2943 (1978).

[17] United States. Griffin v. Carlin, 755 F2d 1516 (CA11, 1985). In the Carlin case, the court held that a prima facie case of disparate treatment may be established by statistics alone if they are sufficiently compelling. In Coates v. Johnson & Johnson, 756 F2d 524 (CA7, 1985), the court held that strong statistical evidence may form a prima facie case "in some cases."

Furnco Construction Corporation v. Waters, 438 US 567, 57 L Ed 2d 957, 98 S Ct 2943 (1978).

[18] United States. Furnco Construction Corporation v. Waters, 438 US 567, 57 L Ed 2d 957, 98 S Ct 2943 (1978).

[19] United States. See Texas Department of Community Affairs v. Burdine, 450 US 248, 67 L Ed 2d 207, 101 S Ct 1089 (1981).

[20] United States. Griggs v. Duke Power Co. 401 US 424, 28 L Ed 2d 158, 91 S Ct 8949 (1971).

[21] United States. Setser v. Novack Investment Company, 657 F2d 962 (CA8, 1981).

[22] United States. Setser v. Novack Investment Company, 657 F2d 962 (CA8, 1981).

[23] United States. See Setser v. Novack Investment Company, 657 F2d 962 (CA8, 1981). An employer's plan is a bona fide one if it is reasonably related to its remedial purpose. The court in the Setser case stated that once an employer has produced evidence that its treatment of a person was a direct consequence of its implementation of a bona fide affirmative action plan, the employer is entitled to a judgment as a matter of law unless the person shows that the purpose of the employer's affirmative action program was not remedial.

[24] 42 USC §2000e-2(h).

United States. See Wygant v. Jackson Board of Education, ——US——, 90 L Ed 2d 260, 106 S Ct 1842 (1986), in which nonminority school teachers

Officers and Employees 111

brought an action against the school board and its members challenging the validity of a provision in a collective bargaining agreement under which board members extended preferential protection against layoffs to some minority employees. The collective bargaining agreement provided that if it became necessary to lay off teachers, those with most seniority would be retained except that at no time would there be a greater percentage of minority personnel laid off than the current percentage of minority personnel employed at the time of the layoff. Some displaced nonminority teachers brought suit alleging a violation of the equal protection clause of the Fourteenth Amendment. The Court held that racial classifications in the context of affirmative action must be justified by a compelling state purpose, and the means chosen by the state to effectuate that purpose must be narrowly tailored. There must be convincing evidence of prior discrimination by a governmental unit before allowing a limited use of racial classifications to remedy such discrimination. The Court held that the policy of the school board did not bear any relationship to harm caused by prior discriminatory hiring practices. If the purpose of the layoff provision was to remedy prior discrimination, the Court held that such purpose would require a court to make a factual determination that the board had a strong basis in evidence for its conclusion that remedial action was necessary.

In Lilly v. City of Beckley, West Virginia, 797 F2d 191 (CA4, 1986), a white male applicant for the position of police officer was successful in presenting a claim for damages based on a suit alleging he was the victim of reverse discrimination. The court stated that although Title VII's prohibition of race discrimination in employment applies to members of racial majorities as well as minorities, the statute does not flatly prohibit implementation of voluntary affirmative programs designed to remedy past discrimination against racial minorities and the resulting racial imbalances. In determining whether an affirmative action plan is justified, the courts apply a test that inquires whether the plan contains safeguards necessary to avoid trammelling the rights of nonminorities, whether the plan is designed to remedy past discrimination, and whether the plan is temporary.

See Firefighters Local Union No. 1784 v. Stotts,—US—, 81 L Ed 2d 483, 104 S Ct 2576 (1984). The Supreme Court pointed out that individual members of a plaintiff class who can demonstrate that they have been actual victims of a discriminatory practice, may be awarded competitive seniority and given their rightful place in the seniority roster. However, according to the Court, to warrant a seniority award, each individual must prove that the discriminatory practice had an impact on him; but even if the individual can show this, the employee is not automatically entitled to have a nonminority employee laid off to make room for him. He may have to wait until a vacancy occurs.

§3:09. —Equal Pay Act.

An employer engaged in commerce or in the production of goods for commerce may not pay different wages to employees of opposite sexes for equal work on jobs the performance of which requires equal skill, effort, and responsibility and which are performed under similar working conditions unless the payment is made pursuant to (1) a seniority system, (2) a merit system, (3) a system which measures earnings by quantity or quality of production, or (4) a differential based on any factor other than sex.[1] The Equal Pay Act is administered by the Equal Employment Opportunity Commission.[2]

A person alleging unequal pay need not show discriminatory intent.[3] The Equal Pay Act creates a type of strict liability; no intent to discriminate need be shown.[4] A person establishes a prima facie case by a showing of payment of different wages to employees of opposite sexes for equal work on the job.[5] Although job titles are entitled to some weight in the assessment of comparative responsibility, the controlling factor under the Equal Pay Act is job content—the actual duties the respective employees are called upon to perform.[6]

Once a prima facie case of unequal pay has been established, the defendant has four affirmative defenses.[7] The defendant must prove that any wage disparity was the result of a seniority system, a merit system, a system which measures earnings by quantity or quality of production, or that the differential was based on any other factor than sex.[8]

A violation of the Equal Pay Act is also a violation of Title VII.[9] The only justifiable pay differentials under Title VII are those attributable to the four affirmative defenses under the Equal Pay Act.[10]

FOOTNOTES

[1] USC §206(d). Activities of nonprofit organizations are included under the act. See 29 USC §203(r) which provides that activities performed for a business purpose are treated as ordinary commercial activities.

United States. See also Williams v. Eastside Mental Health Center, 669 F2d 671 (CA11, 1982); Marshall v. Woods Hole Oceanographic Institution, 458 F Supp 709 (D Mass, 1978); Ritter v. Mount St. Mary's College, 495 F Supp 724 (D Md, 1980). However, in the Ritter case, the court said Congress did not demonstrate a clear, affirmative intention to include religious, nonprofit educational institutions within the scope of the Equal Pay Act.

As enacted in 1963, the Equal Pay Act was inapplicable to state and local governments. However, in 1966, coverage was extended to employees of state and local hospitals, institutions, schools, and public transit systems. In 1974, coverage was extended to virtually all public employees, except public office holders and their staffs.

See also Pearce v. Wichita County, City of Wichita Falls Texas, Hospital Board. 590 F2d 128 (CA5, 1979). The court stated that the Equal Pay Act is severable from the minimum wage provision of the Fair Labor Standards Act. While the Supreme Court in National League of Cities v. Usery, 426 US 833, 49 L Ed 2d 245, 96 S Ct 2465 (1976) ruled that the minimum wage provisions were not applicable to state governmental entities, the court stated in the Pearce case that that reasoning does not apply to the Equal Pay Act. The court further stated that an extension of the Equal Pay Act to states and political subdivisions is a valid exercise of Congress' power under the commerce clause.

In Garcia v. San Antonio Metropolitan Transit Authority, 469 US—, 83 L Ed 2d 1016, 105 S Ct 1005 (1985), the Supreme Court overruled National League of Cities v. Usery, 426 US 833, 49 L Ed 2d 245, 96 S Ct 2465 (1976). The Supreme Court stated in Garcia that there is nothing in the minimum wage provisions that are destructive of state sovereignty.

[2] Executive Order 12144, June 22, 1979.

[3] United States. See Strecker v. Grand Forks County Social Service Board, 640 F2d 96 (CA8, 1980).

[4] United States. Strecker v. Grand Forks County Social Service Board, 640 F2d 96 (CA8, 1980).

[5] United States. Brobst v. Columbus Services International, 761 F2d 148 (CA3, 1985).

EEOC v. Maricopa County Community College Dist., 736 F2d 510 (CA9, 1984).

See Futran v. Ring Radio Company, 501 F Supp 734 (ND Ga, 1980).

[6] United States. Griffin v. Carlin, 755 F2d 1516 (CA11, 1985).

"Substantially equal" does not necessarily mean identical and jobs from different academic disciplines can be substantially equal.

Spaulding v. University of Washington, 740 F2d 686 (CA9, 1984), cert den, 105 S Ct 511 (1984).

See also EEOC v. First Citizens Bank of Billings, 758 F2d 397 (CA9, 1985) in which the court held that the Equal Pay Act does not require that jobs being compared be performed simultaneously. The court stated that the Act applies to situations where an employee of one sex is hired for a particular job to replace an employee of the opposite sex. If a male is hired to replace a female, for example, violations of the act may be proved by comparing the female's salary to that of her male successor. Back pay may be awarded for the period prior to the male's hiring.

See Gunther v. County of Washington, 623 F2d 1309 (CA9, 1979); Williams v. Eastside Mental Health Center, 669 F2d 671 (CA11, 1982); and Odomes v. Nucare Inc, 653 F2d 246 (CA6, 1981). In the Odomes case, the court held that the positions of female nurse's aides and male orderlies were essentially the same. The court stated that only substantial equality of skill, effort, responsibility, and working conditions is required. The issue of whether the jobs are substantially the same is resolved by an overall comparison of the work, not its individual segments.

[7] **United States.** See Strecker v. Grand Forks County Social Service Board, 460 F2d 96 (CA8, 1980); Futran v. Ring Radio Company, 501 S Supp 734 (ND Ga, 1980); Schulte v. Wilson Industries, Inc., 547 F Supp 324 (SD Tex, 1982).

[8] **United States.** See Strecker v. Grand Forks Social Service Board, 640 F2d 96 (CA8, 1980).

[9] **United States.** See Futran v. Ring Radio Company, 501 F Supp 734 (ND Ga, 1980).

[10] **United States.** Schulte v. Wilson Industries, Inc., 547 F Supp 324 (SD Tex, 1982); Futran v. Ring Radio Company, 501 F Supp 734 (ND Ga, 1980). If a violation of the Equal Pay Act is shown, plaintiff is entitled under Title VII to the difference between what she would have earned and what she actually did earn.

§3:10. —Age Discrimination in Employment Act.

An employer engaged in an industry affecting commerce with 20 or more employees for each working day in each of 20 or more calendar weeks in the current or preceding calendar year may not fail or refuse to hire or to discharge any individual or otherwise discriminate against any individual because of the individual's age.[1] The act is limited to persons over the age of

40.[2] Thus, mandatory retirement for persons over age 40 is prohibited.[3]

The purpose of the Age Discrimination in Employment Act is to promote employment of older persons based on their ability rather than on age, to prohibit arbitrary age discrimination in employment, and to help employers and workers find ways of meeting problems arising from the impact of age on employment.[4] However, the act was not intended to prevent employers from changing the job responsibilities of employees over 40 years of age.[5]

Title VII standards are applied to charges of age discrimination.[6] The purposes and structure of the acts are similar. However, Title VII standards are not applied automatically in age discrimination cases.[7] An employer can establish a bona fide occupational qualification as a defense to a charge of age discrimination.[8] However, a business necessity test, not a business convenience test, is used.[9]

FOOTNOTES

[1] USC §§623, 630(b).
United States. See Ritter v. Mount St. Mary's College, 495 F Supp 724 (D Md, 1980), wherein the court held that Congress did not demonstrate a clear, affirmative intention to include religious, nonprofit religious educational institutions within the act.

[2] 29 USC §631.

[3] The retirement benefit must now be equivalent to $44,000 or more.

[4] **United States.** Schwager v. Sun Oil Company of Pennsylvania, 591 F2d 58 (CA10, 1979).
See Monroe v. United Airlines, Inc., 736 F2d 394 (CA7, 1984) for a good discussion of requirements under the act.
See also Thornbrough v. Columbus & Greenville Co., 760 F2d 633 (CA5, 1985).

[5] **United States.** Frazer v. KFC National Management Company, 491 F Supp 1099 (MD Ga, 1980). The court in Frazer stated that the act was also not intended to give employees the right to walk off their jobs and sue their employer because they disliked their changed job responsibilities. If the

employees walk out, the court said they can complain of discharge only if the offered or altered working conditions would have been so difficult or unpleasant that a reasonable person in the employees' shoes would have felt compelled to resign.

[6] **United States.** Schwager v. Sun Oil Company of Pennsylvania, 591 F2d 58 (CA10, 1979); Tuohy v. Ford Motor Company, 675 F2d 842 (CA6, 1982); Tribble v. Westinghouse Electric Corporation, 669 F2d 1193 (CA8, 1982). In the Tribble case, the plaintiff established a prima facie case of age discrimination by showing that plaintiff was in the protected class, that during the period involved plaintiff was confronted by his employer with the alternative of early retirement or termination, that the plaintiff took early retirement under protest, and that after discharge and after plaintiff's application for other positions for which he was qualified, the position remained open and the employer continued to seek applications from persons with similar qualifications. The court found in that case that the employer's offer of a legitimate nondiscriminatory reason for discharging plaintiff—that plaintiff elected to take early retirement due to an intracompany reorganization that eliminated plaintiff's job—was a pretext.

[7] **United States.** Tuohy v. Ford Motor Company, 675 F2d 842 (CA 6, 1982).

[8] **United States.** Tuohy v. Ford Motor Company, 675 F2d 842 (CA 6, 1982); Hodgson v. Greyhound Inc., 499 F2d 859 (CA 7, 1974).

In Trans World Airlines, Inc. v. Thurston, 469 US—, 83 L Ed 2d 523, 105 S Ct 613 (1985), the Supreme Court held that the policy of Trans World Airlines of transferring its captains who were 60 years of age to flight engineers only on a bid basis when other captains were transferred automatically, violated the Age Discrimination in Employment Act. Age was not a bona fide occupational qualification for flight engineers. In Western Air Lines, Inc. v. Criswell, 472 US—, 86 L Ed 2d 321, 105 S Ct 2743 (1985), the Supreme Court held that the bona fide occupational qualification defense is an extremely narrow exception. The defense is available only if the job qualification is reasonably necessary to the overriding interest in public safety and if the employer is compelled to rely on age as a proxy for a safety related job qualification.

[9] **United States.** Hodgson v. Greyhound Inc, 499 F2d 859 (CA 7, 1974). In the Hodgson case, the employer successfully demonstrated that its maximum hiring age policy was founded upon a good faith judgment concerning the safety needs of its passengers and others and that its hiring policy was not the result of an arbitrary belief lacking in objective reason or rationale.

The exception to the Age Discrimination in Employment Act is analyzed in terms of vocations within a general business rather than by duties performed. The state could establish mandatory retirement age of 50 for state police officers even though the plaintiff engaged primarily in administrative duties with no strenuous physical activity. Mahoney v. Trabucco, 738 F2d 35 (CA1, 1984).

§3:11. Vocational Rehabilitation Act.

Section 503 of the Vocational Rehabilitation Act of 1973 provides that persons or firms having contracts with the federal government in excess of $2,500 must take affirmative action to employ and advance qualified handicapped individuals.[1] Reasonable allowances must be made for an employee's handicaps unless doing so would impose an undue hardship upon the employer.[2]

Courts have stated that §503 of the Rehabilitation Act does not give injured parties a private right of action to challenge employment discrimination.[3] Enforcement of the act is through the Department of Labor.[4] If a handicapped individual believes a federal contractor has failed to comply with the act, he or she may file a complaint with the Department of Labor.[5] Upon a finding of failure of compliance, the Department of Labor may withhold payments or may terminate the contract with the employer.[6]

FOOTNOTES

[1] 29 USC §793.

[2] 41 CFR §60-741.5(d).

[3] **United States.** See Rogers v. Frito Lay, Inc, 611 F2d 1074 (CA5, 1980); Meyerson v. State of Arizona, 709 F2d 1235 (CA1, 1983); Painter v. Horne Brothers, Inc, 710 F2d 143 (CA4, 1983).

But see Davis v. Modine Manufacturing Company, 526 F Supp 943 (D Kan, 1981), wherein the court stated that the requirement of including an affirmative action clause in all covered contracts provided a private right of action.

See also Simpson v. Reynolds Metal Company, 629 F2d 1226 (CA7, 1980).

[4] United States. See Meyerson v. State of Arizona, 709 F2d 1235, 1239 (CA1, 1983).
[5] 29 USC §793(b).
[6] United States. Meyerson v. State of Arizona, 709 F2d 1235, 1239 (CA1, 1983).

§3:12. —Vietnam Era Veterans' Readjustment Assistance Act.

Any organization having a contract in the amount of $10,000 or more with the federal government for the procurement of personal property and nonpersonal services (including construction) must take affirmative action to employ and advance in employment qualified disabled veterans and veterans of the Vietnam era.[1] An aggrieved party may file a complaint with the Secretary of Labor.[2] Courts have stated that there is no private right of action to enforce provisions of the act.[3]

FOOTNOTES

[1] 38 USC §2012.
[2] 38 USC §2012(b).
[3] United States. See Butler v. McDonnell-Douglas Saudi Arabia Corporation, 93 FRD 384 (SD Ohio, 1981); De Leon Cruz v. Loubriel, 539 F Supp 250 (D Puerto Rico, 1982).

§3:13. —Retirement Plans for Employees of Nonprofit Enterprises.

Retirement plans for employees are an important form of employee benefit. The tax benefits of retirement plans that qualify under various provisions of the Internal Revenue Code make these specialized plans highly desirable.[1] The employee is not taxed on plan benefits, including earnings of the fund, until they are received.[2] Certain qualified plans receive special tax breaks (in the form of 10-year averaging) upon distributions.[3] For tax years beginning after December 31, 1986, the 10-year averaging provision is eliminated.[4] An election can be made to have a lump sum distribution, received after the employee has reached the age of 59½, subject to 5-year averaging, but the election can be made only one time.[5] Thus, if the election is made for a distribution received in the tax year when the employee reaches age 59½, such an election could not again be made as to any distributions received in subsequent taxable years. In addition, up to $5,000 of qualified plan benefits qualify for exclusion from taxable income as death benefits under §101(b) of the Code.[6] Plan contributions also provide tax deductions to the employer; however, this generally is not a consideration for a tax exempt nonprofit organization.[7]

There are several forms of retirement plans available to employees of nonprofit organizations. These include the qualified pension or profit-sharing plans under §401 of the Code,[8] the individual retirement account (IRA),[9] the simplified employee pension (SEP),[10] and the tax sheltered annuities for § 501(c)(3) organizations.[11] Qualified plans under §401 of the Code must meet the requirements of §§410-412 and 415-416 of the Code regarding minimum participation, vesting, funding standards, top heavy requirements, and limitations on benefits and contributions.[12] These requirements cause substantial accounting and disclosure problems for qualified plans. While the simplified employee pensions are subject to age, service, vesting and nondiscrimination provisions under §408 and §416 of the Code, the accounts are established as individual employee accounts; therefore, any of the extensive accounting and reporting requirements for qualified plans are not applicable to simplified employee pensions.[13]

FOOTNOTES

[1] Qualified pension or profit-sharing plans, available for nonprofit organizations that are incorporated, must meet the requirements of §§401, 410-412, 415-416 of the Internal Revenue Code.
Tax sheltered annuities for §501(c)(3) organizations are subject to the requirements of §403(b) of the Code.
Individual retirement accounts (IRAs) and simplified employee pensions (IRA-SEP) must meet the requirements of §408 of the Code.

[2] IRC (1954), §§401-403, 501(a).

[3] IRC (1954), §402(e). Distributions from a qualified plan that represent contributions made before 1974 qualify for long-term capital gain treatment.

[4] IRC (1986), §402(e) (4) (B).

[5] IRC (1986), §402(e) (4) (B).

[6] IRC (1954), §101(b). The exclusion applies to amounts paid to an employee's beneficiaries after the employee's death. If a lump sum distribution is made from a qualified pension or profit sharing plan or from a §403(b) annuity, the exclusion applies even though the employee's rights to the benefit were nonforfeitable. See IRC (1954), §101(b)(2)(B).
Prior to 1984, up to $100,000 of a distribution from a qualified plan, from an individual retirement account, or from a simplified employee pension, qualified for an estate tax exclusion. However, §§2039(c), (e)-(g), which provided for the exclusion, have been repealed for persons dying after 1984. See §525 of the Deficit Reduction Act of 1984, Pub L No 98-369, 98 Stat 494 (1984).

[7] IRC (1954), §404. However, a contribution deduction may be used to offset any unrelated business taxable income if the employee participant helped produce the unrelated business taxable income.

[8] IRC (1954), §§401, 410-412. Stock bonus plans are also qualified plans; however, a nonprofit organization would not normally use this type plan. See discussion of qualified plans beginning at §3:14.

[9] IRC (1954), §408. See discussion of the IRA at §3:22.

[10] IRC (1954), §408(k). See discussion of the simplified pension plan at §3:23.

[11] IRC (1954), §403(b). See discussion at §3:24.

[12] Government plans and church plans need not meet the coverage and participation rules of §410 of the Code, the vesting provisions of §411, the funding provisions of §412, and the rules prohibiting the assignment of benefits (§401(a)(13)), and the joint and survivor annuity rules (§401(a)(11)). See §§410(c), 411(e), 412(h), 410(a)(25). In addition, these plans need not

meet the reporting requirements as discussed as §3:19. However, these plans must meet the coverage requirements that were in effect on September 1, 1974. This means that the plan must benefit at least 70% of the employees or that at least 70% of the employees be eligible to benefit under the plan and at least 80% of the eligible employees actually are participating in the plan. Employees who worked less than 20 hours a week can be excluded. Vesting requirements in effect on September 1, 1974, must also be met. Vesting is required when an employee reaches normal retirement age, but early vesting is not required except where a plan terminates or contributions to the plan are discontinued.

Church plans are plans established and maintained by a church or a convention or association exempt from tax under §501 of the Code. It does not include a plan established for the benefit of employees who are employed in connection with an unrelated trade or business. An organization is associated with a church if it shares common religious bonds and convictions with that church. See §414(e)(3)(D); Reg §1.414(e)-1. See Lt Rul 8625073 in which the Service ruled that a hospital that is sponsored and wholly controlled by a religious corporation can have its defined contribution money purchase pension plan qualify as a church plan. See Lt Rul 8645052 in which the Service ruled that a religious community of Roman Catholic women dedicated to education, health care, and social services was an organization described in §414(e)(3); thus, its employee benefit plan qualified as a church plan.

[13] See discussion at §3:23.

§3:14. —Qualified Plans.

A nonprofit organization that is incorporated may establish a qualified §401 plan in the form of a pension plan or a profit-sharing plan.[1] In the past the IRS took the position that nonprofit organizations could not establish §401 plans because nonprofit organizations could not generate profits in the sense required for a profit-sharing plan.[2] However, the IRS has conceded that a nonprofit organization may produce a profit, or an excess of revenues over expenses, without causing it to become a for-profit organization.[3] There is the further problem, though, that a nonprofit, tax exempt organization may not distribute any profits to any individuals. To be tax exempt, no part of the earnings may inure to the benefit of an individual.[4]

However, the position of the IRS currently is that contributions to a pension plan on behalf of the organization's employees are a part of the "reasonable" compensation which nonprofit tax exempt organizations are authorized to pay.[5]

To qualify under §401 of the Code, a plan must be created or organized for the exclusive benefit of the employees or their beneficiaries.[6] The plan must satisfy minimum participation standards,[7] and it may not discriminate in favor of employees who are officers, shareholders, or highly compensated employees.[8] It also must satisfy minimum vesting standards,[9] and the employee's interest in the fund must be distributed within a certain time period.[10] The fund must be established so that it is impossible for any part of the corpus or income to be used for, or diverted to, purposes other than for the exclusive benefit of the employees or beneficiaries.[11] If the plan is a pension plan, forfeitures from the fund may not be used to increase the benefits of any employee.[12] If the plan provides for the payment of benefits in the form of an annuity, it must be a qualified joint and survivor annuity unless the employee elects otherwise.[13] The plan may not be assigned or alienated,[14] and, in the case of a merger or consolidation of the employee corporation, each employee must have the same benefits in the succeeding plan (after the merger or consolidation).[15] A plan must provide that the benefits under the plan will begin not later than the 60th day after the latest of (a) the close of the plan year in which the employee attains the earlier of age 65 or the normal retirement age specified under the plan, (b) the 10th anniversary of the year in which the employee commenced participation in the plan, or (c) the date the employee terminates service with the employer.[16] The plan must be limited in the amount of contributions or benefits for employees.[17] A qualified pension or profit-sharing plan must be a definite written arrangement and must be communicated to the employees.[18] The plan must be established in the form of a trust organized and maintained in the United States,[19] or as a custodial account.[20]

A pension plan is one in which the retirement benefits are measured by factors such as years of service and compensation received by the employee.[21] The determination of the amount of retirement benefits and the annual contributions are not dependent upon profits.[22] Pension plans may be either defined benefit plans or defined contribution plans.

A defined benefit plan provides participants with fixed dollar benefits as specified in the plan.[23] These may be in the form of a flat benefit (a stated dollar amount after a certain number of years' service), a fixed benefit (a percentage of compensation), or a unit benefit (a percentage of compensation multiplied by years' of service).[24] The defined benefit plan provides for a definite amount of retirement benefit; it is not a factor of the amount of contributions plus earnings from the fund. Consequently, the employer must bear the risk of loss in this type of plan. Employer contributions must be determined actuarially on the basis of the definitely determinable benefits.[25]

Example 1: A pension plan provides that contributions are to be made by the employer charity sufficient to provide retirement benefits equal to 2% of the employee's average annual compensation multiplied by the employee's years of service to begin at age 65 and payable for the life of the employee. This is a defined unit benefit plan. If the plan provided for the payment of 20% of the employee's last 5 years of salary, it would be a defined fixed benefit plan. If the plan provided for payments to an employee participant in the amount of $500 per month for life beginning at age 65 for all employees who had performed 10 years of service, the plan would be a defined flat benefit plan.

A money purchase pension plan is a defined contribution plan. A defined contribution plan is one that provides for an individual account for each participant and for benefits based solely on the amount contributed to the participant's account plus earnings from the fund.[26] For a money purchase plan, the benefit must be fixed, without being tied to profits.[27] For example, a money purchase plan may provide for a payment annually of 15% of each employee's compensation.[28]

Defined contribution plans include profit-sharing plans. A profit-sharing plan is a plan established and maintained by an employer to provide for participation in the organization's profits by the employees or their beneficiaries.[29] The plan must provide a definite predetermined formula for allocating the contributions made to the plan among the participants and for distributing the funds accumulated under the plan after a fixed number of years, the attainment of a stated age, or upon the prior occurrence of some event such as layoff, illness, disability, retirement, death, or severance of employment.[30] A formula for allocating the contributions among the participants is definite if, for example, it provides for an allocation in proportion to the basic compensation of each participant.[31]

Example 2: A pension plan provides that the employer contribute 12% of an employee's compensation for the year to the plan fund. This is a defined contribution plan called a money purchase pension plan.

Example 3: A pension plan provides that an employer may contribute up to 15% of annual profits to a retirement plan. This is a defined contribution plan that is profit sharing.

A plan must be permanent.[32] Thus, a profit-sharing plan in which the employer does not contribute for a number of years because the organization has not had a profit may cause the plan not to qualify.[33] While the employer is not required to contribute annually to a profit-sharing plan, contributions must be recurring.[34] Nonetheless, contributions to a profit-sharing plan need not be the same amount each year, nor must they be made in accordance with the same ratio each year.[35]

If a plan meets the requirements of §401 of the Code, it need not be submitted to the IRS for approval. However, the IRS will issue a determination letter as to whether a plan meets the requirements for qualification.[36]

A request for a determination letter as to a defined benefit plan is made by filing Form 5300; Form 5301 is used for a defined contribution plan.[37] Both types of plans must also include Form 5302 to provide the IRS with information about the 25 highest paid plan participants.[38] Before a request for a determination letter is filed with the IRS, all interested parties, i.e., present employees, must be notified of the filing so that they may submit comments to the IRS.[39] The notice must be given at least 7 and not more than 21 days before the request is filed.[40]

An employee may make voluntary nondeductible contributions to a qualified pension or profit-sharing plan in amounts up to 10% of his or her compensation.[41] The earnings from these contributions will be tax-free while they are in the fund.[42]

FOOTNOTES

[1] See IRC (1954), §401(a). A pension plan may be either a defined benefit pension plan or a money purchase pension plan.

For a comprehensive description of qualified plans see Boren Qual Def Comp Plans §§1:05-1:11. For sample plans and related documents see Mancoff & Steinberg Qual Def Comp Plans.

[2] See GCM 35865 (1974). The Tax Reform Act of 1986 amended §401(a) of the Internal Revenue Code so that profits are not required for a profit-sharing plan. Section 401(a), as amended, provides that the determination of whether a plan is a profit sharing plan "shall be made without regard to current or accumulated profits of the employer and without regard to whether the employer is a tax-exempt organization."

See §401(a) (27).

[3] See GCM 38283 (1980).

[4] See IRC (1954), §501(a).

[5] See GCM 35638 (1974), GCM 36918 (1976), GCM 38238 (1980).

126   Representing the Nonprofit Organization

[6] IRC (1954), §401(a).
[7] IRC (1954), §401(a)(3).
[8] IRC (1954), §401(a)(4).
[9] IRC (1954), §401(a)(7).
[10] IRC (1954), §401(a)(9). Generally, the interest must be distributed not later than the taxable year in which the employee attains the age of 70½ or in which he or she retires.
[11] IRC (1954), §401(a)(1).
[12] IRC (1954), §401(a)(8). Forfeitures must be used to reduce employer's contributions under the plan. However, if the plan is a profit-sharing plan, forfeitures may be reallocated to provide benefits for other participants in the plan. See Reg §1.401-7(a).
[13] IRC (1954), §§401(a)(11), 417. A spouse must consent in writing to an election not to take a qualified joint and survivor annuity. See IRC (1954), §417(a)(2).
[14] IRC (1954), §401(a)(13).
[15] IRC (1954), §401(a)(12).
[16] IRC (1954), §401(a)(15).
[17] IRC (1954), §401(a)(17).
[18] Reg §1.401-1(a)(2).
[19] Reg §1.401-1(a)(3).
[20] IRC (1954), §401(f).
[21] Reg §1.401-1(b)(1)(i).
[22] Reg §1.401-1(b)(1)(i).
[23] See IRC (1954), §414(j).
[24] TIR-1403 (1975).
[25] Reg §1.401-1(1(b)(1)(i).
[26] IRC (1954), §414(i).
[27] Reg §1.401-1(b)(1)(i).
[28] IRC (1954), §404(a)(3).
[29] Reg §1.401-1(b)(1)(ii).
[30] Reg §1.401-1(b)(1)(ii).
[31] Reg §1.401-1(b)(1)(ii).
[32] Reg §1.401-1(b)(2).
[33] Reg §1.401-1(b)(3).
[34] Reg §1.401-1(b)(2).
[35] Reg §1.401-1(b)(2).

[36] See Rev Proc 80-30, 1980-1 CB 685.
[37] Rev Proc 80-30, 1980-1 CB 685; Rev Proc 84-23, 1984-12 IRB 11.
[38] Rev Proc 80-30, 1980-1 CB 685, 688.
[39] IRC (1954), §7476(b)(2).
[40] See Rev Proc 80-30, 1980-1 CB 685. The notice must give a brief description of the plan, identifying the class of parties to whom the notice is addressed, a description of the class of employees eligible to participate, whether or not the IRS has issued a previous determination as to the qualified status of the plan, a statement that any person to whom the notice is addressed may submit comments to the IRS, the dates by which the comments must be received, the numbers of interested parties needed in order for the Department of Labor to comment, and a description of a reasonable procedure by which additional informational material will be available to interested parties. A sample notice is included in Rev Rul 80-30, 1980-1 CB 685, 697.

The IRS has provided a model money purchase plan and a model profit-sharing plan that would automatically qualify under §401 of the Code. These were Forms 5612, 5613, 5614, 5615. However, because of the many changes in the requirements relating to qualified plans in recent years, these model plans are now obsolete.

[41] See Rev Rul 80-350, 1980-2 CB 133. The 10% is applied on an annual basis. An employee can make up an underpayment in a succeeding year. The limitation is 10% of aggregate compensation for all years since the employee became a participant in the plan.

[42] They are tax-free because the fund is tax exempt. See IRC (1954), § 501(a).

§3:15. ——Participation and Vesting Requirements.

Not all employees are required to be covered by a qualified plan. Employees that have not attained the age of 21 or that have not completed one year of service (whichever occurs later) can be excluded.[1] A defined benefit plan may exclude any employees hired within 5 years before normal retirement age.[2] An educational institution that provides for 100% vesting after one year of service may exclude persons under the age of 26.[3] A plan that provides for 100% vesting after 3 years of service may exclude employees with less than 3 years of service.[4]

A year of service means a 12-month period during which the employee has worked 1,000 hours.[5] An employee must be eligible to join the plan no later than the earlier of the first day of the first plan year beginning after the date on which the employee satisfied the minimum age and service requirements, or 6 months after the date on which he or she satisfied the requirements, unless the employee was separated from service before one of these dates.[6] All years of service with the employer are counted in computing the period of service unless the employee has had a 1-year break in service.[7] A break in service occurs when the employee fails to complete more than 500 hours of service during a consecutive 12-month period.[8] If an employee has a break in service, the employer may disregard all prior years of service (before the break in service) until the employee has again completed a year of service.[9] In determining the 3 years of service for the 3-year 100% vesting schedule, any time earned before a break in service need not be considered.[10]

At least 70% of the employees that cannot be excluded as noted above must either be covered by the plan, or in the alternative, be eligible to participate in the plan with 80% of the eligible employees being participants.[11] If these tests cannot be met, the plan can still be qualified if the IRS finds that the plan requirements do not discriminate in favor of officers, shareholders, or highly compensated employees.[12]

For plan years beginning after December 31, 1988, the coverage rules are modified. After this date, qualified plans must meet one of three coverage tests: (a) at least 70% of all nonhighly compensated employees must be covered, (b) the percentage of nonhighly compensated employees covered by the plan must be at least 70% of the percentage of highly compensated employees covered by the plan, or (c) the plan must satisfy an average benefit percentage test.[13] The average benefit percentage test is met if the plan benefits employees who qualify under a classification set up by the employer which is found by the Internal Revenue Service not to be discriminatory in favor of highly compensated employees and if the average benefit percentage for nonhighly compensated employees is at least 70% of the average benefit percentage for highly compensated employees.[14] Qualified plans must also meet a minimum participation requirement. A plan must benefit at least the lesser of (a) 50 employees or (b) 40% or more of all employees.[15]

An employee's benefits in a qualified plan must vest according to one of the three following vesting schedules: (a) 10-year vesting, (b) 5- to 15-year vesting, or (c) rule of 45.[16] The 10-year vesting schedule provides that an employee who has at least 10 years of service must have a nonforfeitable right to 100% of his or her accrued benefits derived from employer contributions.[17] The 5- to 15-year vesting schedule provides that an employee who has completed at least 5 years of service must have a nonforfeitable right to 25% of his accrued benefits derived from employer contributions, with an additional 5% for every additional year of service up to 10 years and an additional 10% for every year of service after 10 years.[18] Under this schedule the employee would be 100% vested at 15 years of service.[19] The rule of 45 provides that an employee who has completed at least 5 years of service and whose age and years of service equals or exceeds 45 must have a nonforfeitable right to 50% of the accrued benefits derived from employer contributions.[20] When the employee has completed 6 years of service and his age and years of service equals or exceeds 47, the employee will have a nonforfeitable right to 60% of the accrued benefits.[21] The percentage increases 10 points for each additional year of service and as the age and years of service increase by 2, until the employee will be 100% vested when the years of service equal or exceed 20 and the sum of the employee's age and service equals or exceeds 55.[22] An alternative vesting schedule may be used, in addition to the three above, if the schedule provides a percentage of vested rights that is not less than the percentage that would be provided under one of the three schedules discussed above.[23]

Vesting is accelerated for plan years beginning after December 31, 1988. Pursuant to the Tax Reform Act of 1986, a participant's benefits must vest at least as rapidly as under one of two alternative minimum vesting schedules. A participant must either have a nonforfeitable right to 100% of the participant's accrued benefits derived from employer contributions upon the completion of 5 years of service or must be 20% vested after 3 years of service with an additional 20% vesting for each succeeding year of service thereafter so that there will be 100% vesting upon the completion of 7 years of service.[24]

If a plan is deemed to be "top-heavy," more rapid vesting is required.[25] A top-heavy plan is, in the case of a defined benefit plan, one in which the present value of the cumulative accrued benefits under the plan applicable to key employees exceeds 60% of the present value of the total cumulative accrued benefits,[26] and, in the case of a defined contribution plan, one in which the accounts for key employees exceeds 60% of all accounts under the plan.[27] For a top-heavy plan, there must be 100% vesting after 3 years of service or 20% vesting after 2 years of service with an additional 20% for each additional year of service so that the employees will be 200% vested after 6 years of service.[28]

FOOTNOTES

[1] IRC (1954), §410(a)(1)(A). For plan years before 1984, the age limitation was age 25.

[1]RC (1954), §410(a)(2)(A).

[3] IRC (1954), §410(a)(1)(B)(ii). For plan years before 1984, the age limitation was age 30.

[4] IRC (1954), §410(a)(1)(B)(i).

[5] IRC (1954), §410(a)(3)(B).
[6] IRC (1954), §410(a)(4)(B).
[7] IRC (1954), §410(a)(5)(B).
[8] IRC (1954), §411(a)(5)(A).
[9] IRC (1954), §410(a)(5)(B).
[10] IRC (1954), §410(a)(5)(B).
[11] IRC (1954), §410(b)(1)(A).
[12] IRC (1954), §410(b)(1)(B).
[13] IRC (1986), §410(b)(1).
[14] IRC (1986), §410(b)(2).
[15] IRC (1986), §401(a)(26).
[16] IRC (1954), §411(a)(2).
[17] IRC (1954), §411(a)(2)(A).
[18] IRC (1954), §411(a)(2)(B).
See Boren Qual Def Comp Plans §3:14.
[19] IRC (1954), §411(a)(2)(B).
See Boren Qual Def Comp Plans §3:15.
[20] IRC (1954), §411(a)(2)(C).
[21] IRC (1954), §411(a)(2)(C).
[22] IRC (1954), §411(a)(2)(C).
[23] TIR 1334 (1975).
[24] IRC (1986), §411(a)(2).
[25] See IRC (1954), §416(a).
[26] IRC (1954), §416(g).
[27] IRC (1954), §416(g).
See Boren Qual Def Comp Plans §3:25.
[28] IRC (1954), §416(b).
Boren Qual Def Comp Plans §3:26.

§3:16. ——Funding of Qualified Plans.

Qualified plans, except profit-sharing plans,[1] must meet funding requirements as set out in §412 of the Code.[2] A plan satisfies the funding requirements if it does not have an "accumulated funding deficiency."[3] A qualified plan must maintain a funding standard account which reflects charges for contributions required under the plan and credits for amounts contributed.[4] For money purchase plans under a defined contribution plan, the amount of funding required is simple to compute; it is the amount required by the plan (10% of each participant's compensation, for example). For a defined benefit plan, however, costs, liabilities, rates of interest, and other factors under the plan must be determined on the basis of actuarial assumptions and reasonable methods which, in combination, offer the actuary's best estimate of anticipated experience under the plan.[5] An actuary determines the amount of funding necessary for a defined benefit plan.[6]

If a plan does not satisfy the minimum funding requirements, an initial penalty tax of 5% of the accumulated funding deficiency is imposed on the employer.[7] If the employer does not correct the deficiency within the earlier of the dates of the mailing of a notice of deficiency with respect to the initial tax or the date on which the initial tax is assessed, an additional penalty of 100% of the accumulated funding deficiency is imposed.[8]

The IRS may waive the minimum funding requirements for a year in which there would be substantial business hardship; however, the minimum funding requirements may not be waived for more than 5 of any 15 consecutive plan years.[9]

FOOTNOTES

[1] IRC (1954), §412(h)(1). Stock bonus plans are also excluded from funding requirements; however, nonprofit organizations would seldom, if ever, use such a plan.

[2] IRC (1954), §412(a).

For a comprehensive discussion of funding standards, see Boren Qual Def Comp Plans ch 9.

[3] IRC (1954), §412(a)(2).

[4] IRC (1954), §412(b); Reg §1.412(b)-1.

[5] IRC (1954), §412(c).

[6] See Reg §301.6059-1(d).
[7] IRC (1954), §4971(a).
[8] IRC (1954), §4971(b).
[9] IRC (1954), §412(d).

§3:17. —Limitations on Contributions.

A plan will not be a qualified plan under §401 of the Code if it provides for benefits or contributions in excess of those specified in §415 of the Code.[1] For defined benefit plans, the limitation is placed upon the benefits provided the employee. These cannot exceed the lesser of $90,000 or 100% of the participant's average compensation for the highest 3 consecutive years during which the employee was an active participant in the plan.[2] The $90,000 will be adjusted for cost of living beginning in 1986.[3] For defined contribution plans, the contribution may not exceed the lesser of $30,000 or 25% of the participant's compensation.[4] The $30,000 will also be adjusted for cost of living beginning in 1986.[5]

The maximum deduction an employer may take for contributions to a profit-sharing plan is 15% of the compensation of plan participants.[6] However, if a profit-sharing plan is combined with a pension plan, the 15% is increased to 25%.[7]

FOOTNOTES

[1] See IRC (1954), §415(a).
For a comprehensive discussion of limitations on contributions under IRC §415, see Boren Qual Def Comp Plans ch 12.
[2] IRC (1954), §415(b).
[3] IRC (1954), §415(d).
[4] IRC (1954), §415(c).
[5] IRC (1954), §415(d).

[6] IRC (1954), §404(a)(3).
[7] IRC (1954), §404(a)(7).

§3:18. —Integration with Social Security.

Qualified plans may not discriminate in favor of employees who are officers, shareholders, or highly compensated employees;[1] however, a plan that excludes employees whose compensation is covered by social security or that integrates a qualified plan with social security is not, because of that fact, discriminatory.[2] A plan is integrated that provides for different contributions or benefits based on that part of compensation which is excluded from social security coverage under the Federal Insurance Contributions Act (FICA).[3] The plan can be discriminatory if the discrimination is based upon proportionately greater benefits for employees earning above a specified salary amount. The proportionate differences in benefits which result from the integration must be offset by social security benefits which are provided by employer contributions, on behalf of its employees, to social security.[4] A classification system is not discriminatory where the integration level applicable to an employee is the employee's covered compensation.[5] For plan years beginning after December 31, 1988, a minimum contribution is required with respect to earnings below the social security wage base.[6] As a result, the integrated benefit will generally be limited to 50% of the nonintegrated benefit.[7]

The amount of contributions which may be considered as attributable to employer contributions is the covered compensation under the social security act times the tax rate applicable to employers for social security purposes.[8] Before 1984, this could not exceed 7%.[9] For 1984 to 1987, the rate is 5.7%.[10]

Example: X, a nonprofit organization has established a qualified money purchase plan for its employees. It contributes 15% compensation annually to the fund, but has chosen to integrate the plan with social security. X has three employees, with total compensation of $100,000, as follows: A, $60,000, B, $30,000, and C, $10,000. Thus, X would contribute $15,000 to the pension plan in 1984. For 1984, taxable wages in excess of $37,800 were not subject to social security taxes. The excess salaries over $37,800 would be multiplied by 5.7%. Only contributions in excess of this amount, or $13,735 ($15,000—$1,265) would be probated among the employees. The pro rata allocation would be based upon the ratios of each individual salary to total salaries, or 60% for A, 30% for B, and 10% for C. The $15,000 contribution would be prorated among the three employees as follows:

Employee	Salary	FICA Pay	Excess	Excess × 5.7%	Remainder Pro Rata	Total Allocation	% of Pay
A	$ 60,000	$37,800	$22,000	$1,265	$ 8,241	$ 9,506	15.8
B	30,000	37,800	0	0	4,120	4,120	13.7
C	10,000	37,800	0	0	1,374	1,374	13.7
	$100,000			$1,265	$13,735	$15,000	

FOOTNOTES

[1] IRC (1954), §401(a)(5).

[2] IRC (1954), §401(a)(5).

[3] See Reg §1.401-3(e)(1). The Federal Insurance Contributions Act is Chapter 21 of the Internal Revenue Code.

For an in-depth discussion of integrating plan contributions with social security, see Boren Qual Def Comp Plans ch 6.

[4] Reg §1.401-3(e)(1).

[5] Reg §1.401-3(e)(2)(ii). See IRC (1954), §401(l).

[6] IRC (1986), §401(l).

[7] IRC (1986), §401(l).

[8] See Rev Rul 71-446, 1971-2 CB 187, 194.

[9] See Rev Rul 71-446, 1971-2 CB 187, 194.

[10] IRC (1954), §3111(a).

§3:19. ——Reporting Requirements for Qualified Plans.

A nonprofit organization that maintains a qualified plan under §401 of the Code must file an annual return providing information to the IRS concerning the qualification, financial condition, and operation of the plan.[1] For a defined benefit plan, a report by an actuary must also be submitted.[2] The actuarial report must contain a description of the funding method and the actuarial assumptions used to determine costs under the plan, as well as a certification of the contribution necessary to eliminate any accumulated funding deficiency.[3] A defined benefit plan must also file Form PBGC-1 with the Pension Benefit Guaranty Corporation and make a premium insurance payment each year to guarantee, within certain limits, that there are sufficient assets in the plan to pay plan benefits.[4]

Annual reports must be filed with the IRS for all types of qualified plans on either Form 5500 (for plans with at least 100 participants) or Form 5500-C (for plans with fewer than 100 participants).[5] Plans with fewer than 100 participants may file a registration statement, Form 5500-R, and only file Form 5500-C every 3 years.[6] If the plan is funded by an insurance company, Schedule A must be attached to the annual return.[7] Schedule B (containing actuarial information) must be included for defined benefit plans subject to the minimum funding requirements.[8] For any employees who have vested benefits and who are no longer working for the employer, Form SSA must be filed.[9]

A copy of the plan must be furnished to each participant of the plan within 90 days after the employee becomes a participant, and within 120 days after the end of the year.[10]

FOOTNOTES

[1] IRC (1954), §6058(a). Defined benefit plans and defined contribution plans providing medical benefits, or benefits in the event of sickness, acci-

OFFICERS AND EMPLOYEES   137

dent, disability, death or unemployment or vacation benefits must also file annual reports with the Secretary of Labor. The annual report must contain financial statements regarding the plan prepared by independent qualified public accountants. See 29 CFR §2520.103-1(b). The Secretary may waive the requirement of examination and report of an independent qualified public accountant for employee benefit plans with fewer than 100 participants. See 29 CFR §2520.104-46.

Reports required to be filed with the Secretary of Labor should be mailed to Pension and Welfare Benefit Programs. United States Department of Labor, 200 Constitution Avenue NW, Washington, D.C. 20216.

See IRS Pub 1048 (Jan. 83) for filing requirements for employee benefit plans.

[2] IRC (1954), §6059(a).

[3] IRC (1954), §6059(b).

[4] See copy of Form PBGC-1. This is not required for defined contribution plans because these plans do not guarantee any benefits.

[5] See Reg §301.6058-1(a)(1).

[6] 29 CFR §2520.103-2(c).
See copies of Forms 5500, 5500-C, 5500-R.

[7] See 29 CFR §2520.103-2(b).

[8] Reg §301.6059-1(a).

[9] Reg §301.6057-1(a)(4).

[10] See 29 CFR §2520.104b-2.

§3:20.   ——Plan Termination.

Before a qualified plan is terminated, certain requirements must be met or the plan may become disqualified from its inception.[1] A plan must be permanent in order to qualify under §401 of the Code; consequently, termination without a valid reason may cause the plan to be disqualified from its inception on the grounds that it was not intended to be permanent.[2]

A plan may be terminated for a sound business reason, such as financial problems of the employer.[3] A plan may also be discontinued even though there is no business necessity for its

138 Representing the Nonprofit Organization

termination so long as the termination is nondiscriminatory and there is no evidence of bad faith.[4] A plan may continue even though the employer is no longer in existence.[5] Even though the employer would no longer be making contributions to the plan, the fund would continue in existence until all benefits have been paid the participants.[6]

Upon termination of a plan, all participants must become 100% vested in their accrued benefits to the extent funded.[7]

The IRS must be notified of the termination of a qualified plan.[8] An employer may request a determination letter from the IRS concerning termination of a plan.[9] Form 5310 is used for this purpose. If a plan must file with the Department of Labor, a copy of a letter of sufficiency of assets from the Pension Benefit Guaranty Corporation (PBGC) must be attached to Form 5310.[10]

FOOTNOTES

[1] See Rev Rul 66-151, 1966-2 CB 121.

For a comprehensive discussion of plan terminations see Boren Qual Def Comp Plans ch 17.

[2] See Reg §1.401.

[3] See Rev Rul 69-25, 1969-1 CB 113.

[4] See Rev Rul 72-239, 1971-1 CB 107.

[5] See Rev Rul 69-157, 1969-1 CB 115.

[6] Rev Rul 69-157, 1969-1 CB 115.

[7] IRC (1954), §411(d)(3).

[8] IRC (1954), §6057(b).

[9] See Rev Rul 80-30, 1980-1 CB 685.

[10] See Rev Rul 80-30, 1980-1 CB 685. See also 29 CFR §2617.3.

See copy of a letter of sufficiency in Mancoff & Steinberg Qual Def Comp Plans §8:15. If the letter of sufficiency of assets is not attached, the IRS will not process the termination unless the applicant requests in writing that the application be processed without PBGC action. To secure a letter of sufficiency of assets, write Administrator of Pension and Welfare Benefit Programs, United States Department of Labor, 200 Constitution Avenue NW, Washington, D.C. 20216.

Form 5310 can be used as a single form for both the IRS and the PBGC upon termination of a plan. The form can be filed in duplicate with the IRS and the PBGC, or it may be filed separately. See Rev Proc 83-14, 1983-1 CB 675.

The annual premium required to be paid by employers with defined benefit plans (paid with the annual filing of Form PBGC-1) provides termination insurance for these plans. The PBGC must be notified at least 10 days prior to termination of a plan.

§3:21. ——Taxation of Benefits.

An employee is not taxed on benefits from a qualified plan until the benefits are received.[1] Payments from a qualified plan may be in the form of lump sum distributions or they may be in the form of an annuity payable in a stated definite amount over a stated number of years or for life. If the payments are made other than in a lump sum distribution, they are taxed pursuant to §72 of the Code in the same manner as an annuity.[2] If the employee made no contributions, the entire amount would be taxable. If the employee made contributions to the plan, these contributions would be the employee's investment in the contract. A percentage of the payments (computed by dividing the employee's investment by the total expected benefits from the plan to the employee) would be excluded from taxable income.[3] If the employee will recover the amount of his own contributions within 3 years, the employee may exclude all payments from income until he recovers his contributions.[4] The excess will be taxed in full.[5]

For annuities whose starting date is after July 1, 1986, the 3-year recovery provision is repealed.[6] Any distributions received after December 31, 1986, will be subject to a pro rata recovery of employee contributions.[7]

If an employee receives a lump-sum distribution within one tax year from a qualified plan, the payment qualifies for a special 10-year averaging tax.[8]

The 10-year averaging tax has been replaced with a one time election to use 5-year averaging for a lump-sum distribution, for taxable years beginning after December 31, 1986.[9] The tax is computed by reducing the amount distributed by a minimum distribution allowance (which is the lesser of $10,000 or one-half of the total amount, reduced by 20% of the amount by which the total amount exceeds $20,000) and dividing by 10.[10] This amount is then increased by the zero bracket amount for a single taxpayer ($2,300).[11] Tax is computed on the remaining amount using the tax table for single taxpayers. The tax so computed is then multiplied by 10. This tax is added to the regular tax on other income of the participant in that year. Form 4972 is used to calculate the tax.[12] For a lump-sum distribution paid by reason of death, $5,000 of the amount may be excluded as a death benefit under §101(b) of the Code.[13]

Example: In 1985, A receives a lump-sum distribution in the amount of $100,000, from a qualified plan established by X Charity in 1980. The distribution would be taxed as follows:

Total distribution	$100,000
Less Employee Contributions	5,000
Taxable Amount	95,000
Less: Minimum Distribution Allowance (lesser of $10,000 of ½ of $95,000) minus 20% of $95,000) − 20,000) ($10,000 minus 20% of $75,000 provides no reduction)	0
	$95,000
Divide $95,000 by 10	9,500
Add zero bracket amount	2,300
	$11,800
Tax using rates for single individuals	$1,383
Multiply by 10	$13,830

The tax of $13,830 would be added to the A's tax on other income computed in the regular manner, but excluding the lump-sum distribution. Tax on the lump-sum distribution is only 14.5% of the total distribution less the employee's contributions. (If A's beneficiaries had received the distribution as a result of A's death, an additional $5,000 could be excluded from the taxable amount; only $90,000 would then be subject to tax.)

A lump-sum distribution from a qualified plan will not be included in taxable income for the year if the amount is rolled over into an individual retirement account, an annuity plan under §403(a), or another qualified plan, within 60 days of receipt.[14] However, the amount of any employee contributions cannot be rolled over.[15]

A loan to the employee or plan participant from a qualified plan is treated as a distribution from the plan and subject to tax unless the loan does not exceed the lesser of (a) $50,000 or (b) the greater of ½ of the present value of the employee's nonforfeitable accrued benefits under the plan, or $10,000, and is repaid within 5 years.[16] For loans made, renewed, renegotiated, modified, or extended after December 31, 1986, the $50,000 limitation on the amount of the loan is reduced by the highest outstanding balance of loans from the plan during the prior one-year period.[17] If the loan is made to a key employee or is secured by §403(b) annuities, no deduction is permitted for interest paid on the loans.[18] A pledge of the participant's interest in the plan is considered to be a loan for these purposes.[19] (The 5-year repayment requirement does not apply to home loans.)[20] The 5-year repayment exception only applies to a loan made to acquire a home that is the principal residence of the participant for a loan made, renewed, renegotiated, modified, or extended after December 31, 1986.[21] If funds are withdrawn from a qualified plan before death or disability or before the participant reaches age 59½, there is a 10% penalty tax on the withdrawal for distribu-

142 Representing the Nonprofit Organization

tions after December 31, 1986.[22] However, the penalty tax is not applicable if distributions are made in the form of an annuity payable over the life of the participant, are made after the participant has attained age 55 and has satisfied the conditions for early retirement, or are used for payment of medical expenses.[23] There is a new excise tax of 15% on distributions in excess of $112,500, reduced by any payment of the 10% penalty tax.[24] Once the participant has attained the age of 70½, any amounts required to be distributed that are not distributed will be subject to a penalty tax of 50% of the undistributed amount.[25]

FOOTNOTES

[1] IRC (1954), §§402 and 403.

For a comprehensive discussion of taxation of benefits see Boren Qual Def Comp Plans §5:21.

[2] See IRC (1954), §402(a).

[3] IRC (1954), §72(b).

[4] IRC (1954), §72(d).

[5] See IRC (1954), §402(e)(1).

[6] IRC (1954), §72(d) has been repealed by the Tax Reform Act of 1986, §1122(c).

[7] IRC (1986), §72(b) as amended.

[8] IRC (1954), §402(e)(1). The portion of any lump-sum distribution allocable to contributions made before 1974 qualify for capital-gain treatment. See IRC (1954), §§402(a)(2), 403(a)(2).

[9] IRC (1986), §402(e). Capital gain treatment that was available for the pre-1974 portion of a lump sum distribution is phased out over a 5-year period.

[10] IRC (1954), §402(e)(1)(C).

[11] IRC (1954), §402(e)(1)(C).

[13] See IRC (1954), §101(b).

[14] IRC (1954), §402(a)(5). See discussion of individual retirement accounts at §3:22.

[15] IRC (1954), §402(a)(5)(B).

[16] IRC (1954), §72(p).
[17] IRC (1986), §72(p)(2)(A).
[18] IRC (1986), §72(p)(3).
[19] IRC (1954), §72(p)(1)(B).
[20] IRC (1954), §72(p)(2)(B)ii).
[21] IRC (1986), §72(p)(2)(B)(ii).
[22] IRC (1986), §72(t)(1).
[23] IRC (1986), §72(t)(2).
[24] IRC (1986), §4981A.
[25] IRC (1986), §4974(a). This provision does not apply to individuals who attained age 70½ before January 1, 1988.

§3:22. —Individual Retirement Accounts.

Employees can be encouraged to establish their own retirement accounts. An individual may create an individual retirement account through tax deductible contributions of up to $2,000 annually (or $2,250 for married filing jointly if spouse is included).[1] The amount deductible for contributions to an individual retirement account is the lesser of $2,000 or 100% of the individual's compensation for the year.[2] However, for a married individual filing a joint return, the deduction is increased to the lesser of $2,250 or 100% of compensation.[3] This assumes the spouse is not working; if the spouse is working, the spouse would also qualify for the lesser of $2,000 or 100% of compensation deduction.

Earnings of an individual retirement account are not taxed until they are received by the beneficiary of the account.[4] Distributions from an individual retirement account are taxed in full; lump-sum distributions are not subject to the 5-year averaging provisions.[5]

Beginning in 1987, contributions to individual retirement accounts will no longer be deductible for taxpayers covered by a qualified plan (or whose spouse is so covered) if those taxpayers have adjusted gross income of $50,000 on a joint return or $35,000 on a single return.[6] For taxpayers with adjusted gross income between $40,000 and $50,000 on a joint return and between $25,000 and $35,000 on a single return, there is a phase-out of the amount that may be deducted.[7] For taxpayers with adjusted gross income between these amounts, the deduction limit is determined as follows: $2,000 is multiplied by a fraction, the numerator of which is the taxpayer's adjusted gross income, less $40,000 for a joint return and less $25,000 for a single return, and the denominator of which is $10,000. The product is subtracted from $2,000.[8] The deductible amount is rounded to the next lowest $10.[9] The deduction will not be less than $200 until the deduction is completely phased out (at adjusted gross income of $50,000 for a joint return and $35,000 for a single return.)[10]

Assume a taxpayer and spouse are covered by a qualified plan. Their adjusted gross income is $46,000 and they file a joint return. The maximum deduction they can claim for a contribution to an individual retirement account would be $800, computed as follows: $2,000 − [($46,000 − $40,000/$10,000) × $2,000].

Assume a single individual covered by a qualified plan has adjusted gross income of $29,000. The maximum deduction would be $1,200, computed as follows: $2,000 − [($29,000 − $25,000/$10,000) × $2,000]. Assume the single individual's adjusted gross income is $34,500. While the computation would cause the maximum deduction to be $100, computed as follows: $2,000 − [($34,500 − $25,000/$10,000) × $2,000] the deduction will be $200 as there is no deduction below $200 until the deduction is completely phased out.

The spousal deduction of $2,250 is reduced in the same proportions as noted above.[11]

A taxpayer may make nondeductible contributions to individual retirement accounts beginning in 1987 to the extent the deduction is reduced by the phase-out provisions.[12] However, the total combined contributions, deductible and nondeductible, may not exceed $2,000 (or $2,250 for a spousal account).[13] For example, if a taxpayer's deduction to an individual retirement account is limited to $800 in a taxable year, he could contribute a nondeductible amount of $1,200 (or $1,450 for a spousal account). Earnings on the additional nondeductible contributions will not be taxed until withdrawn.[14]

If an individual withdraws an amount from an individual retirement account and that individual has previously made both deductible and nondeductible contributions, the amount included in taxable income as to the withdrawal will be the amount withdrawn multiplied by a fraction, the numerator of which is the individual nondeductible contributions and the denominator of which is the balance of all individual retirement accounts of the individual.[15]

Excess contributions (above the amount permitted as a tax deduction) are subject to a penalty tax of 6%.[16] In addition, if amounts are withdrawn from an individual retirement account before the owner reaches the age of $59\frac{1}{2}$ (except in the case of disability), there is a penalty tax of 10% of the amount of the premature distribution.[17] For distributions made after December 31, 1986, there is a new excise tax of 15% on distributions in excess of $112,500. The tax is reduced by any payment of the 10% penalty tax on early withdrawals.[18] The distribution must also be included in the recipient's taxable income for the year.[19]

To establish an individual retirement account, Form 5305 or Form 5305–A is executed; contributions are deposited with a bank or savings and loan association.[20] Contributions are deductible if they are made by the date for filing the income tax return.[21] Deductions are not allowed, once the individual has attained the age of $70\frac{1}{2}$ before the close of the individual's taxable year.[22]

Distributions from individual retirement accounts must

begin at age 70½. Distributions must commence no later than April 1 of the calendar year following the year in which the owner attains age 70½ regardless of whether the owner has retired.[23] For failure to make the minimum required distribution at age 70½, there is a 50% penalty tax on the amount that should have been distributed less the amount actually distributed.[24]

An individual may not borrow any money on an individual retirement account.[25] In addition, if an individual uses any portion of the account as security for a loan, that portion is treated as being distributed to the individual.[26]

FOOTNOTES

[1] IRC (1954), §408(a)(1).
See IRS Pub 590 (Nov. 83) for detailed discussion of individual retirement arrangements.
[2] IRC (1954), §219(b).
[3] IRC (1954), §219(c).
[4] IRC (1954), §408(e).
[5] IRC (1954), §408(d)(1).
[6] IRC (1986), §219(g)(3).
[7] IRC (1986), §219(g)(2).
[8] IRC (1986), §219(g)(2).
[9] IRC (1986), §219(g)(2)(C).
[10] IRC (1986), §219(g)(2)(B).
[11] IRC (1986), §219(g)(1).
[12] IRC (1986), §408(o).
[13] IRC (1986), §408(o)(2)(B).
[14] IRC (1986), §408(e).
[15] IRC (1986), §408(d)(1) and (o)(4).
[16] IRC (1954), §4973(a).
[17] IRC (1954), §408(f).
[18] IRC (1986), §4981A.

[19] IRC (1954), §408(d).
[20] See Forms 5305, 5305A.
[21] IRC (1954), §219(f)(3).
[22] IRC (1954), §219(d).
[23] IRC (1986), §§408(a)(6) and 408(b)(3).
[24] IRC (1986), §§4974(a).
[25] IRC (1954), §408(e)(3).
[26] IRC (1954), §408(e)(4).

§3:23. —Simplified Employee Pension

Those nonprofit organizations that do not want to be subjected to the many reporting requirements regarding qualified plans under §401 of the Code but nonetheless want to establish a retirement plan for their employees may set up a form of an individual retirement account, called a simplified employee pension.[1] A nonprofit organization need not be incorporated to establish a simplified employee pension arrangement. When the simplified employee pension procedure is utilized, the employer makes contributions directly to the individual plan of its employees.[2] Beginning in 1984, an employer may contribute the lesser of 15% of the employee's compensation or $30,000.[3] The simplified employee pension is defined as a defined contribution plan.[4] Such a plan is subject to some of the restrictions applicable to qualified plans, such as age and period of service requirements, nondiscrimination and top-heavy provisions.[5]

A simplified employee pension plan is established with a bank or savings and loan association using Form 5305-SEP as an agreement to provide benefits to all employees.[6] A copy of this form must be given to each participant in the plan.[7] Beginning in 1987, an employer must include each employee who has attained age 21, has performed services for the employer during at least three of the immediately preceding five years, and has received at least $300 in compensation from the employer for the year.[8] Contributions may not discriminate in favor of highly compensated employees, officers of the organization, or shareholders.[9] Further, there can be no prohibition imposed by the employer on withdrawals by the employee nor may employer contributions be conditioned on the retention in the pension of any portion of the amount contributed.[10] Employer contributions must be determined under a definite written allocation formula which specifies the requirements which an employee must satisfy to share in an allocation and the manner in which the amount allocated is computed.[11] A simplified employee pension plan may be integrated with social security taxes so that the employer payment of social security taxes on the employee's salary is considered an employer contribution under the simplified employee pension plan.[12]

Beginning in 1987, employees may elect to have contributions made to simplified employee pensions on their behalf or to receive the contributions in cash without causing the amounts contributed to the simplified employee pension to be deemed to have been received.[13] Elective deferrals under simplified employee pensions are treated as other qualified cash or deferral arrangements; thus, there is a $7,000 limitation on any such cash deferrals.[14] The election to have contributions made to a simplified employee pension or to receive the amounts in cash is available only if the employer has 25 or fewer employees and if the election is available to all employees and at least 50% of the employees elect to have amounts contributed to a simplified employee pension.[15]

Integration with social security is subject to the nondiscrimination rules applicable to qualified plans.

A participant in a simplified pension plan must include the payments to the fund as income; however, the participant is allowed a deduction in determining his or her adjusted gross income for contributions to the plan equal to the lesser of 15% of compensation or the amount contributed by the employer, up to $30,000.[16] Distributions from the fund are treated in the same manner as an individual retirement account. Like the individual retirement account, a participant is subject to a penalty tax of 6% for excess contributions and a 10% penalty for premature withdrawals (before age 59$^{1}/_{2}$).[17]

An employee that is a participant in a simplified employee pension established by his employer may also establish an individual retirement account subject to the limitations as noted in §5:22.[18]

For tax years beginning in 1987, an employee that is a participant in a simplified employee pension established by his employer may not establish an individual retirement account if his or her adjusted gross income exceeds $50,000 on a joint return or $35,000 on a single return.[19] For taxpapers with adjusted gross income between $40,000 and $50,000 on a joint return and between $25,000 and $35,000 on a single return, there is a phase-out of the amount that may be deducted.[20]

The advantage of the simplified employee pension is its simplicity. An employer may establish an account for its employees at a bank or savings and loan association and not be subject to the annual reporting and disclosure problems applicable to a qualified plan.[21] The disadvantages of the plan are that all employees above the age of 25 who have 3 years of service must be included in the plan[22] (recall that qualified plans need only include 70% of covered employees[23]) and that all covered employees are 100% vested in any contributions made by the employer on their behalf. (Recall that there is no immediate vesting in employer contributions to a qualified plan.[24]) However, the fact that qualified plans under §401 that are top-heavy must provide more rapid vesting makes the latter requirement less of a disadvantage for the simplified employee pension plans.[25]

FOOTNOTES

[1] IRC (1954), §408(k). For an in-depth discussion of simplified employee pension plans (SEPs). See Boren Qual Def Comp Plans §§18:10–18:15.

[2] IRC (1954), §408(k).

[3] IRC (1954), §408(j). See also IRC (1954), §415(c)(1)(A).

[4] IRC (1954), §416(i)(6).

[5] See IRC (1954), §§408, 416(i)(6).

[6] See Form 5305-SEP.

[7] Reg §1.408–9(b). See also 29 CFR §12520.104–48, which prescribes disclosure requirements to participants in a simplified pension plan if the plan is created without proper use of Form 5305-SEP.

[8] IRC (1954), §408(k)(2).

[9] IRC (1954), §408(k)(3).

[10] IRC (1954), §408(k)(4).

[11] IRC (1954), §408(k)(5).

[12] IRC (1954), §408(k)(3)D). See example of integration of a pension plan with social security at §3:18.

[13] IRC (1986), §408(k)(6).

[14] IRC (1986), §408(k)(6)(C).

[15] IRC (1986), §408(k)(6)(A) and (B).

[16] IRC (1954), §219(b)(2). Before 1985, the limitation was the lesser of 15% of compensation up to $15,000.

[17] See discussion at §3:22.

[18] See IRC (1954), §§4973(a), 408(f).

[19] IRC (1986), §219(g)(5)(A)(v).

[20] IRC (1986), §219(g)(2).

[21] See reporting and disclosure problems of qualified plans discussed at §3:19.

[22] See IRC (1954), §408(k)(2).

[23] See discussion at §3:15.

[24] See vesting requirements of qualified plans at §3:15.

[25] See discussion at §3:15. For a top-heavy plan, there must be 100% vesting after 3 years of service or vesting based on a 20% per year basis after 2 years of service so that there would be 100% vesting after 6 years.

§3:24. —Tax-Sheltered Annuities for Employees of §501(c)(3) Organizations.

Section 501(c)(3) organizations may purchase annuity contracts that are not a part of a qualified employee annuity plan[1] for their employees pursuant to §403(b) of the Code; the employee will not be taxed on all or a part of the employer contributions.[2] Tax on the annuity will be deferred until the employee receives payments from the annuity.[3]

The employee may exclude from taxable income for the year up to 20% of included compensation multiplied by years of service, less amounts contributed in the past by the employer to annuity contracts, to the extent the amounts were excluded from the employee's taxable income.[4] The amount is further limited by the provisions of §415 of the Code which imposes the same limitations that are provided for qualified plans.[5] However, some recipients of §403(b) annuities are subject to special elections with respect to the §415 limitation, causing the limitation to be less onerous.[6]

Beginning in 1987, there is an overall annual limitation on the elective amount that may be contributed to a §403(b) annuity of $9,500.[7] However, for employees of education organizations, hospitals, home health service agencies, health and welfare services agencies, churches, and conventions or associations of churches, who have completed 15 years of service with the organization, the limitation is increased to $7,000 plus the lesser of (a) $3,000, (b) $15,000 reduced by amounts not included in gross income for prior taxable years because of this special provision and (c) the excess of $5,000 multiplied by the years of service over the employer's contributions to §403(b) and §401(k) plans in previous years.[8]

Example 1: A, an employee of X charity, a §501(c)(3) organization, had salary of $20,000, $22,000, and $25,000 for A's first 3 years of employment by X. X contributed

$4,000, $4,800, and $6,000 to a tax-sheltered annuity for A during these 3 years. A may exclude from income the following amounts:

	Year 1	Year 2	Year 3
Salary	$20,000	$22,000	$25,000
20% of salary	4,000	4,400	5,000
Times Years of Service	4,000	8,800	15,000
Less Contributions Excluded in Prior Years' Allowance	0	4,000	8,800
Exclusion Allowance for Year	$ 4,000	$ 4,800	$ 6,200
Limited to Contribution	$ 4,000	$ 4,800	$ 6,000

Example 2: Assume A has a salary of $30,000 in Year 4. The exclusion allowance would be $9,200 (20% of $30,000 times 4 less $14,800, the amounts excluded in prior years). However, applying the limitations of §415, contributions would be limited to the lesser of 25% of compensation up to $30,000; thus, the limitation would be $7,500 (25% of $30,000 salary). If A is an employee of an education organization, a hospital, a home health service agency, or a church, convention, or association of churches, A may substitute for the §415 limitation the lesser of (a) 25% of A's compensation of $30,000 plus $4,000, or $11,500, (b) the exclusion allowance of $9,200 or (c) $15,000. The lesser would be $9,200; thus, A could exclude this amount from taxable income.

Amounts received from a §403(b) annuity are taxed in the same manner as a regular annuity under §72 of the Code.[9] If the employee made no contributions, the entire amount would be taxable.[10] If the employee made contributions to the plan, these contributions would be the employee's investment in the contract. A percentage of the payments, computed by dividing the employee's investment by the total expected benefits from the annuity, would be excluded from taxable income.[11] For annuities whose starting date is before July 1, 1986, if the employee can recover the amount of his contributions within 3 years, the employee may exclude all payments from income until his contributions are recovered.[12] The remainder would then be taxed in full. If the amounts are received by the employee's beneficiaries by reason of death of the employee, $5,000 of the distribution is excluded from taxable income under §101(b) of the Code.[13]

An employee's rights under a 403(b) annuity must be nonforfeitable[14] and nontransferable.[15]

For plan years beginning after December 31, 1988, tax-sheltered annuities are subject to the general coverage and nondiscrimination requirements applicable to qualified pension plans except for those maintained by churches.[16]

Section 457 of the Code permits state and local governments and tax-exempt organizations to establish unfunded deferred compensation plans by which employees may elect to defer receipt of current compensation up to an annual maximum amount of $7,500 or 33⅓ percent of compensation.[17] The maximum deferral can be increased to $15,000 annually for the three years before the tax year in which the participant reaches retirement age.[18] Amounts that can be deferred under §457 are reduced by any amounts contributed to a §403(b) annuity and are reduced, dollar for dollar, by elective deferrals under a qualified cash or deferred arrangement.[19] Thus, an employee's elective deferrals under a simplified employee pension (see §5:23) would reduce the amount an employee could defer under §457.

Beginning in 1987, early withdrawals from a §403(b) annuity, in like manner as early distributions from a qualified retirement plan or an individual retirement account, will be subject to a penalty tax of 10%.[20]

154 Representing the Nonprofit Organization

FOOTNOTES

[1] IRC (1954), §403(b)(1).

[2] IRC (1954), §403(b)(1). See IRS Pub 571 (March 83) for a detailed discussion of tax-sheltered annuity programs for employees of §501(c)(3) organizations.

[3] IRC (1954), §403(b)(1), (2).

[4] IRC (1954), §403(b)(2). An employee of a church or convention or association of churches whose adjusted gross income is less than $17,000 has an alternative exclusion allowance of the lesser of (a) $3,000, or (b) the employee's compensation. See IRC (1954), §403(b)(2)(D).

[5] IRC (1954), §415(a)(2).

[6] See IRC (1954), §415(c)(4). An employee of an educational organization, a hospital, a home health service agency, or a church, convention or association of churches may elect to exclude the lesser of (a) 25% of compensation plus $4,000, (b) the amount of the exclusion allowance under §403(b)(2), or (c) $15,000. See IRC (2954), §415(c)(4)(B). If one of these employees is separated from service, the employee may elect to exclude the exclusion allowance under §403(b)(2) times the number of years of service ending on the date of separation with the employer (not to exceed 10) less the amounts contributed in the past by the employer to any annuity contracts. See IRC (1954), §415(c)(4)(A).

[7] IRC (1986), §402(g)(4).

[8] IRC (1986), §402(g)(8).

[9] IRC (1954), §403(b).

[10] IRC (1954), §72(a).

[11] IRC (1954), §72(b).

[12] IRC (1954), §72(d). Any distributions received after December 31, 1986, will be subject to a pro rata recovery of employee contributions. The 3-year recovery provision was repealed for all annuities whose starting date is after July 1, 1986.

[13] IRC (1954), §101(b).

[14] IRC (1954), §403(b)(1).

[15] IRC (1954), §401(g).

[16] IRC (1986), §403(b)(10).

[17] IRC (1986), §457(b). Section 457 plans were available only to employees of state and local governments. The Tax Reform Act of 1986 amended §457 to make such plans available to employees of tax exempt organizations.

[18] IRC (1986), §457(b)(3).
[19] IRC (1986), §457(c).
[20] IRC (1986), §72(t)(1) and §4974(c).

§3:25 Checklist of Points To Remember.

__ 1. The officers of a corporation generally include a president, one or more vice presidents, a secretary, and a treasurer.[1]

__ 2. Officers are elected or appointed at the time and in the manner prescribed in the articles of incorporation or in the bylaws.[2]

__ 3. The term of office should be set out in the articles of incorporation or in the bylaws but should not exceed three years.[3]

__ 4. As a general rule, officers of a corporation are appointed annually by the board of directors.[4]

__ 5. Any two offices, except the offices of president and secretary, may be held by the same person.[5]

__ 6. Officers are agents of the corporation and have whatever authority is delegated to them by the board of directors.[6]

__ 7. As delegatees of the board of directors, officers are fiduciaries of the corporation and, within the scope of their delegated management functions, are subject to the same fiduciary duties as are directors.[7]

__ 8. The president is normally recognized as the general manager of the corporation and, as such, often has authority to bind the corporation as to its ordinary business transactions by virtue of the office.[8]

__ 9. While corporate officers have their duties created

by the charter or the bylaws and, thus, are distinguished from regular employees who are hired by the officers, officers are considered to be employees by the Internal Revenue Service.[9] Nonetheless officers differ from regular employees in many respects. Officers are in a quasi-fiduciary relationship to members of the corporation; employees are not.[10]

__ 10. Because officers share liability with directors, any indemnification provided corporate directors should include corporate officers.[11]

__ 11. An officer and an employee of a corporation generally may be removed with or without cause; however, removal without cause may not be contrary to any contract right of the officer or employee.[12]

__ 12. Officers and employees are protected in their employment by certain state and federal statutes providing for nondiscrimination in employment.[13]

__ 13. Nonprofit organizations that are engaged in activities affecting commerce and that have 15 or more employees on each working day in each of 20 or more calendar weeks in the current or preceding year are subject to the Civil Rights Act of 1964, referred to as Title VII. Title VII provides for nondiscrimination in employment regarding a person's race, color, religion, sex, or national origin.[14]

__ 14. A nonprofit organization may not pay different wages to employees of opposite sexes for equal work on jobs the performance of which requires equal skill, effort, and responsibility and which are performed under similar working conditions unless the payment is made pursuant to a

seniority system, a merit system, a system which measures earnings by quantity or quality or production, or a differential based on any factor other than sex.[15]
- 15. An employer may not discriminate in employment because of the age of an individual if that individual is between the ages of 40 and 70. However, an employer can establish a bona fide occupational qualification regarding age.[16]
- 16. Employers having contracts with the federal government in excess of $2,500 must take affirmative action to employ and advance qualified handicapped individuals. Those with contracts in the amount of $10,000 or more with the federal government for the procurement of personal property and nonpersonal services (including construction) must take affirmative action to employ and advance in employment qualified disabled veterans and veterans of the Vietnam era.[17]
- 17. Retirement plans for employees that qualify under various provisions of the Internal Revenue Code provide tax benefits for employees. The employee is not taxed on the plan benefits, including income earned by the fund, until they are received.[18] Nonprofit organizations that are incorporated may establish qualified plans in the form of pension plans or profit-sharing plans. While the IRS took the position in the past that nonprofit organizations could not establish these plans because the organizations could not generate a profit, the IRS has now conceded that a nonprofit organization may have a profit in the form of an excess of revenues over expenses.[19]
- 18. Qualified plans must meet the requirements of §§401, 410–412, and 415–416 of the Internal Rev-

enue Code. These sections provide for participation, vesting, funding, contribution, nondiscrimination, and reporting and disclosure requirements.[20] Distributions from qualified plans are taxed as annuities under §72 of the Code. A lump-sum distribution from a qualified plan qualifies for a special 10-year averaging tax.[21]

__ 19. Individual employees can establish their own retirement accounts through tax deductible contributions of the lesser of $2,000 ($2,250 for a spousal account) or 100% of compensation to individual retirement accounts (IRAs). Contributions and earnings of the account are not taxed until they are received by the beneficiary. Distributions are taxed in full; they are not subject to the 10-year averaging provisions.[22]

__ 20. An employer may contribute to an individual retirement account for each employee over the age of 25 who has 3 years of service in lieu of establishing a qualified retirement plan for its employees. Contributions may not exceed the lesser of 15% of compensation or $30,000 for each employee.[23] All qualified employees must be participants in the plan. While the employee includes the contributions in income, the employee can deduct the lesser of 15% of compensation or $30,000.[24] A covered employee may also contribute an additional deductible amount of the lesser of $2,000 ($2,250 for a spousal account) or 100% compensation to an individual retirement plan.[25]

__ 21. Pursuant to §403(b) of the Code, employers of §501(c)(3) organizations may purchase annuity contracts that are not a part of a qualified employee annuity plan for their employees.[26]

The employee may exclude from taxable income for the year up to 20% of included compensation multiplied by years of service, less amounts contributed in the past by the employer to tax deferred annuity accounts to the extent the amounts were excluded from the employee's taxable income. However, the amounts excluded are further limited by §415 of the Code. The employee is not taxed on the annuity until benefits are received.[27]

FOOTNOTES

[2] See §3:01.
[3] See §3:01.
[4] See §3:01.
[5] See §3:01.
[6] See §3:02.
[7] See §3:02.
[8] See §§3:02, 3:03.
[9] See §3:04.
[10] See §3:04.
[11] See §3:05.
[12] See §3:06.
[13] See §3:07.
[14] See §3:08.
[15] See §3:09.
[16] See §3:10.
[17] See §3:11.
[18] See §3:13.
[19] See §3:14.
[20] See §3:13.
[21] See §3:21.
[22] See §3;22.

[23] See §3:23.
[24] See §3:23.
[25] See §3:23.
[26] See §3:24.
[27] See §3:24.

CHAPTER 4

LEGAL PROBLEMS OF NONPROFIT ENTERPRISES

§ 4:01. Legal Action Involving Nonprofit Enterprises.
§ 4:02. Right of Association.
§ 4:03. —Discriminatory Practices of Private Associations.
§ 4:04. —Judicial Intervention in Religious Associations.
§ 4:05. —Standing of Association To Seek Judicial Relief.
§ 4:06. Tort Liability of Nonprofit Enterprises.
§ 4:07. —Charitable Immunity.
§ 4:08. Application of the Copyright Act to Nonprofit Enterprises.
§ 4:09. —Sources of Copyright Ownership.
§ 4:10. —Copyright Protection.
§ 4:11. —Public Performances of Copyrighted Music by Nonprofit Enterprises.
§ 4:12. —Fair Use of Copyrighted Works.
§ 4:13. Securities Laws.
§ 4:14. —Exemptions for Securities Issued by Nonprofit Enterprises.
§ 4:15. —Sale of Securities Donated to a Nonprofit Organization.
§ 4:16. —Compliance with State Securities Laws.
§ 4:17. Application of Antitrust Laws to Nonprofit Enterprises.
§ 4:18. Unfair Competition.
§ 4:19. Labor Laws.
§ 4:20. —Selection of Labor Representative.
§ 4:21. —Duty To Bargain in Good Faith.
§ 4:22. —Subject Matter of Bargaining.
§ 4:23. —Unfair Labor Practices.
§ 4:24. —Strikes.
§ 4:25. —Right To Work Laws.
§ 4:26. Checklist of Points To Remember.

§4:01. Legal Action Involving Nonprofit Enterprises.

A nonprofit corporation can sue or be sued in its corporate name.[1] Like a profit corporation, the nonprofit corporation must have a designated registered agent for service of process.[2] Some state statutes provide that the president and vice-presidents of the corporation may also be agents for process of service.[3] If a nonprofit corporation fails to designate an agent for service, most states provide that process may be served upon the Secretary of State in the state in which the nonprofit organization is incorporated.[4]

In contrast to the nonprofit corporation, there are problems in initiating legal proceedings by or against unincorporated nonprofit associations.[5] At common law an unincorporated association could not sue nor be sued in its name.[6] Because an association is not an entity separate and distinct from its members, each member had to be named as a party, and process had to be served upon each member individually.[7] One other method was to employ the class action suit.[8] Some states have enacted statutes providing that unincorporated associations may sue or be sued in the association name without the necessity of serving the individual members or of making them parties to the suit.[9] However, many of these statutes are limited to associations "doing business" within the state.[10] Consequently, a charitable nonprofit association may not be covered by such a statute. There is a further question as to whether a judgment against the association causes liability on the part of the members.[11]

For those nonprofit organizations that are in trust form, litigation is by or against the trustee as the trustee has legal title to the trust property.[12]

FOOTNOTES

[1] See Model Nonprofit Corporation Act §5(b) (1964).

[2] Model Nonprofit Corporation Act §8 (1964). See also §1:07.
[3] See Tex Civ Stat §1396–2.07.
[4] See Tex Civ Stat §1396–2.07; Ohio Rev Code 1702.06(H).
[5] See Brunson, Some Problems Presented by Unincorporated Associations in Civil Procedure, 7 S C L Rev 394 (1955).
[6] Brunson, Some Problems Presented by Unincorporated Associations in Civil Procedure, 7 S C L Rev 394 (1955).
[7] Brunson, Some Problems Presented by Unincorporated Associations in Civil Procedure, 7 S C L Rev 394 (1955).
[8] Brunson, Some Problems Presented by Unincorporated Associations in Civil Procedure, 7 S C L Rev 394 (1955).
[9] See Conn Gen Stat §52–76; Del Code Ann tit 10, §3904; and Tex Civ Stat §6133.

See Fed Rules Civ Proc 17(b) which provides that while capacity to sue or be sued is determined by the law of the state in which the district court is held, an unincorporated association which has no capacity to sue by the law of the state may nonetheless sue and be sued in its common name for the purpose of enforcing for or against it a substantial right under the Constitution or laws of the United States.

[10] **Texas.** See Realty Trust Co v. First Baptist Church of Haskell, 46 SW2d 1009 (Tex Civ App, 1932) in which the court held that the Texas statute providing for suits against unincorporated associations was not applicable to a suit against an unincorporated religious society because the religious society was not "doing business" within the state.

[11] See Del Code Ann tit 10, §3904 which provides that a judgment against an unincorporated association is also a judgment against the members.

However, see Ga Code Ann §3–121 which provides that such a judgment will not bind an individual member unless the member was named as a party in the lawsuit.

[12] Scott, Law of Trusts §261–265 (3d Ed).

§4:02. Right of Association.

The right of an individual to join others in the various pursuits fostered by nonprofit organizations has been recognized as a mode of expression, called the freedom of association, which is protected by the First and Fourteenth Amendments to the United States Constitution.[1] Although the First Amendment does not explicitly include a right of association,[2] the activities engaged in by many nonprofit organizations are constitutionally protected.[3] The Supreme Court has stated that implicit in the right to engage in activities protected by the First Amendment is a corresponding right to associate with others in pursuit of a wide variety of political, social, economic, educational, religious, and cultural ends.[4] The Supreme Court has also stated that "it is beyond debate that freedom to engage in association for the advancement of beliefs and ideas is an inseparable aspect of the liberty assured by the due process of the Fourteenth Amendment which embraces freedom of speech."[5] Freedom of association has received protection as a fundamental element of personal liberty.[6] The Supreme Court has recognized that effective advocacy of public and private points of view, particularly controversial ones, is undeniably enhanced by group association.[7] Consequently, there is a close nexus between the freedoms of speech and assembly.[8]

Courts have recognized the relationship between freedom to associate and privacy in one's associations;[9] consequently the requirement by a state to disclose the names of its members has been held to an interference with the freedom of association.[10]

The extent to which a court will interfere in the operations of a private association or corporation is not clear. As a general rule, courts do not interfere in the internal affairs of private associations because of the public interest in maintaining an individual's freedom of association and freedom of choice in private matters.[11] However, because of the economic control possessed by professional and trade associations and by labor unions and the limited power of the individual members of such organizations to control the affairs of the association, the courts have exercised jurisdiction to prevent arbitrary exclusion or expulsion from these types of organizations.[12]

FOOTNOTES

[1] **United States.** See National Association for the Advancement of Colored People v. Button, 371 US 415, 9 L Ed 2d 405, 83 S Ct 328 (1963). Freedom of association presupposes a freedom not to associate. See Roberts v. United States Jaycees, — US —, 78 L Ed 2d 137, 104 S Ct 3244, 52 USLW 5077 (1984).

[2] The First Amendment to the United States Constitution reads:

"Congress shall make no law respecting an establishment of religion, or prohibiting the free exercise thereof; or abridging the freedom of speech, or of the press; or the right of the people peaceably to assemble, and to petition the Government for a redress of grievances."

[3] **United States.** See National Association for the Advancement of Colored People v. Alabama, 357 US 449, 2 L Ed 2d 1488, 78 S Ct 1163 (1958).

[4] **United States.** Roberts v. United States Jaycees, — US —, 78 L Ed 2d 137, 104 S Ct 3244, 52 USLW 5077 (1984).

[5] **United States.** National Association for the Advancement of Colored People v. Alabama, 357 US 449, 2 L Ed 2d 1488, 78 S Ct 1163 (1958).

[6] **United States.** Roberts v. United States Jaycees, — US —, 78 L Ed 2d 137, 104 S Ct 3244, 52 USLW 5077 (1984).

[7] **United States.** National Association for the Advancement of Colored People v. Alabama, 357 US 449, 2 L Ed 2d 1488, 78 S Ct 1163 (1958).

[8] **United States.** National Association for the Advancement of Colored People v. Alabama, 357 US 449, 2 L Ed 2d 1488, 78 S Ct 1163 (1958).

[9] **United States.** National Association for the Advancement of Colored People v. Alabama, 357 US 449, 2 L Ed 2d 1488, 78 S Ct 1163 (1958).

[10] **United States.** National Association for the Advancement of Colored People v. Alabama, 357 US 449, 2 L Ed 2d 1488, 78 S Ct 1163 (1958).

[11] See Judicial Control of Actions of Private Association, 76 Harv L Rev 983, 989 (1963).

[12] See Judicial Control of Actions of Private Associations, 76 Harv L Rev 983, 989 (1963).

§4:03 —*Discriminatory Practices of Private Associations.*

In the past, courts have held that private discrimination, however repugnant, could be practiced.[1] While the equal protection clause of the Fourteenth Amendment reaches state action,[2] it is no shield against merely private conduct, however discriminatory or wrongful.[3] Without a finding of state action, courts have had no authority to compel private clubs to maintain a nondiscriminatory admission policy.[4] A finding that a private association has no involvement with the state and, thus, can discriminate, does not eliminate the discrimination; it is merely a determination that regardless of the discrimination, the federal government is not permitted to interfere.[5]

In recent years, courts have been more prone to find state action. The right to serve alcoholic beverages through a license from the state has been held to be the requisite state action so that a discriminatory admission policy by a private club could be prohibited by the court.[6]

The Supreme Court recently ruled that a state statute, making the denial to any person of the full and equal enjoyment of public accommodations because of race, color, creed, national origin, or sex an unfair discriminatory practice, could be applied to a private club without being a violation of the members' right of association.[7] The Court did, however, distinguish the application of the statute to a completely private club, ruling that the club in question was neither small nor selective and that admission of unwelcome members would not change the message communicated by the group's speech.[8]

The Supreme Court also recently addressed the issue of race discrimination by a nonprofit private educational institution by denying it tax exempt status.[9] While the Internal Revenue Code denies tax exemption by statute to social clubs that discriminate on the basis of race, color, or religion,[10] there has been no statutory prohibition as to other tax exempt organizations. However, the Supreme Court has taken the position that racial discrimination in education is contrary to public policy; thus, according to the Court, it would be incompatible with the concepts underlying tax exemption to grant tax-exempt status to racially discriminatory private educational entities.[11]

Those private associations that control a practice or trade (membership in the organization is required in order to practice a particular trade) have been subjected to control by the courts.[12] To permit these types of organizations to exclude or to expel members arbitrarily is repugnant to one's sense of justice. Thus, courts have reviewed the application procedures of private associations when membership is an economic necessity.[13] As an example, a medical society cannot arbitrarily deny membership to an applicant when that society controls access to local hospital facilities and, thus, can deprive the applicant of his or her ability to practice medicine.[14] A state may forbid a labor organization from denying membership because of race, color or creed; such a statute has been held not to be an interference with the association's right of selection of membership nor an abridgement of associational property rights and right of contract.[15]

Courts do review the expulsion of a member of a private association if minimum standards regarding termination are not followed based both upon either a property right or a contractual right in the member.[16] The power to expel a member is in the nature of a forfeiture; thus, there is a presumption against it.[17] Membership in a nonprofit organization generally may be terminated only by voluntary act of the member or by an act of the organization pursuant to authority granted it by its charter, articles of association, or bylaws. If nonprofit associations establish effective nonjudicial methods of control and internal procedures, courts are less likely to hear individual and group disputes.[18] Thus, as a general rule, if the constitution and bylaws of a voluntary association provide a system for trial and appeal of internal controversies between members, the courts will require that members exhaust such procedures

168 Representing the Nonprofit Organization

before resorting to the courts.[19] However, such remedies need not be exhausted by a member if the attempt would be futile.[20] Further, if an association does not establish rules, it risks judicial intervention.[21]

FOOTNOTES

[1] **United States.** Seidenberg v. McSorleys' Old Ale House, Inc., 317 F Supp 593 (SD NY, 1970).
Illinois. See Davis v. Attic Club, 56 Ill App 3d 58, 371 NE2d 903 (1977).

[2] The Fourteenth Amendment provides:

"No state shall make or enforce any law which shall abridge the privileges or immunities of citizens of the United States; nor shall any state deprive any person of life, liberty, or property, without due process of law; nor deny to any person within its jurisdiction the equal protection of the laws."

[3] **United States.** See Seidenberg v. McSorleys' Old Ale House, Inc., 317 F Supp 593 (SD NY, 1970); and Moose Lodge No. 107 v. Irvis, 407 US 163, 23 L Ed 2d 627, 92 S Ct 1965 (1972).

But see §501(c)(i) of the Internal Revenue Code which prohibits discrimination on the basis of race, color, or religion for certain social clubs. Social clubs cannot be tax exempt if they discriminate on these bases. See further discussion at §7:18 (Fraternal beneficiary societies that in good faith limit their membership to persons of a particular religion in order to further the teachings of that religion and not to exclude persons of a particular race or color are exempt from §501(c)(i).)

[4] **United States.** See Dezell v. Day Island Yacht Club, 796 F2d 324 (CA9, 1986), in which a female applicant was denied membership in a yacht club on the basis of sex. The court held that a plaintiff must demonstrate state action to assert jurisdiction under the equal protection clause of the Fourteenth Amendment.

See Seidenberg v. McSorleys' Old Ale House, Inc., 317 F Supp 593 (SD NY, 1970); Moose Lodge No. 107 v. Irvis, 407 US 163, 23 L Ed 2d 627, 92 S Ct 1965 (1972).

[5] **United States.** Seidenberg v. McSorleys' Old Ale House, Inc., 317 F Supp 593 (SD NY, 1970).
Indiana. See Lozanoski v. Sarafin, 485 NE2d 669 (Ind App, 1985) in which the court stated that courts in Indiana will not interfere with the internal

affairs of private organizations unless a personal liberty or property right is jeopardized.

⁶ **United States.** Seidenberg v. McSorleys' Old Ale House, Inc., 317 F Supp 593 (SD NY, 1970). The court found state action in this case because the state's participation through regulation, control, price fixing, place of time and sale setting by the licensing process was deemed to be sufficient involvement by the state. But see, Moose Lodge No. 107 v. Irvis, 407 US 163, 23 L Ed 2d 627, 92 S Ct. 1965 (1972). The Supreme Court ruled that regulation by a state liquor board through its granting of liquor licenses was not state action. However, in that case the plaintiff, a black, had not sought admission to the club (as had the plaintiff in the Seidenberg case), but rather was challenging the club policy with respect to serving guests of members.

See also, Sullivan v. Little Hunting Park, Inc., 396 US 299, 24 L Ed 2d 386, 90 S Ct 400 (1960); Tillman v. Wheaton-Haven Recreation Association, Inc., 410 US 431, 35 L Ed 2d 403, 93 S Ct 1090 (1973). In the Wheaton-Haven Recreation Association case, the Supreme Court found that a nonprofit corporation organized to operate a swimming pool open to all white persons within a designated area was not a private club; consequently, it could not reject the membership application of a black. The Court held that the provisions of 42 USC §§1981, 1982 applied and guaranteed a nonwhite resident who purchased or held property within the area the same rights as those enjoyed by white residents.

⁷ **United States.** Roberts v. United States Jaycees, — US —, 78 L Ed 2d 137, 104 S Ct 3244, 52 USLW 5077 (1984). The Court declared that the Minnesota Human Rights Act, Minn Stat §363.03(3), could be constitutionally applied to the Jaycees to prohibit their local organizations from denying membership to women. The Court stated that freedom of association is not an absolute right. According to the Court, infringements on that right may be justified by regulations adopted to serve compelling state interests, unrelated to the suppression of ideas, that cannot be achieved through means significantly less restrictive of associational freedoms. The Court determined that Minnesota's compelling interest in eradicating discrimination against its female citizens justified the impact that application of the statute to the Jaycees would have on the male members' associational freedoms. It justified the exclusion of the Kiwanis Club from the act because of a determination that the Kiwanis Club is sufficiently private.

See Ohio Civil Rights Commission v. Dayton Christian Schools, — US —, 91 L Ed 2d 512, 106 S Ct 2718 (1986), in which the Supreme Court reversed the decision of the Sixth Circuit, 766 F2d 932 (CA6, 1985). The Supreme Court ruled that the elimination of sex discrimination is a compelling state interest that would bring a religious institution within the ambit of state authorities. The Court determined that the state commission would violate no constitutional rights of the school by merely investigating the circumstances of the discharge of a pregnant teacher if only to ascertain whether the ascribed religious-based reason was in fact the reason for the discharge. The Court noted that Dayton Schools could raise its constitutional objections at the state proceedings.

[8] **United States.** Roberts v. United States Jaycees, — US —, 78 L Ed 2d 137, 104 S Ct 3244, 52 USLW 5077 (1984). The Court stated that local chapters of the Jaycees lacked the distinctive characteristics that might have afforded constitutional protection to their members' decision to exclude women.

[9] **United States.** See Bob Jones University v. United States, — US —, 76 L Ed 2d 157, 103 S Ct 2017 (1983).

[10] See IRC (1954), §501(c)(i).

[11] **United States.** Bob Jones University v. United States, — US —, 76 L Ed 2d 157, 103 S Ct 2017 (1983). But see Allen v. Wright, — US —, 77 L Ed 2d 1365, 105 S Ct 51, 52 USLW 5111 (1984) in which the Supreme Court held that the parents of black public school children who alleged in a nationwide class action suit that the IRS had not adopted sufficient standards and procedures to fulfill its obligation to deny tax exempt status to racially discriminatory private schools did not have standing to file the suit. The Court stated that only those who are personally denied equal treatment by the challenged discriminatory conduct could bring suit. The overall stigmatizing injury caused by racial discrimination is not sufficient grounds for persons who have not applied to a private school. (The IRS has guidelines and procedures for determining whether particular schools are in fact racially nondiscriminatory. See Rev Proc 75–50, 1975–2, CB 587. A failure to comply with the guidelines will ordinarily result in a proposed revocation of tax exempt status.)

See Virginia Education Fund v. Commissioner, 58 AFTR2d 86–5620 (CA4, 1986), in which the Fourth Circuit affirmed a holding of the Tax Court, 85 TC 743, that an organization that solicits funds for distribution to segregated private schools for whites desiring to avoid integration of public schools will be denied tax status. The court held that a fund's entitlement to tax exempt status depends upon the entitlement of its donees to tax exemption.

See Research Consulting Associates v. Electric Power Research Institute, Inc., 626 F Supp 1310 (D Mass, 1986), which followed Allen v. Wright in denying standing to an organization to challenge the tax exempt status of a research institute. The court in Research Consulting Associates cited the Allen case in noting that an organization challenging the tax exempt status of a nonprofit organization must allege personal injury "fairly traceable" to the nonprofit's alleged conduct and must allege that the plaintiff will likely be redressed by the requested relief. The court was of the opinion that it is

LEGAL PROBLEMS OF NONPROFIT ENTERPRISES 171

difficult to trace financial losses of a for-profit organization to the tax exempt status of a nonprofit organization or that enjoining the grant of tax exempt status to such nonprofit would likely redress the injury complained of by the for-profit organization.

[12] See Judicial Protection of Membership in Private Associations, 14 West L Rev 346 (1961).

United States. Lathrop v. Donohue, 367 US 820, 6 L Ed 2d 1191, 81 S Ct 1826 (1961). The Supreme Court held in the Lathrop case that a requirement that a person be an enrolled dues paying member of a state bar association does not abridge a person's rights of freedom of association.

[13] **United States.** See Marrese v. American Academy of Orthopaedic Surgeons, 470 US —, 84 L Ed 2d 274, 105 S Ct 1327 (1985) in which denial of membership in a professional organization was challenged as being in violation of the Sherman Act as a group boycott.

Judicial Protection of Membership in Private Association, 14 West L Rev 346 (1961).

[14] **Arizona.** See Blende v. Maricopa County Medical Society, 96 Ariz 240, 393 P2d 926 (1964).

Illinois. Treister v. American Academy of Orthopaedic Surgeons, 396 NE 2d 1225 (Ill App, 1979).

In Siqueria v. Northwestern Memorial Hospital, 132 Ill App 3d 293, 477 NE2d 16 (1985), the court discussed due process requirements in expelling a doctor from membership in a voluntary association. The court noted that while an expulsion from membership in a voluntary association may affect economic and property interests thereby triggering due process protections, voluntary associations need not accord members due process to the extent protected under the United States Constitution. The court stated that voluntary associations should afford members subject to disciplinary actions a hearing before a fair and impartial tribunal which may be provided for under the organization's bylaws.

New Jersey. Falcone v. Middlesex County Medical Society, 34 NJ 582, 170 A2d 791 (1961).

[15] **United States.** Railway Mail Association v. Corsi, 326 US 88, 89 L Ed 2072, 65 S Ct 1483 (1945).

[16] See Judicial Protection of Membership in Private Associations, 14 West Res L Rev 346 (1963).

[17] See further discussion at §2:11.

Georgia. In Bartley v. Augusta Country Club, Inc., 254 Ga 144; 326 SE2d 442 (1985), the court held that disciplinary actions against members of a private club are governed by the bylaws of the club. There is no constitutional question, according to the court.

[18] **Florida.** In Everglades Protective Syndicate v. Makinney, 391 So 2d 262 (Fla App, 1981), the court held that the governing body of a private, social club is the final arbiter of the sufficiency of causes for expulsion. The court stated that almost any reason to expel a member is sufficient if the governing body of the nonprofit, private association so determines. The court distinguished the rights of members of professional clubs where membership is related to earning one's livelihood or professional advancement. The Florida court stated that "neither due process nor concepts of fundamental fairness compel the conclusion that an individual is entitled to the association of one or more other individuals against his or their will." According to the court, a private, social club, or any other voluntary group of individuals, has the right to select its own members. The court stated that membership in this context is not a constitutional right. Because it is a bare privilege, it is terminable at the will of either the group or the individual.

Texas. See Raulston v. Everett, 561 SW2d 635 (Tex Civ App, 1978).

[19] **Florida.** See Travis v. Lost Tree Village Corporation, 388 So2d 319 (Fla App, 1980). The court stated that intervention of a court is premature if the opportunity for a hearing was given a member who was expelled.

Tennessee. See Wilson v. Miller, 250 SW2d 575 (1952).

[20] **Tennessee.** Wilson v. Miller, 250 SW2d 575 (1952).

[21] See Judicial Protection of Membership in Private Associations, 14 West L Rev 346 (1963).

§4:04. —Judicial Intervention in Religious Associations.

Courts generally will not interfere in the internal affairs of a church for the "purpose of determining whether they are regular or in accordance with the policy, discipline or usages of the organization."[1] Courts have held that religious organizations may establish their own rules and regulations for internal discipline and that state governments should refrain from involving themselves in ecclesiastical affairs or controversies.[2] According to the courts, denominations and not courts should interpret their own body of church policy.[3]

Courts do exercise their equitable jurisdiction in church controversies for the protection and preservation of civil or property rights of the members, often to prevent an unauthorized alienation of property or the wrongful diversion of church funds.[4] However, the Supreme Court has stated that even when rival church factions seek resolution of a church property dispute in the civil courts, there is substantial danger that the state will become entangled in essentially religious controversies.[5] Because of this danger, the First Amendment severely limits the role that civil courts may play in resolving church property disputes.[6] Civil courts cannot analyze whether the ecclesiastical actions of a church judicatory regarding matters of discipline, faith, internal organization, or ecclesiastical rule, custom, or law, are arbitrary.[7] The Supreme Court has stated that it is the "essence of religious faith that ecclesiastical decisions are reached and are to be accepted as matters of faith whether or not rational or measurable by objective criteria."[8]

FOOTNOTES

[1] **United States.** See First English Lutheran Church v. Evangelical Lutheran Synod of Kansas, 135 F2d 701 (CA10, 1943).

See, however, Tony & Susan Alamo Foundation v. Secretary of Labor, 471 US —, 85 L Ed 2d 278, 105 S Ct 1953 (1985) in which the Supreme Court held that a religious foundation is subject to the minimum wage, overtime and record keeping requirements of the Fair Labor Standards Act. The Court held that payments to workers for the foundation in the form of food, clothing, shelter, and other such benefits were wages. The workers were drug addicts, derelicts, and/or criminals; nonetheless, the Court held they were "employees" of the foundation. Income for the foundation was derived from its operation of a number of commercial businesses, which it supervised and staffed with these workers. The Court held that when religious or educational organizations perform activities for a business purpose, the business activities will be treated under the Act the same as when they are performed by the ordinary business enterprise. The Court did not hold that the Act does not apply to the foundation's evangelical activities or to individuals engaged in volunteer work for other religious organizations.

[2] **Massachusetts.** Wheeler v. Roman Catholic Archdiocese of Boston, 389 NE2d 966 (1979).

174 Representing the Nonprofit Organization

[3] **Massachusetts.** Wheeler v. Roman Catholic Archdiocese of Boston, 389 NE2d 966 (1979).

[4] **United States.** First English Lutheran Church v. Evangelical Lutheran Synod of Kansas, 135 F2d 701 (CA10, 1943). The First English Lutheran Church of Oklahoma City wanted to withdraw from the Synod of Kansas and affiliate with the Midwest Synod. The Synod of Kansas refused to consent and enjoined the deacons and trustees of the church from exercising control over church property. The court stated that the Synod of Kansas had no beneficial interest in the property. It belonged to the church at Oklahoma City.

Alabama. See Caples v. Nazareth Church, 245 Ala 656, 18 So 2d 383 (1944). In church disputes, the court will generally award the property to the group adhering most closely to the church's doctrine.

[5] **United States.** See Serbian Eastern Orthodox Diocese v. Milivojevich, 426 US 696, 49 L Ed 2d 151, 96 S Ct 2372 (1976).

See Ohio Civil Rights Commission v. Dayton Christian Schools, — US —, 91 L Ed 2d 512, 106 S Ct 2718 (1986), in which the Supreme Court reversed the Court of Appeals stating that the elimination of sex discrimination is a sufficiently important state interest to bring a case involving a religious school within the ambit of the authorities. The Court noted that religious schools cannot claim to be wholly free from some state regulation. The Court held that the state commission violated no constitutional rights by merely investigating the circumstances of the discharge of the school teacher if only to ascertain whether the ascribed religious-based reason was in fact the reason for the discharge. The Court did note that Dayton Christian Schools could raise its constitutional claims at the proceedings.

[6] **United States.** Serbian Eastern Orthodox Diocese v. Milivojevich, 426 US 696, 49 L Ed 2d 151, 96 S Ct 2372 (1976).

[7] **United States.** See Presbyterian Church v. Hull Church, 393 US 440, 21 L Ed 2d 658, 89 S Ct 601 (1969).

[8] **United States.** Serbian Eastern Orthodox Diocese v. Milivojevich, 426 US 696, 49 L Ed 2d 151, 96 S Ct 2372 (1976).

§4:05. —Standing of Association To Seek Judicial Relief.

The standing of an association to seek judicial relief from injury to itself and to its members is still somewhat unresolved. Courts have stated that an association has standing in its own right to seek judicial relief from injury to itself and to vindicate whatever rights and immunities the association itself may enjoy.[1] An association may also assert the rights of its members so long as the challenged infractions adversely affect its members' associational ties.[2] Injury to an organization may be established by a showing that the organization will suffer diminished financial support or membership.[3] However, an association must assert its own legal rights and interests and not those of third parties.[4] Thus, an association may not bring an action for damages based on harms to particular members of the association unless the association also alleges monetary damages to itself or an assignment of the damage claims of its members.[5] In the case of individual harm, the individual members claiming injury generally must be parties to the suit, and the association has no standing to claim damages on their behalf.[6]

FOOTNOTES

[1] **United States.** See Warth v. Seldin, 422 US 490, 511, 45 L Ed 2d 343, 95 S Ct 2197, 2211 (1975).

[2] **United States.** Warth v. Seldin, 422 US 490, 45 L Ed 2d 343, 95 S Ct 2197 (1975).

[3] **United States.** See National Association for the Advancement of Colored People v. Alabama, 357 US 449, 2 L Ed 2d 1488, 78 S Ct 1163 (1958).

[4] **United States.** See Havens Realty Corporation v. Coleman, 455 US 363, 379, 71 L Ed 2d 214, 102 S Ct 1114, 1124 (1982).

[5] **United States.** See Valley Forge Christian College v. Americans United for the Separation of Church and State, Inc., 454 US 464, 476, 70 L Ed 2d 700, 102 S Ct 752, 761 (1982); Minority Employees of the Tennessee Department of Employment Security, Inc. v. State of Tennessee, 573 F Supp 1346 (MD Tenn, 1983).

[6] **United States.** Minority Employees of the Tennessee Department of Employment Security, Inc. v. State of Tennessee, Department of Employment Security, 573 F Supp 1346 (MD Tenn, 1983).

§4:06. Tort Liability of Nonprofit Enterprises.

Nonprofit corporations are generally held to the same standards of legal liability for negligence and other torts as are other business enterprises. Corporations and trusts are usually held liable for the torts of their agents or employees under the doctrine of respondeat superior or course of employment.[1] Members of unincorporated associations can be individually liable for torts committed in the name of the association.[2]

In a few states, those nonprofit corporations that are charitable in nature have some immunity from liability.[3]

FOOTNOTES

[1] Under the doctrine of respondeat superior, the principal is liable for the wrongful acts of his agent which occurred within the scope of employment.
United States. See President and Directors of Georgetown College v. Hughes, 130 F2d 810 (CA DC, 1942). As the court pointed out in the Georgetown College case, corporations and trust cannot be guilty of tort as a controlling premise. Corporate charters and trust indentures do not authorize corporate representatives or trustees to commit assaults, libel, slander, and negligent torts. However, lack of authority has given way to respondeat superior and course of employment. As the court noted, the law of ultra vires action (those acts beyond the scope of power of a corporation as defeating liability) has moved from authorized action to conduct incidental to the enterprise and the actual or apparent function of the actor as the line of demarcation. (130 F2d at 832).

[2] **United States.** See State Farm Mutual Automobile Insurance Company v. Mackechnic, 114 F2d 728 (CA8, 1940).

[3] **New Jersey.** See Schultz v. Roman Catholic Archdiocese of Newark, 95 NJ 530, 472, A2d 531 (1984), in which the Supreme Court of New Jersey affirmed the doctrine of charitable immunity in New Jersey. The court held that charitable immunity barred a claim of a beneficiary of a charitable institution based upon the charity's alleged negligence. While the common-law doctrine of charitable immunity was abolished in New Jersey in 1958 [see Benton v. YMCA, 26 NJ 67, 141 A2d 298 (1958)], the legislature of New

Jersey reestablished the doctrine by statute. The New Jersey Charitable Immunity Act, NJSA §§2A:53A–7 to 2A:53A–10, provides that no nonprofit organization established exclusively for religious, charitable, educational, or hospital purposes shall be liable for damages to any person who is a beneficiary of the works of the nonprofit organization. A nonprofit organization has no immunity as to those outside its benefaction. In addition, hospitals are liable up to $10,000. (See NJSA §2A:53A–8.)

New York. See Schultz v. Boy Scouts of America, Inc., 65 NY2d 189, 491 NYS2d 90, 480 NE2d 679 (1985), in which a New York court applied the New Jersey law of charitable immunity to bar recovery against a charitable institution located in New Jersey.

[3] **South Carolina.** See Fitzer v. Greater Greenville South Carolina Young Men's Christian Ass'n, 282 SE2d 230 (1981). South Carolina has now repudiated the doctrine. As stated by the Supreme Court in the Fitzer case, the doctrine of charitable immunity has no place in today's society.

Wisconsin. See, e.g., Duncan v. Steel, 116 NW2d 154 (1962). Immunity provides absolution from liability. As Prosser stated, it avoids liability within the limits of the immunity. Prosser, Law of Torts, (4th Ed, p. 970). According to Prosser, charitable immunity in its complete form exists only in Maine, New Mexico, and South Carolina Prosser, Law of Torts §133 (4th Ed).

§4:07. —Charitable Immunity.

In the past, charitable corporations were immune from liability for torts committed by their employees. The foundation of immunity was the dictum of Lord Cottenham in the old English case of Feoffees of Heriot's Hospital v. Ross.[1] However, this dictum was later repudiated by the English courts.[2] Nonetheless, Massachusetts and Maryland adopted the doctrine apparently in ignorance of the English reversal.[3]

Lord Cottenham based the doctrine of charitable immunity on a trust fund theory—to give damages from a trust fund would divert the fund to a different purpose from what the donor intended. The doctrine, as applied in the United States, was based on one of three theories: (1) public policy, (2) protection of trust funds, and (3) an implied waiver by injured persons through an acceptance of benefits from a charity.[4]

The public policy theory asserts that it is against public policy to hold a charity liable for tort damages because the benefits of a charity are greater than the detriment suffered by an injured party.[5] The trust fund theory assumes that charitable organizations derive no profit or private gain from the acts of their agents and employees; thus, the doctrine of respondeat superior should not be applicable.[6] The implied waiver theory assumes that a beneficiary of benefits from a charity, by accepting the tendered aid, implicitly agrees that that is all he or she may accept and waives any right of recourse for any wrong done.[7] Under this theory, a stranger may recover damages from a charity; a beneficiary of its services may not. (The stranger group includes those who are not receiving direct benefits from the charity, such as visitors and invitees.)[8]

The charitable immunity doctrine has diminished considerably in importance.[9] As one court stated, the rule of immunity is out of step with the general trend of legislative and judicial policy in distributing losses incurred by individuals through the operation of an enterprise among all who benefit by it rather than in leaving them wholly to be borne by those who sustain them.[10] Courts have pointed out that if there is danger of dissipation of a charity's assets, insurance is available to guard against it, and prudent management should provide such protection.[11]

The doctrine of charitable immunity has been abrogated in most states.[12] Some states have a qualified immunity.[13]

FOOTNOTES

[1] **England.** 12 Clark & Fin 507, 513, 8 Eng Reprint 1508 (1846).
See also Duncan v. Findlater, 6 Clark & Fin 894, 7 Eng Reprint 934 (1839).

[2] **England.** See Docks Trustees v. Gibbs, LR 1 HL 93 (1866); Foreman v. Mayor of Canterbury, LR 6 QB 214 (1871).

LEGAL PROBLEMS OF NONPROFIT ENTERPRISES 179

[3] **Maryland.** Perry v. House of Refuge, 63 Md 20, 52 Am Rep 495 (1885).
Massachusetts. McDonald v. Massachusetts General Hospital, 120 Mass 432, 21 Am Rep 529 (1876).

[4] **Idaho.** See Bell v. Presbytery of Boise, 421 P2d 745 (1966).
Kentucky. Roland v. Catholic Archdiocese of Louisville, 301 SW 2d 574 (Ky App, 1957).

[5] See Charitable Immunity: A Diminishing Doctrine, 23 Wash and Lee L Rev 109 (1966).

[6] See A Survey of Charitable Hospital Immunity, 19 Univ of Pitt L Rev 119 (1957).

[7] **United States.** President and Directors of Georgetown College v. Hughes, 130 F2d 810, 825, (CA DC, 1942). The Court of Appeals in the Georgetown College case discussed the theory but determined that there is no reason to treat stranger and beneficiaries differently. That court ruled that the incorporated charity should respond in damages for torts of its employees in the same manner as business corporations and private individuals.

[8] **United States.** President and Directors of Georgetown College v. Hughes, 130 F2d 810, 825 (CA DC, 1942).

[9] **United States.** President and Directors of Georgetown College v. Hughes, 130 F2d 810 (CA DC, 1942).
See also Charitable Immunity: A Diminishing Doctrine, 23 Wash and Lee L Rev. 109 (1966).

[10] **United States.** President and Directors of Georgetown College v. Hughes, 130 F2d 810, 827 (CA DC, 1942).

[11] **United States.** See President and Directors of Georgetown College v. Hughes, 130 F2d 810, 823 (CA DC, 1942).

[12] See e.g.:
  Idaho. Bell v. Presbytery of Boise, 421 P2d 745 (1966).
  Indiana. Harris v. YWCA, 237 NE2d 242 (1965).
  New Hampshire. Merrill v. City of Manchester, 332 A2d 378 (1974).
  Pennsylvania. Hoffman v. Misericordia Hospital of Philadelphia, 267 A2d 867 (1970).
  South Carolina. Fitzer v. Greater Greenville, 282 SE2d 230 (1981).
  Texas. Howle v. Camp Amon Carter, 470 SW2d 629 (1971).

[13] **Kentucky.** See Roland v. Catholic Archdiocese of Louisville, 301 SW2d 574 (Ky App, 1957); St Walburg Monastery v. Geltner's Administrator, 275 SW2d 784 (1955); and Forrest v. Red Cross Hospital, 265 SW2d 80 (Ky App, 1954).
  Wisconsin. Duncan v. Steele, 116 NW2d 154 (1962) and Hooten v. Civil Air Patrol, 161 F Supp 478 (ED Wis, 1958).

§4:08. Application of the Copyright Act to Nonprofit Enterprises.

Nonprofit enterprises are often involved in transactions and controversies involving copyright law; thus, the principal sections of the copyright statutes are summarized.

Copyright law in the United States was modified by the Copyright Act of 1976 which became effective January 1, 1978.[1] Under prior law, the right of an artist or author to his or her creation had common law protection which continued indefinitely until the work was published.[2] Protection was regulated by the states. However, the federal government has now preempted the field; thus, state provisions regarding copyright law are no longer effective.[3] As a result, there is now a single system of statutory protection for all copyrightable works whether published or unpublished.[4]

Copyright protection applies to original works of authorship fixed in any tangible medium of expression.[5] It does not extend to ideas, procedures, processes, systems, methods of operation, concepts, principles, or discoveries.[6] Consequently, a work would ordinarily be in the form of writing; however, works of art are also copyrightable.[7] Works of authorship subject to copyright include: literary works; musical works (including any accompanying words); dramatic works (including any accompanying music); pantomimes and choreographic works; pictorial, graphic, and sculptural works; motion pictures and other audiovisual works; and sound recordings.[8]

Property rights of the artist or author are protected for the artist's or author's life plus fifty years after death.[9] A copyright owner has the exclusive right to reproduce the copyrighted work, to prepare derivative works, to distribute the work publicly, to perform the copyrighted work publicly, and to display the copyrighted work publicly.[10] Once a work is sold, the exclusive right to sell is terminated; a copyright owner cannot in that event control future disposition of sold copies of the work.[11] When the artist sells his work, he also loses the display right in the work; however, he does not lose the right to reproduce the work.[12] In addition, one who has merely rented a work or who has it on loan does not acquire a display right.[13]

Example 1: A museum purchases a painting from an artist. The museum has the right to display the work but may not make reproductions of the work without permission from the artist.

Example 2: A museum has a painting on loan from a person other than the artist. The museum must ascertain the rights of the lender. If the lender does not own the painting, the lender may not have display rights and, in that event, may not transfer display rights to the museum. The museum would have to secure permission from the artist to display the work.

FOOTNOTES

[1] 17 USC §§101–810.

[2] **United States.** See Wells v. Universal Pictures Co., 166 F2d 690 (CA2, 1948).
See also Notes of Committee on the Judiciary, HR No. 94–1476, 17 USC §301.

[3] 17 USC §301(a).
See Callmann Unfair Comp, Trademarks & Monopolies §15.08 (4th Ed).

[4] See Notes of Committee on the Judiciary, HR No. 94–1476, 17 USC §301.

[5] 17 USC §102(a).

[6] 17 USC §102(b).

[7] 17 USC §102(a).

[8] 17 USC §102(a).
For a discussion of copyright protection of sound recordings, see Callmann Unfair Comp, Trademarks & Monopolies §15.10 (4th Ed).

[9] 17 USC §302(a).
For "works made for hire" the copyright endures for a term of 75 years

after the year of its first publication or a term of 100 years from the year of its after the year of its first publication or a term of 100 years from the year of its creation, whichever expires first. See 15 USC §302(c). See discussion of "work made for hire" at §4:09.

Under previous law, statutory copyright protection began on the date of publication (or the date of registration in unpublished form) and continued for 28 years from that date; the copyright was subject to renewal for a second 28 years, making a total potential term of 56 years.

[10] 17 USC §106.

[11] See 17 USC §109.
See Notes of Committee on the Judiciary, HR No. 94–1476 at 15 USC §109.
See also Callmann Unfair Comp, Trademarks & Monopolies §4.64 (4th Ed).
United States. See American International Pictures, Inc. v. Foreman, 576 F2d 661 (CA5, 1978).

[12] 15 USC §109(b).
See Callmann Unfair Comp, Trademarks & Monopolies §4.64 (4th Ed).

[13] 17 USC §109(c).

§4:09. —Sources of Copyright Ownership.

The owner, or coowners, of a work are the source of copyright ownership.[1] However, if a work is made for hire, the employer is considered to be the author and is regarded as the initial owner of the copyright unless there is an agreement to the contrary.[2] A "work made for hire" includes a "work prepared by an employee within the scope of the employment," and certain categories of commissioned works, which are produced as a result of a special order.[3] Commissioned works are "works made for hire" only if there is an express agreement in writing signed by the parties stating that the work is to be considered a work made for hire.[4]

> *Example:* An employee of a nonprofit organization prepares a work of art or writes a book within the scope of employment. The copyright would be owned by the nonprofit organization unless the parties agreed otherwise in

a written agreement. However, if the nonprofit organization had commissioned a person to prepare a work of art or to write a book, the nonprofit organization would be the source of copyright ownership only if there was a written agreement to that effect.

A copyright in a contribution is separate and distinct from a copyright in the collective work as a whole, and in the absence of an express transfer, the owner of the collective work obtains only certain limited rights to each contribution.[5] In the absence of an express transfer, the author of the separate individual article which appears in a collection retains all rights in the article except the right to reproduce and distribute the contribution as part of the collective work.[6].

Example: An author submits an article for publication to a literary magazine published by a nonprofit organization. Unless the author transfers his or her copyright in the article, the nonprofit organization would have a copyright only in the collective work.

FOOTNOTES

[1] 17 USC §201(a).
[2] 17 USC §201(b).
[3] 17 USC §101.
[4] 17 USC §101.
[5] 17 USC §201(c).
[6] 17 USC §201(c).

§4:10. —Copyright Protection.

To secure copyright protection, the owners of the work should place a notice on all visually perceptible copies that are distributed to the public.[1] The required elements for notice are: (1)

the symbol © (the letter "c" in a circle), or the word "Copyright," or the abbreviation "Copr.," (2) the year of first publication of the work, (3) the name of the owner of copyright in the work, or an abbreviation by which the name can be recognized, or a generally known alternative designation of the owner.[2] The year may be omitted for pictorial, graphic, or sculptural works where the work is reproduced in greeting cards, stationery, dolls, jewelry, or other such articles.[3]

Notice of copyright must be affixed to copies of a work in such a manner and location as to give reasonable notice of the claim of copyright.[4] The Register of Copyrights prescribed by regulation specific methods of affixation and positions of the notice on various types of work to satify the requirement.[5] For two-dimensional pictorial, graphic, or sculptural works, a notice can be placed on either the front or the back of the work or on a permanent mounting, matting, or framing.[6] For three-dimensional works, a label on any visible portion, including a permanent base, is sufficient.[7]

The notice of copyright should be placed on all publicly distributed copies of work.[8] Publication includes distribution of copies of work to the public by sale or other transfer of ownership and by rental or leasing.[9] Public display, by itself, does not constitute publication.[10] Thus, a nonprofit organization could exhibit a work of art without the notice.[11]

Under prior law, publication without the statutory notice caused the work to fall into the public domain; once a work goes into public domain, there is no copyright protection.[12] Under present law, a work becomes a part of the public domain if the copyright owner has authorized publication of the work without the notice of copyright and fails to register a claim for copyright in the United States Copyright Office within 5 years of publication without the notice.[13] Distribution of only a relatively small number of copies without the notice will not cause copyright to be lost if efforts are made to add the notice later.[14]

Within three months after a work has been published with a

copyright notice in the United States, the copyright owner must deposit two copies with the Library of Congress.[15] Registration of published or unpublished works, which is separate from depositing the work with the Library of Congress, is permissive; it can be made at any time during the copyright term.[16] A claim can be registered by depositing copies of the work with the Copyright Office with a completed application form and a fee.[17]

Registration is not a condition to copyright; however, it is required if a suit for infringement is instituted.[18] If infringement occurs after registration, the copyright owner is entitled to extraordinary remedies of attorney's fees and statutory damages.[19] If an infringement suit occurs before registration, the owner is entitled only to an injunction and actual damages.[20] Further, a certificate of registration is given prima facie weight in a judicial proceeding if the registration was made within 5 years after first publication of the work; thereafter, the court has discretion as to what weight the certificate will be given.[21]

Application forms for registration may be obtained from the Copyright Office.[22] There are five application forms: Form TX (for nondramatic literary works); Form PA (for works of the performing arts); Form VA (for works of the visual arts); Form SR (for sound recordings); and Form RE (for renewal of registrations). Form GR/CP (an adjunct application to be used for registration of a group of contributions to periodicals) is also available.

FOOTNOTES

[1] 17 USC §401(a).

[2] 17 USC §401(b). The notice would be as follows: © 1985 John Smith. **United States.** In order for a work to be protected under the Universal Copyright Convention, it must contain the letter "c" enclosed in a circle, together with the date and name of the owner. See Ross Products, Inc. v. New York Merchandise Company, 233 F Supp 260 (SD NY, 1964).

See Copyright Office Circular 38 which contains general information

186 Representing the Nonprofit Organization

about international copyright protection for United States authors. Circular 38 explains the use of the phrase "All Rights Reserved" which often follows the copyright notice. The term provides some advantages for copyright protection for United States authors in South American countries that are parties to the Buenos Aires Convention of 1910 though not members of the Universal Copyright Convention.

[3] 17 USC §401(b).

[4] 17 USC §401(c).

[5] 17 USC §401(c).

[6] 37 CFR §201.20(i)(1).

[7] 37 CFR §201.20(i)(2).

[8] 17 USC §401(a).

[9] 17 USC §101.

[10] 17 USC §101.

[11] See 17 USC §101 which provides that the offering to distribute copies to a group of persons for the purpose of further distribution, performance, or public display constitutes publication. Public display by itself, however, does not constitute performance. **United States.** See Brown v. Tabb, 714 F2d 1088 (CA11, 1983); Burke v. Todd, 598 F2d 688 (CA1, 1979), cert den, 444 US 869, 62 L Ed 2d 93, 100 S Ct 144 (1980), for a discussion of the common law (prior to the 1976 Copyright Act) regarding performance or exhibition constituting a publication. A mere performance or exhibition of a work did not result in a publication. A limited publication that communicated the contents of a work for a limited purpose and without the right of reproduction, distribution, or sale did not cause the work to lose its copyright by becoming the public domain; however, any circulation had to be restricted both as to persons and purposes.

[12] **United States.** See Bell v. Combined Registry Company, 397 F Supp 1241 (ND Ill, 1975), affd, 536 F2d 164 (CA7, 1976).

[13] 17 USC §405(a). However, any person who innocently infringes a copyright in reliance upon an authorized copy from which the copyright notice has been omitted incurs no liability for actual or statutory damages for any infringing acts committed before receiving actual notice that registration for the work has been made, if that person proves that he or she was misled by the omission of notice. See 17 USC §405(b).

United States. In Canfield v. Ponchatoula Times, 759 F2d 493 (CA5, 1985), the court discussed the notice requirements. The court held that a newspaper claiming a copyright ownership in an advertisement must give specific notice for the advertisement in addition to any copyright notice which purported to cover the newspaper as a whole. In addition, the notice must include a person claiming a copyright in the advertisement other than the collective work copyright owner.

[14] 17 USC §405(a).

[15] 17 USC §407(a). The Register of Copyrights may exempt by regulation any categories of material from the deposit requirements. See 17 USC §407(c).

At any time after publication of a work, the Register of Copyrights may make written demand for the required deposit on any of the persons obligated to make the deposit. Unless deposit is then made within three months after the demand is received, the person on whom the demand was made is liable to a fine of not more than $250 for each work plus the retail price of the copies demanded. If the person willfully or repeatedly fails to comply with the demand, the fine can be $2500. See 17 USC §407.

[16] 17 USC §408(a).

[17] 17 USC §408(b). See 17 USC §409 for the requirements for an application for copyright registration.

[18] 17 USC §411(a).

[19] See 17 USC §412.

[20] 17 USC §412.

[21] 17 USC §410(c).

[22] The address is Informational Publications Section, Copyright Office, Washington, D.C. 20559.

§4:11. —Public Performances of Copyrighted Music by Nonprofit Enterprises.

Under the 1947 Copyright Act, a copyright owner had the exclusive right to perform a copyrighted work publicly "for profit."[1] Consequently, most performances at nonprofit organizations were exempt from copyright protection, and there was no need for a nonprofit organization to secure permission to use copyrighted works. However, the 1976 Copyright Act removed the "for profit" limitation in its broad grant of power to copyright owners.[2] Nonetheless, the 1976 Copyright Act has specific limitations on the grant of power causing many performances by nonprofit organizations to remain exempt from copyright protection.[3] Consequently, in many instances nonprofit organizations still need not seek permission from the composer or publisher to use copyrighted music.[4]

Section 106 of the Copyright Act of 1976 grants copyright owners the exclusive right to perform a copyrighted work publicly.[5] However, everything in §106 is made subject to and must be read in conjunction with §§107–118.[6] The approach of the 1976 Act is to set forth the copyright owner's exclusive rights in broad terms and then to provide various limitations. One of the limitations is §110 which exempts certain nonprofit performances from copyright protection.[7]

The exemptions include, among others: (1) performances in the course of face-to-face teaching activities of a nonprofit educational institution; (2) performance of a nondramatic literary or musical work by or in the course of a transmission if the performance or display is a regular part of the systematic instructional activities of a nonprofit educational institution or governmental body when the performance is directly related to the teaching content of the transmission and the transmission is made primarily for reception in classrooms, for handicapped persons, or for officers or employees of governmental bodies as part of their official duties or employment; (3) performance of a nondramatic literary or musical work or of a dramatic musical work of a religious nature, or display of work, in the course of services at a place of worship or other religious assembly; (4) a nonprofit performance of a nondramatic literary or musical work (otherwise than transmission to the public) when there is no payment of any fee to any of the performers, promoters, or organizers and no admission charge is made (an admission charge will not destroy the exempt status if the proceeds are used exclusively for charitable purposes); (5) performance of a nondramatic musical work by a nonprofit agricultural or horticultural organization or by a governmental body in the course of an annual agricultural or horticultural fair or exhibition conducted by the nonprofit organization; and

(6) performance of a nondramatic musical work in the course of a transmission by certain designated carriers to the blind or other handicapped persons who are unable to read.[8] Performances of nondramatic literary or musical works in the course of a social function which is organized and promoted by a nonprofit veterans' organization or a nonprofit fraternal organization to which the general public is not invited (but not including the invitees of the organizations) are exempt if the proceeds from the performance are used exclusively for charitable purposes and not for financial gain.[9]

The exemption of nonprofit performances of nondramatic literary or musical works when there is no payment of any fee to a performer, promoter or organizer provides an exemption for the same general activities and subject matter covered by the "for profit" limitation of the former act: nonprofit public performances of nondramatic literary and musical works.[10] However, an important condition for the exemption is that the performance must be given without payment of any fee or other compensation for the performance to any of the performers, directors, or organizers. The exemption is not lost if the performer, directors, or organizers are paid a salary for duties encompassing the performance and are not paid directly.[11] While there is a further condition that no direct or indirect admission charge be made, this condition is not applicable if the net proceeds are used exclusively for educational, religious, or other charitable purposes and not for private financial gain.[12] Under this exception, the copyright owner is permitted to object to the use of his or her copyrighted work; however, a notice of objection must be served at least 7 days before the date of the performance and must comply with service requirements set out in the Register of Copyrights.[13]

Because of the exemptions from copyright coverage §§107-110, much of the music used by nonprofit organizations is still not subject to coverage by the Copyright Act.[14] However, each use should be carefully examined. Penalties for violation of the Copyright Act can be extensive.[15]

FOOTNOTES

[1] 61 Stat 652, 653 (1947). The Copyright Act of 1947 granted the copyright holder the exclusive right to "deliver or authorize the delivery of the copyrighted work in public for profit."

[2] 17 USC §106.

[3] See exemptions at 17 USC §§107–118.

[4] See USC §§107-118.

[5] Section 106 provides:
"Subject to section 107 through 118, the owner of copyright under this title has the exclusive rights to do and to authorize any of the following:

(1) to reproduce the copyrighted work in copies of phonorecords. . . .

(4) in the case of literary, musical, dramatic, and choreographic works, pantomimes, and motion pictures and other audiovisual works, to perform the copyrighted work publicly, and. . . ."

[6] Notes of Committee on the Judiciary, HR No. 1476, 94th Cong, 2d Sess 5, reprinted in 1976 US Code Cong & Ad News 5659, 5674.

[7] See 17 USC §110.

[8] There are ten general exceptions listed in 17 USC §110.

[9] 17 USC §110(10).

[10] 17 USC §110(4).

[11] 17 USC §110(4).

[12] 17 USC §110(4).

[13] 17 USC §110(4). As a practical matter, this provision is ineffective as a restraint upon the use of copyrighted music because it is unlikely that the copyrighted owner will learn of the performance in sufficient time to object properly.

[14] See Phelan, The Continuing Battle with the Performing Rights Societies: The Per Se Rule, the Rule of Reason Standard, and Copyright Misuse, 25 Texas Tech Law Review 349 (1984), for a discussion of the nonprofit exemptions regarding the use of music and the requirement by the performing rights societies, Broadcast Music, Inc. (BMI) and American Society of Composers, Authors, and Publishers (ASCAP), that users of music, including nonprofit organizations, obtain a blanket license in order to use any of the music copyrighted by members of these organizations.

[15] See 17 USC §504.

An infringer is liable for either the copyright owner's actual damages and additional profits of the infringer or statutory damages in a sum of not less than $250 or more than $10,000 as the court considers just. In the case of a willful offense, a court can increase statutory damages up to $50,000. In addition, an infringer is liable for attorney's fees of the copyright owner if the copyright owner prevails in the lawsuit. See 29 USC §505. A person who willfully infringes a copyright for purposes of commercial advantage or private financial gain can be subjected to criminal fines including imprisonment for not more than one year. See 29 USC §506.

§4:12. —Fair Use of Copyrighted Works.

The "fair use" of a copyrighted work is not an infringement of the copyright.[1] Fair use is the use by reproduction of copyrighted works for criticism, comment, news reporting, teaching (including multiple copies for classroom use), scholarship, or research.[2] In determining whether a use of copyrighted material is a fair use, the following factors are considered:

(1) the purpose and character of the use, including whether such use is of a commercial nature or is for nonprofit educational purposes,
(2) the nature of the copyrighted work,
(3) the amount and substantiality of the portion used in relation to the copyrighted work as a whole; and
(4) the effect of the use upon the potential market for or value of the copyrighted work.[3]

Fair use permits the photocopying of a complete work in some instances.[4] It permits library photocopying in proper circumstances, which includes an evaluation of all the applicable criteria and the facts of the particular case.[5] "Use" is not the same as infringement.[6] Fair use is most often defined as the "privilege in others than the owner of a copyright to use the copyrighted material in a reasonable manner without his consent, notwithstanding the monopoly granted to the owner."[7] The reproduction of copyrighted material for purposes of classroom teaching can constitute fair use; however, a finding of a nonprofit educational purpose does not automatically compel a finding of fair use.[8]

The question of how much copying for classroom use is permissible was of major concern to Congress and, although it did not include a section in the 1976 Copyright Act on the subject, it did approve a set of guidelines with respect to it.[9] These guidelines were intended to represent minimum standards of fair use; they are not binding.[10]

The guidelines indicate that multiple copies for classroom use are permissible if three tests, brevity, spontaneity, and cumulative effect, are met.[11] Spontaneity assumes that the copying was made as a result of a decision to use a work so close in time to its need that it would be unreasonable to expect a timely reply to a request for permission.[12] Cumulative effect requires that the copied material be for only one course in the school.[13]

A library or archive that provides reproducing equipment must display a notice next to equipment that the making of copies may be subject to the copyright law.[14]

FOOTNOTES

[1] 17 USC §107.

United States. See Sony Corporation v. Universal City Studios, — US —, 80 L Ed 2d 148, 104 S Ct 774, 784 (1984). The Supreme Court has stated that copyright protection has never accorded the copyright owner complete control over all possible uses of his work. As the Court stated, any individual may reproduce a copyrighted work for a "fair use," the copyright owner does not possess the exclusive right to such a use. The Supreme Court stated in the Sony case that an unlicensed use of the copyright is not an infringement unless it conflicts with one of the specific exclusive rights conferred by the copyright statute. (104 S Ct 791). The Court stated that time-shifting by private viewers through videotape recorders is not a violation of the copyright act.

[2] 17 USC §107.

[3] 17 USC §107.

[4] **United States.** See Williams & Wilkins Company v. United States, 487 F2d 1345, 1353 (Ct Cl 1973).

[5] **United States.** Williams & Wilkins Company v. United States, 487 F2d 1345, 1356 (Ct Cl, 1973).

LEGAL PROBLEMS OF NONPROFIT ENTERPRISES   193

⁶ **United States.** Sony Corporation v. Universal City Studios, — US —, 80 L Ed 2d 148, 104 S Ct 774, 784 (1984).
⁷ **United States.** Marcus v. Rowley, 695 F2d 1171, 1174 (CA9, 1983).
⁸ **United States.** Marcus v. Rowley, 695 F2d 1171, 1175 (CA9, 1983).
⁹ Conf Rep No. 1733, 94th Cong, 2d Sess 70, reprinted in 1976 US Cong & Ad News 5810, 5811.
¹⁰ **United States.** See Marcus v. Rowley, 695 F2d 1171, 1178 (CA9, 1983).
¹¹ **United States.** Marcus v. Rowley, 695 F2d 1171, 1178 (CA9, 1983). The court in the Marcus case found a violation of the copyright act when a school teacher copied almost 50% of the plaintiff's teaching materials into a booklet which she prepared for use in her classes. She used the booklet for three school years. The court stated that fair use does not cover such extensive use of copyrighted material.

See also Encyclopaedia Britannica Education Corporation v. Crooks, 447 F Supp 243 (WD NY, 1978) wherein the court also found excessive copyrighting which could not be defended under the doctrine of fair use.

In drafting the 1976 Copyright Act, the Copyright Committee recognized that there is a need for greater certainty and protection for teachers concerning limited copying. See Notes of Committee on the Judiciary, H R No. 1476, 94th Cong, 2d Sess 5, reprinted in 1976 US Code Cong & Ad News 5659, 5674. In order to meet that need, §504(c) of the Act was amended to provide teachers and other nonprofit users of copyrighted material with broad insulation against unwarranted liability for infringement. Section 504, which provides remedies for infringement, provides that if an infringer believed and had reasonable grounds for believing his use of the copyrighted work was a fair use, the court *must* remit statutory damages if the infringer is an employee of a nonprofit educational institution, library, or archives and was acting within the scope of employment when the infringing act occurred.

¹² **United States.** Marcus v. Rowley, 695 F2d 1171, 1178 (CA9, 1983).
¹³ **United States.** Marcus v. Rowley, 695 F2d 1171, 1178 (CA9, 1983).
¹⁴ See 17 USC §108.

§4:13. Securities Laws.

Directors of nonprofit organizations must be aware of possible application of federal or state securities laws should they issue, for consideration, stocks, bonds, or other security certificates. The Securities Act of 1933[1] provides that unless an exempted security or an exempted transaction is involved, no offer to sell or buy a security may be made by the mails or in interstate commerce unless a registration statement has been filed.[1] In addition, after a registration statement has been filed, no prospectus may be used unless the prospectus meets the requirements of the act.[3] Further, no delivery of securities after a sale may be made unless a registration statement as to the securities is in effect, and any deliveries must be preceded or accompanied by a prospectus that meets the requirements of the act.[4]

Securities that are covered by the act include much more than stock certificates.[5] Debentures and memberships in a foundation have been held to be securities.[6] Application blanks used by a nonprofit association in procuring contributions to the association that indicated the contributors would receive 30% of profits per annum from the agricultural operations of the association have been held to be securities and covered by the act.[7] Mortgage bonds of a charitable hospital have been held to be securities; their sale must be in compliance with the act.[8]

There have been questions as to whether an interest in a pooled income fund is a security covered by the act.[9] A pooled income fund may be deemed to be an investment contract which is a security under the act and required to be registered.[10] A pooled income fund provides income to noncharitable beneficiaries; thus, a part of the earnings inure to the benefit of private individuals. Because the fund's donor receives income from the fund, the transfer could be characterized as a sale. However, the SEC has taken the position that if a pooled income fund qualifies its donors for deductible charitable contributions, it is not required to register.[11] Nevertheless, each donor must receive written disclosure that describes the pooled income fund's operation in detail, and all fund raisers must be either volunteers or persons employed by the charity.[12] A pooled income fund may be a security under state securities laws.[13] There are civil and criminal penalties for failure to comply with the Securities Act. Even if a security is exempt from registration, the antifraud provisions of the act will apply if interstate commerce or use of the mails is involved, either directly or indirectly.[14]

In order to comply with the antifraud provisions of the federal securities laws, a disclosure statement describing in detail the fund, debenture, or other form of security should be issued to prospective purchasers.[15] The statement must contain no misleading information and must not omit any material facts concerning the transaction.[16]

FOOTNOTES

[1] 15 USC §§77a–77aa.
See Prifti Securities Pub & Private Offerings § 31:02 (Rev Ed).

[2] 15 USC §77e(a). If a security is not sold in interstate commerce or by use of the mails, it may nonetheless be subject to registration under state securities laws.

[3] 15 USC §§77c(b), 77j. A prospectus must contain information required by rules or regulations of the SEC as being necessary or appropriate in the public interest or for the protection of investors.
See 15 USC §77j(c); 17 CFR §§229.500–229.601, §§230.420-230.432.
United States. See Securities and Exchange Commission v. Manor Nursing Centers, 458 F2d 1082, 1098 (CA2, 1972) wherein the court stated that a prospectus must contain, with specified exceptions, all the information contained in the registration statement. In turn, the registration statement must contain information concerning the use of the proceeds, the estimated net proceeds, the price at which the security will be offered to the public and any variation therefrom, and all commissions or discounts paid to underwriters, directly or indirectly. Any developments subsequent to the effective date of the registration statement that would make information in the regis-

196 Representing the Nonprofit Organization

[4] 15 USC §77e.

[5] See 15 USC §77b. Securities are defined as notes, stock, treasury stock, evidences of indebtedness, certificates of interest or participation in any profit-sharing agreement, collateral-trust certificates, preorganization certificate or subscription, transferable share, investment contract, voting-trust certificate, certificate of deposit for a security, and fractional interest in oil, gas, or other mineral rights.

See Prifti Securities Pub & Private Offerings §31:05 (Rev Ed).

[6] **United States.** Securities and Exchange Commission v. American Foundation for Advanced Education of Arkansas, 222 F Supp 828 (WD La, 1963).

[7] **United States.** Securities and Exchange Commission v. Universal Service Association, 106 F2d 232 (CA 7, 1939).

[8] **United States.** Securities and Exchange Commission v. Children's Hospital, 214 F Supp 883 (D Ariz, 1963).

[9] 15 USC §§77k, 771-1.

[10] 15 USC §77q.

United States. See Securities and Exchange Commission v. W J Howey Company, 328 US 293, 90 L Ed 1244, 66 S Ct 1100 (1946) which defines an investment contract as a transaction in which a person invests money in a common enterprise and expects profits solely from the efforts of a promoter or a third party.

[11] See Pooled Income Funds, Release No. 33–6175, 34–16478, IC–11016 (1980). The fund must qualify for tax deductions under §642(c)(5) of the Internal Revenue Code.

[12] Pooled Income Funds, Release No. 33–6175, 34–16478, IC–11016 (1980). The antifraud provisions of the federal securities acts do apply to pooled income funds.

See 15 USC §§77-1, 77q.

[13] The majority of the states have adopted the Uniform Securities Act which provides that if securities are issued by an organization that meets the not-for-profit requirements of the act §402(a)(9), the securities are exempt from registration. State statutes should always be consulted on this issue.

See discussion of state statutes at §4:16.

[14] 15 USC §77q.

See Prifti Securities Pub & Private Offerings §9:07 (Rev Ed).

[15] See 15 USC §77q(a).

[16] 15 USC §77q(a).

See also 17 CFR §240.10b–5.

§4:14. —Exemptions for Securities Issued by Nonprofit Enterprises.

The principal exemptions from registration under the Securities Act of 1933 are found under §§3 and 4 of the Act.[1] Section 3 exempts securities issued by an entity organized and operated exclusively for religious, educational, benevolent, fraternal, charitable, or reformatory purposes and not for pecuniary profit, and in which no part of the net earnings may inure to the benefit of any person, private stockholder, or individual.[2] Section 4 exempts certain transactions not involving a public offering.[3]

Directors of nonprofit enterprises must not assume that because §3 of the Securities Act of 1933 exempts securities issued by certain nonprofit organizations, they have no problems relating to the securities act. The exemption under §3 is limited; the courts have held that anyone who asserts an exemption has the burden of proving its availability.[4] Courts have also held that a single substantial for-profit purpose will destroy the exemption.[5] If any of the net earnings from a particular sale of debentures or other securities will inure to the benefit of any private individual, the issuance is not exempt.[6] Further, the exemption does not cover all nonprofit organizations. In addition, even though an issuance by a charity may be exempt from registration, the antifraud provisions of the act are nonetheless applicable.[7] Thus, the possible application of the securities act must be considered whenever a nonprofit organization decides to sell securities, or forms of securities.

FOOTNOTES

[1] 15 USC §§77c, 77d.
See Prifti Securities Pub & Private Offerings §§1:03, 1:04 (Rev Ed).

198 Representing the Nonprofit Organization

[2] 15 USC §77c(4). Note that not all nonprofit organizations are covered by this exemption. **United States.** See Bastian v. Lakefront Realty Corporation, 581 F2d 685 (CA7, 1978) where the court held that a corporation, engaged solely in the business of owning, maintaining, and leasing property used only as a social and athletic club, did not have the basis for an exemption under the act. The club had 500 shareholders and only club members could own stock.

See also Securities and Exchange Commission v. American Foundation for Advanced Education of Arkansas, 222 F Supp 828 (WD La, 1963). The court held that the sale of debentures and membership in an educational foundation would not be exempt from the act because the purchasers of the debentures received a monetary benefit in the form of the foundation paying the cost of board, room, tuition, and other college fees; thus, profits of the foundation were returned to the members. To come under the exemption, none of the net earnings of the organization may inure to the benefit of any private individual.

If a nonprofit organization is covered by the exemption, the exemption becomes permanent because it applies to the security and not to the transaction. Thus, a nonprofit organization meeting the requirement of 15 USC §77(c)(4) need not determine whether its exempted securities are being distributed or traded or whether the person selling them is an issuer, an affiliate of the issuer, a nonaffiliate, or a broker-dealer.

[3] 15 USC §77d.

[4] **United States.** Securities and Exchange Commission v. American Foundation for Advanced Education of Arkansas, 222 F Supp 828 (WD La, (1963).

[5] **United States.** See Better Business Bureau of Washington v. United States, 326 US 279, 90 L Ed 67, 66 S Ct 112 (1945); Securities and Exchange Commission v. American Foundation for Advanced Education of Arkansas, 222 F Supp 828 (WD La, 1963).

[6] **United States.** See Securities and Exchange Commission v. Children's Hospital, 214 F Supp 883 (D Ariz, 1963); Securities and Exchange Commission v. American Foundation for Advanced Education of Arkansas, 222 F Supp 828 (WD La, (1963). The court in the Children's Hospital case stated that a charitable corporation can engage in income producing activities and still be a corporation operated exclusively for charitable purposes as long as the income producing activities were purely incidental to the principal charitable purposes to which the income was devoted. However, because a substantial purpose of the organization of the hospital was to entice promoters by providing them with large profits from the enterprise, there could be no exemption under the Securities Act. The court also stated that if it is

known that the character of the corporation will change from a noncommercial to a commercial one, any securities should be registered immediately.
[7] See 15 USC §77q.

§4:15. Sale of Securities Donated to a Nonprofit Organization.

Securities donated to a nonprofit enterprise are not exempt securities; thus, any sale of these securities by the nonprofit organization can present problems under the securities laws. Any securities received by a nonprofit organization as a donation may be restricted securities.[1] If so, in order to sell the securities, the donee nonprofit organization must follow the requirements of SEC Rule 144.[2]

The problem regarding securities of outsiders held by nonprofit organizations related to §4 of the Securities Act of 1933.[3] While §3 of the Act[4] exempts securities issued by nonprofit entities organized and operated exclusively for religious, educational, benevolent, fraternal, charitable, or reformatory purposes, from the broad registration and prospectus requirements of §5 of the act, securities of outsiders are generally not exempt securities; consequently, their sale, including those by nonprofit organizations, will be subject to the act if they are "restricted" securities.[5]

Under §4 of the 1933 Act, transactions by any person other than an issuer, underwriter, or dealer are exempt from the registration and prospectus requirements of the 1933 Act.[6] Thus, only transactions by an issuer, underwriter, or dealer are covered by the act. The definition of an "underwriter" can be far-reaching, however.[7] Rule 144 was designed to permit the public sale of limited amounts of securities owned by persons who would otherwise be deemed underwriters. A limited number of securities owned by persons controlling, or controlled by, the issuer and by persons who have acquired "restricted" securities of the issuer may be sold without registration if the provisions of Rule 144 are followed.[8]

Under Rule 144, a nonprofit organization that has acquired "restricted" stock must hold the stock at least 2 years prior to sale.[9] However, the donee nonprofit institution may count the donor's holding period as part of its own.[10] There must be adequate current public information about the issuer corporation at the time of the sale.[11] Only a limited amount of the securities may be sold during any three month period and the donor and donee must group their sales together for these purposes for 2 years following the gift.[12] The securities must be sold without soliciting orders to buy the securities, without the seller making any payment to anyone other than the seller's broker, and only in brokers' transactions or transactions directly with a market maker.[13] A notice of the proposed sale must be sent to the SEC and to the principal securities exchange on which the securities are listed.[14]

If the securities have been held for more than 3 years (the donee may add the donor's holding period to its own to determine whether it has held the stock for 3 years), the compliance problems in selling the restricted securities under Rule 144 are substantially reduced.[15] If the 3-year holding period is in effect, the donee may sell the stock immediately with no volume limitation, and without manner of sale and notice of sale requirements.[16]

FOOTNOTES

[1] Such securities may have been issued pursuant to Regulation D (17CFR §§230.501–230.506) which provides certain issuers with limited offering exemptions from the registration and prospectus delivery requirements of §5 of the Securities Act of 1933 (15 USC §77e). However, some of Regulation D securities will be restricted shares and, if so, a resale must comply with Rule 144 (17 CFR §230.144). Regulation D provides that stock can be issued in limited amounts without registration under three different provisions: Rules 504 (17 CFR §230.504), 505 (17 CFR §230.505), 506 (17 CFR §230.506). Rule 504 permits any issuer, other than an investment company

or an Exchange Act nonreporting company, to offer and sell a maximum of $500,000 of securities to an unlimited number of persons during a 12-month period without requiring that any specific information be furnished to the purchasers. If the stock is registered pursuant to state securities laws, there are no prohibitions on resale; consequently, this stock could be resold by the donee nonprofit organization without the requirement of complying with Rule 144. Rule 505 permits the sale of securities, by any investor, except an investment company, of up to $5 million in a 12-month period to 35 nonaccredited investors and to an unlimited number of accredited investors without the requirement of registration. If the investors are accredited investors, no specific information need be furnished the purchasers; however, if any securities are offered to any purchaser other than an accredited investor, Rule 502 (17 CFR §230.502) requires that the same type of information as that required in Part I of Form S–18 (which is an abbreviated registration statement for nonexempt issues up to $5 million by smaller companies) be furnished to the extent material to an understanding of the issuer, its business, and the securities being offered. Rule 506 permits any issuer an unlimited amount of offerings without registration to an unlimited number of accredited investors but to not more than 35 nonaccredited investors. If any nonaccredited investors are offered any securities, Rule 502 requires that the same type of information as would be required to be included in Part I of a registration statement filed under the 1933 Act be furnished to the extent material to an understanding of the issuer, the business, and the securities being offered.

In summary, all offerings issued pursuant to Rules 505, 506 are restricted securities and a resale must comply with Rule 144. Offerings under Rule 504 are restricted unless the securities were registered in the states that require delivery of a disclosure document.

Even though securities are exempt from registration when issued pursuant to Regulation D, the offerings are not exempt from the antifraud or civil liability provisions of the 1933 Securities Act; thus, issuers must provide material information that would be necessary to make the information required not misleading. In addition, sales must not be accomplished through general advertising or solicitation and the issuer must inform the purchasers of the restrictions on resale (17 CFR §230.502). Further, a notice of sale must be filed with the SEC (17 CFR §230.503).

An accredited investor includes the following: certain defined banks, insurance companies and investment companies; defined private business development companies; nonprofit organizations described in §501(c)(3) of the Internal Revenue Code with assets in excess of $5 million; affiliates of the issuer; an individual whose net worth exceeds $1 million, or whose net income for the present and the past two years exceeds $200,000.

See 17 CFR §230.501.
For further discussion of Regulation D, see Prifti Securities Pub & Private Offerings §§4:05–4:11 (Rev Ed).

[2] 17 CFR §230.144. However, as noted in footnote 1, stock issued pursuant to Rule 504 of Regulation D that has been registered under state securities laws is not restricted stock and, thus, the donee may sell that stock without the requirement of complying with Rule 144.
See 14 CFR §230.504(b)(1).

[3] 15 USC §77d.

[4] 15 USC §77c.

[5] See discussion in footnote 1.

[6] 15 USC §77d(1).

[7] "Underwriter" is defined in 15 USC §77b(11) as any person who has purchased from an issuer with a view to, or offers or sells for an issuer in connection with, the distribution of any security, or participates or has a direct or indirect participation in any such undertaking, or participates or has a participation in the direct or indirect underwriting of any such undertaking.

[8] See 17 CFR §230.144; Prifti Securities Pub & Private Offerings §4:12 (Rev Ed).

[9] 17 CFR §230.144(d).

[10] 17 CFR §230.144(d)(v).

[11] 17 CFR §230.144(c).

[12] 17 CFR §230.144(e).

[13] 17 CFR §230.144(f).

[14] 17 CFR §230.144(h).

[15] 17 CFR §230.144(k).

[16] 17 CFR §230.144(k).

§4:16. —Compliance with State Securities Laws.

Even though sale of a security by a nonprofit enterprise may be exempt from the Federal Securities Act, it may nonetheless be subject to state securities provisions.[1] The 1933 Securities Act did not remove state jurisdiction over securities.[2]

Most states have adopted the Uniform Securites Act.[3] This Act is broader than the Federal Securities Act and exempts from registration those securities of nonprofit entities that are organized and operated exclusively for religious, educational, benevolent, fraternal, charitable or reformatory purposes or as a chamber of commerce or trade or professional association.[4] However, some of the states that have adopted the Uniform Securities Act have nonetheless limited the exemption for the various nonprofit organizations.[5]

Some states have exempted securities of a broader range of nonprofit organizations. Texas statutes exempt any securities issued and sold by a domestic corporation without capital stock and not organized nor engaged in business for profit.[6] Illinois exempts securities of entities organized and operated not for pecuniary profit and exclusively for religious, educational, benevolent, fraternal, agricultural, charitable, trade, social or reformatory purposes,[7] California exempts any securities of an issuer organized exclusively for education, benevolent, fraternal, religious, charitable, social, or reformatory purposes and those organized as a chamber of commerce or trade or professional association.[8]

Some states have a more narrow exemption than the federal act or the Uniform Securities Act. For example, Florida statutes exempt securities issued by corporations organized exclusively for religious, educational, benevolent, fraternal, charitable, or reformatory purposes but with the provision that no person may directly or indirectly offer or sell securities except by an offering circular containing full and fair disclosure of all material information including a description of the securities offered and the terms of the offering; a description of the nature of the issuer's business; a statement of the purpose of the offering and the intended application by the issuer of the proceeds of the sale; and financial statements of the issuer prepared in conformance with generally accepted accounting principles.[9]

FOOTNOTES

[1] See 15 USC §77r.

[2] 15 USC §77r.

[3] See Prifti Securities Pub & Private Offerings §6:16 (Rev Ed).

See, as examples: Ala Code §§8-6-1 to 8-6-23; Ark Stat Ann §§67-1235 to 67-1337; Ind Code §§23-2-1-1 to 23-2-1-24; Kan Stat Ann §§17-1252 to17-1275 Ky Rev Stat §§292.310-292.550; Mont Code Ann §§3-10-101 to 3-10-308; Or Rev Stat §§59.005-59.995; Utah Code Ann §§61-1-1 to 61-1-30; Wyo Stat §§17-4-101 to 17-4-129.

[4] Like the Federal Securities Act, the Uniform Securities Act does not exempt securities of nonprofit organizations from antifraud and civil liability provisions of the act.

[5] See, as examples: NJ Stat Ann §49:3-50(9), See 7A Unif Laws Ann 638, Uniform Securities Act §402. Mont Code Ann §30-10-104.

See also Pa Stat Ann, tit 70, §1-202(e). The Pennsylvania statute provides that the fact that amounts received from memberships or dues will or may be used to construct or otherwise acquire facilities for use by members of the nonprofit organization does not disqualify the organization from the exemption. However, the exemption will not apply to the securities of any nonprofit organization if any promoter expects or intends to make a profit directly or directly from any business or activity associated with the organization or operation of the nonprofit organization. Pa Stat Ann tit 70, §1-202(e).

[6] Tex Civ Stat §581-6(E). Notes, bonds, or other evidences of indebtedness of religious, charitable or benevolent corporations are also exempt securities in Texas. See Tex Civ Stat §581-6(J).

The sale of any security or membership issued by a corporation or association organized exclusively for religious, educational, benevolent, fraternal, charitable or reformatory purposes and not for pecuniary profit, and no part of whose earnings will inure to the benefit of any stockholder, shareholder, or individual member, and where no commission or remuneration is paid or is to be paid or given in connection with the disposition is an exempt transaction under the Texas statute. See Tex Civ Stat §581-5(K).

[7] Ill Rev Stat ch 121½, par 137.3(H).

[8] Cal Corp Code §25100(j).

The California statute also provides that the fact that amounts received from memberships or dues will or may be used to construct or otherwise acquire facilities for use by members of the nonprofit organization does not disqualify the organization for the exemption. However, the exemption will not apply to the securities of any nonprofit organization if any promoter

expects or intends to make a profit directly or indirectly from any business or activity associated with the organization or operation of the nonprofit organization or from remuneration received from the nonprofit organization. (Cal Corp Code §25l00(j).
[9] Fla Stat Ann §517.051(4).

§4:17. Application of Antitrust Laws to Nonprofit Enterprises.

While nonprofit enterprises have often escaped liability under the antitrust laws, there actually is nothing in the language of the Sherman Act that would prevent its application to the nonprofit organization.[1] The Supreme Court has stated that it is "beyond debate that nonprofit organizations can be liable under the antitrust laws."[2] However, because the Sherman Act regulates "commerce" that affects trade among the several states,[3] the courts have examined practices of nonprofit organizations to determine whether a particular activity is commercial in nature.[4] Consequently, in this context, an incidental restraint of trade by a nonprofit organization that has no intent or purpose to affect the commercial aspects of a business or profession has not, in the past, been subject to antitrust laws.[5]

Some recent applications of the antitrust laws to nonprofit enterprises have indicated a current tendency by the courts to find commercial involvement.[6] The increasing importance of private associations in the affairs of individuals and organizations has led to substantial expansion of judicial control over the internal affairs of associations not for profit and, in that context, a broader application of the antitrust laws to nonprofit organizations.[7] While the courts, in applying the antitrust laws to the nonprofit organization, still generally look toward a nexus between the practice of the organization and commercial or business activities, a court could nonetheless impose liability under the act without finding a direct involvement in commerce.[8]

Activities of a nonprofit enterprise that are not commercial in nature have been evaluated under the antitrust laws using a "rule of reason" standard.[9] Those activities which are premised on public service or public welfare have been evaluated using this standard.[10] However, certain conduct, such as price fixing, is deemed to be a per se violation of the Sherman Act regardless of the fact that a nonprofit organization is involved.[11]

FOOTNOTES

[1] See 15 USC §§7, 15. There is no distinction in the statutes between business and nonprofit organizations and no other language in the statute that would limit jurisdiction to particular corporation.

Section 13c of the Sherman Act (15 USC 13c) provides that the price discrimination provisions of the Act (15 USC §§13–13b, 21a) will not apply to purchases of supplies for their own use by schools, colleges, universities, public libraries, churches, hospitals, and charitable institutions not operated for profit. However, this provision has limited application.

See Callmann Unfair Comp, Trademarks & Monopolies §1:02 (4th Ed).

[2] **United States.** See American Society of Mechanical Engineers v. Hydrolevel Corporation, 456 US 556, 72 L Ed2d 330, 102 S Ct 1935 (1982).

[3] 15 USC §§1, 2.

[4] **United States.** See Goldfarb v. Virginia State Bar, 421 US 657, 44 L Ed2d 572, 95 S Ct 2004 (1975); National Society of Professional Engineers v. United States, 435 US 679, 55 L Ed2d 637, 98 S Ct 1355 (1978); Arizona v. Maricopa County Medical Society, 457 US 332, 73 L Ed2d 48, 102 S Ct 2466 (1982).

[5] **United States.** In Association for Intercollegiate Athletics for Women v. National Collegiate Athletic Ass'n, 735 F2d 577 (CA DC, 1984), the court stated that practices by nonprofit organizations that economically disadvantage consumers are prohibited even though such practices are designed to advance independent social or political values; however, the court noted that the achievement of an essential noncommercial activity may justify some anticompetitive impact.

See Apex Hosiery Company v. Leader, 310 US 469, 84 L Ed 1311, 60 S Ct 982 (1940). The Supreme Court stated in the Apex case that the Sherman Act does not condemn all combinations and conspiracies which interrupt interstate transportation. According to the Court in Apex, the end sought by the antitrust laws is the prevention of restraints to free competition in businesses and commercial transactions. The Court in Apex recognized that the act was aimed primarily at combinations having commercial objectives and stated that it should be applied only in a very limited extent to organizations, like labor unions, that normally have other objectives.

See also Majorie Webster Junior College, Inc. v. Middle States Association of Colleges & Secondary Schools, Inc., 432 F2d 650 (CA DC, 1970) wherein the court stated that the proscriptions of the Sherman Act were tailored for the business world, not for noncommercial aspects of the liberal arts and the learned professions. The court ruled that an incidental restraint of trade, absent an intent or purpose to affect the commercial aspects of the profession, was not sufficient to warrant application of the antitrust laws. The court was of the opinion that the process of accreditation was an activity distinct from the sphere of commerce; according to the court, it "goes rather to the heart of the concept of education itself." The court felt that Congress did not intend this concept to be modeled by the policies underlying the Sherman Act.

[6] **United States.** See American Society of Mechanical Engineers v. Hydrolevel Corporation, 456 US 556, 72 L Ed2d 330, 102 S Ct 1935 (1982); Arizona v. Maricopa County Medical Society, 457 US 332, 73 L Ed2d 48, 102 S Ct 2466 (1982); National Society of Professional Engineers v. United States, 435 US 679, 55 L Ed2d 637, 102 S Ct 1355 (1978); Goldfarb v. Virginia State Bar, 421 US 657, 44 L Ed2d 576, 95 S Ct 2004 (1975).

See also Federal Prescription Service v. American Pharmaceutical Association, 484 F Supp 1195 (D DC, 1980).

[7] See Majorie Webster Junior College, Inc. v. Middle States Association of Colleges and Secondary Schools, 432 F2d 650 (CA DC, 1970).

[8] **United States.** See Hennessey v. National Collegiate Athletic Association, 564 F2d 1136 (CA5, 1977) in which the NCAA asserted that it was a voluntary, nonprofit organization whose activities and objectives were educational, carried out with respect to amateur athletics and, thus, should be exempt from the Sherman Act. The court rejected that argument, stating that while it was sound prior to 1975, the Goldfarb case Goldfarb v. Virginia State Bar, 421 US 773, 44 L Ed2d 572, 95 S Ct 2004 (1975), supported the view that such a blanket exclusion could no longer be accepted. According to the Fifth Circuit in Hennessey, Congress did not intend that the Sherman Act should be read with so wide an exemption.

See National Collegiate Athletic Association v. Board of Regents of University of Oklahoma and University of Georgia Athletic Association, 463 US 1311, 82 L Ed 2d 70, 104 S Ct 1 (1984) in which the Supreme Court held the practices of the NCAA to be a violation of the Sherman Act. The Court stated

208 Representing the Nonprofit Organization

in footnote 22 in that case that "the sweeping language of §1 of the Sherman Act applies without doubt to nonprofit entities." The Court noted that the economic significance of the NCAA's nonprofit character was questionable inasmuch as the NCAA is organized to maximize revenues. At any rate, it noted that the NCAA was not relying on its nonprofit character as a basis of challenge of the lower court. In a dissenting opinion, Justice White noted that although the NCAA does not enjoy blanket immunity from the antitrust laws, the Sherman Act is aimed at combinations that have commercial objectives and should be applied to a very limited extent to organizations that normally have other objectives.

In the Goldfarb decision, the Court declared that a minimum fee schedule enforced by a bar association constituted price fixing. However, in a footnote (footnote 17), the Court preserved a distinction between professions and businesses in antitrust analysis. The Court noted, in the footnote, that the public service aspect and other features of the professions could require that a particular practice, which would properly be viewed as a violation of the Sherman Act in another context, should be treated differently. The more recent Supreme Court cases involving nonprofit organizations as cited above—National Society of Professional Engineers v. United States, Arizona v. Maricopa County Medical Society, American Society of Mechanical Engineers v. Hydrolevel Corporation, and National Collegiate Athletic Association v. Board of Regents of University of Oklahoma and University of Georgia Athletic Association—have all applied the Sherman Act to the nonprofits. However, each of the cases involved what the Court deemed to be commercial activity on the part of the nonprofit.

In the American Society of Mechanical Engineers case, the Supreme Court substantially broadened the reach of the antitrust laws by applying the agency law doctrine of apparent authority to hold the nonprofit association liable under the Sherman Act for the unauthorized anti-competitive acts of its members. In that case an official of a competitor of the plaintiff was vice-president of the nonprofit corporation's subcommittee that drafted and interpreted a segment of the organization's code governing safety devices for use in water boilers. The subcommittee determined that Hydrolevel's product was unsafe. The official's company, Hydrolevel's competitor, used the subcommittee's response to discourage customers from buying Hydrolevel's products. The Supreme Court held the nonprofit organization responsible for the anti-trust violation of its member.

While all of the recent pronouncements of the Supreme Court holding nonprofit organizations liable under the Sherman Act involve some aspect of commercial activity, there is a question whether the Court might carry its rulings further and hold charitable nonprofit organizations liable. In this context, the united charities controversies present questions concerning application of the Sherman Act. Other charities have already challenged, to date without success, the authority of businesses to solicit only on behalf of the United Way. See Moye v. Chrysler Corporation, 465 F Supp 1189 (ED Mo, 1979) in which the plaintiff challenged the right of an employer to deny payroll deductions for the United Black Community Fund when deductions were permitted for the United Way. See also National Black United Fund v. Devine, 667 F2d 173 (CA DC, 1981) where the National Black United Fund challenged the United Way as being controlled by larger charities. It contended that the larger, more conservative donors were biased both against new charities and against organizations seeking to serve the black community. The Civil Service Commission rejected the application of the National Black United Fund to participate in a combined federal campaign and an on the job solicitation directed at federal governmental employees. The Court held the National Black United Fund did not provide evidence of how its activities would be adversely affected if it were required to associate with the local United Way.

While neither of these cases involved a challenge against the united charities based on antitrust violations, it is conceivable that the courts might consider such a challenge in light of the recent Supreme Court cases. However, in this context, the courts might still take the position that the competition does not originate in the market place or as a sector of the economy and, thus, might rule that charitable solicitation has no nexus to commercial or business activities.

[9] The rule of reason is a standard, based upon common-law tradition, used to analyze transactions that provide restraints upon trade. The facts peculiar to the business, the history of the restraint, and the reasons why it was imposed are analyzed to determine the competitive effects of an agreement. If the restraint is found to be unreasonable in terms of its impact on competitive conditions, the agreement is in violation of the Sherman Act.

United States. See Board of Trade of City of Chicago v. United States, 246 US 231, 62 L Ed 683, 35 S Ct 242 (1918); National Society of Professional Engineers v. United States, 435 US 679, 55 L Ed2d 637, 98 S Ct 1355 (1978) for a discussion of the application of the rule of reason standard to practices of trade and professional associations.

The Chicago Board of Trade case was the first case to suggest that an arrangement which advanced the public interest could be reasonable and, thus, not a violation of the Sherman Act even though detrimental to competition.

However, Justice Stevens stated in National Society of Professional Engineers that unreasonableness under the rule of reason standard can only be based upon (a) the nature or character of the contracts or (b) on the surrounding circumstances giving rise to the inference or presumption that they were intended to restrain trade and enhance prices. Justice Stevens stated that under either branch of the test, the inquiry should be confined to a consideration of the impact on competitive conditions.

[10] **United States.** See Boddicker v. Arizona State Dental Association, 549 F2d 626 (CA9, 1977); Feminist Women's Health Center v. Mohammed, 415 F Supp 1258 (ND Fla, 1976). In the Feminist Women's Health Center case the court stated that the defendant had the burden of proving that it had a good faith motive to protect the public health and welfare.

See also National Society of Professional Engineers v. United States, 435 US 679, 55 L Ed2d 637, 98 S Ct 1355 (1978) which retains the rule of reason standard to evaluate ethical norms that serve to regulate and promote competition for professional associations but which rejects its application to price fixing agreements imposed by professional associations upon its members. These agreements, according to the Supreme Court, are per se violations of the Sherman Act.

[11] **United States.** See Arizona v. Maricopa County Medical Society, 457 US 332, 72 L Ed 2d 330, 102 S Ct 2466 (1982); United States Dental Institute v. American Association of Orthodontists, 396 F Supp 565 (ND Ill, 1975). If the challenged conduct is inconsistent with the public welfare, the per se rules will cause such practices to fall under the prohibitions of the Sherman Act.

According to the Supreme Court in the Maricopa County Medical Society case, price fixing agreements not premised on public service or ethical norms are per se violations of the Sherman Act. But see National Collegiate Athletic Association v. Board of Regents of University of Oklahoma and University of Georgia Athletic Association, — US —, 79 L Ed 2d 674, 104 S Ct 1, 52 USLW 4928 (1984) in which the Court analyzed the price fixing activities of the NCAA using the Rule of Reason standard. The Court stated it would be inappropriate to apply a per se rule because it involved an industry in which horizontal restraints on competition were essential if the product was to be available at all. Nonetheless, the Rule of Reason standard did not produce a different result. The practices of the NCAA were held to violate the Sherman Act.

§4:18. *Unfair Competition.*

Whereas the Sherman Act forbids restraints on competition, the unfair competition law imposes restraints on that competition; it polices unfair practices.[1] However, those practices are still competition; thus, they are outside the antitrust laws.[2]

LEGAL PROBLEMS OF NONPROFIT ENTERPRISES 211

Unfair methods of competition in commerce and unfair or deceptive acts or practices in commerce are unlawful under the unfair competition laws.[3] The Federal Trade Commission is given authority under the unfair competition act to monitor organizations for unfair business practices.[4]

The unfair competition laws do not apply to most activities of nonprofit organizations.[5] Section 4 of the act provides that the act applies to a corporation, trust, or association that is "organized to carry on business for its own profit or that of its members."[6] Consequently, the Federal Trade Commission can regulate nonprofit organizations if they are in fact profitmaking enterprises.[7] However, Congress did not intend to bring within the reach of the Commission any and all nonprofit organizations regardless of their purposes and activities.[8] The courts have held that the act does not apply to a charitable nonprofit organization even though the organization does conduct profit making activities so long as the income is devoted exclusively to the purposes of the corporation and is not distributed to members or shareholders.[9] However, the Commission may regulate nonprofit trade associations that carry on a business for their own profit or for that of their members.[10] In addition, the Federal Trade Commission may monitor nonprofit organizations that take unfair competitive advantage of their nonprofit status.[11]

FOOTNOTES

[1] See 15 USC §45.
United States. See Mid-West Underground Storage, Inc v. Porter, 717 F2d 493 (CA 10, 1983).
[2] **United States.** Mid-West Underground Storage, Inc v. Porter, 717 F2d 493 (CA10, 1983).
[3] 15 USC §45.
[4] See 15 USC §§41–58.
Callmann, Unfair Comp, Trademarks & Monopolies §24:01 (Rev Ed).
[5] **United States.** Community Blood Bank of Kansas City Area v. Federal

Trade Commission, 405 F2d 1011 (CA8, 1969). Cf., Callmann, Unfair Comp, Trademarks & Monopolies §1:02 (4th Ed).

[6] 15 USC §44. This provision differs from the antitrust laws which make no distinction whatever between profit and not-for-profit organizations. See, e.g., 15 USC §§7, 12. See also discussion at §2:17.

[7] 15 USC §44.

[8] United States. See Community Blood Bank of Kansas City Area v. Federal Trade Commission, 405 F2d 1011 (CA8, 1969). The court stated in the Community Blood Bank case that the test to be applied is whether the nonprofit organization engages in business for profit within the traditional and generally accepted meaning of that word. The court noted that Congress did not intend to provide a blanket exclusion of all nonprofit organizations; it was aware that some corporations are organized ostensibly not for profit, such as trade associations, but are merely vehicles through which a pecuniary profit can be realized for the associations or for their members (405 F2d 1017). The Court in Community Blood Bank was of the opinion that the limiting language of §4 of the act indicated an intention that the question of whether a nonprofit organization was covered should be determined on an ad hoc basis (405 F2d 1018).

[9] United States. See Community Blood Bank of Kansas City Area v. Federal Trade Commission, 405 F2d 1011, 1019 (CA8, 1969).

[10] United States. See Federal Trade Commission v. National Commission on Egg Nutrition, 517 F2d 485 (CA7, 1975). In this case a nonprofit corporation composed of egg producers published statements in the form of paid advertisements asserting that there was no scientific evidence that eating eggs increased the risk of heart disease or a heart attack. The Court ruled that the Federal Trade Commission had jurisdiction to show that the advertisements were materially misleading. The organization was a trade association which, according to the court, could be a vehicle through which pecuniary profit could be realized for it or for its members.

[11] United States. Community Blood Bank of Kansas City Area v. Federal Trade Commission, 405 F2d 1011 (CA8, 1969).

§4:19. Labor Laws.

Nonprofit organizations involved in interstate commerce are subject to the National Labor Relations Act;[1] consequently, the directors and officers may be required to engage in collective bargaining.[2] The National Labor Relations Act (NLRA) provides for the regulation of practices occurring in relations between employer and employees which cause labor disturbances affecting interstate commerce and establishes a single tribunal, the National Labor Relations Board (NLRB) to administer the provisions of the act, with opportunity for judicial review in a designated court.[3]

There was a question as to whether nonprofit organizations were subject to the NLRA.[4] However, in 1970 the NLRB pointed to what it viewed as an increased involvement in commerce by educational institutions and concluded that it had jurisdiction over nonprofit educational institutions.[5] The act itself does not exclude nonprofit organizations.[6] Until 1974, nonprofit hospital corporations or associations were exempt from the act.[7] However, with the 1974 amendments to the act, removing the nonprofit hospital exemption,[8] the NLRB concluded that any statutory basis it may have had for declining jurisdiction over nonprofit organizations on the basis of an organization's charitable function or worthy purpose was removed.[9] The only basis upon which the NLRB now declines jurisdiction is that the activities of the organization do not have a sufficient impact on interstate commerce.[10] The NLRB takes the position that it must treat profit and nonprofit organizations alike; the sole basis for declining or asserting jurisdiction over a nonprofit organization should be the same as for a profit organization.[11]

The NLRB has established jurisdictional limitations over some nonprofit organizations.[12] The Board will assert jurisdiction over those private nonprofit colleges, universities, and symphony orchestras that have a gross annual revenue from all sources (excluding only contributions which, because of limitation by the grantor, are not available for use for operating expenses) of not less than $1 million.[13] It previously ruled that it will assert jurisdiction over child care centers if their gross income is $250,000 or more.[14]

The Supreme Court has limited the scope of the NLRA as it

relates to nonprofit educational institutions in two of its recent decisions. The Court has stated that to require church-operated schools to grant recognition to unions as bargaining units for their teachers would implicate the guarantees of the First Amendment regarding freedom of religion.[15] In addition, it has ruled that full-time faculty members are managerial employers and are excluded from the Act.[16] According to the Court, a faculty member's professional interests cannot be separated from those of the institution; thus, a faculty member cannot be an employee entitled to representation by a union.[17]

FOOTNOTES

[1] 29 USC §§151–168.

[2] The National Labor Relations Act states that the inequality of bargaining power between employees who do not possess full freedom of association or actual liberty of contract, and employers who are organized in the corporate or other forms of ownership association substantially burdens and affects the flow of commerce, and tends to aggravate recurrent business depressions by depressing wage rates and the purchasing power of wage earners in industry; the right of employees to organize and bargain collectively safeguards commerce from injury. See 29 USC §151.

[3] See 29 USC §§153, 160.

[4] The NLRB ruled in 1951 that it would not exercise jurisdiction over nonprofit educational institutions because to do so would not affect the purpose of the act. See Trustees of Columbia University in the City of New York, 97 NLRB 424 (1951).

[5] See Cornell University, 183 NLRB 329 (1970).

[6] Section 2(1) of the National Labor Relations Act defines a "person" subject to the act as one or more individuals, labor organizations, partnerships, associations, corporations, legal representatives, trustees, trustees in cases under Title 11, or receivers. See 29 USC §152(1).

Section 2(2) does exclude from the definition of "employer" the United States or any wholly owned government corporation and any state or political subdivision thereof. See 29 USC §152(2). Thus, the NLRA applies to private industry and not to public employment. (However, federal employees are covered by 5 USC §§7101–7901 which regulates collective bargaining among federal employees.)

United States. See Beauboeuf v. Delgado College, 428 F2d 470 (CA5, 1970), where the court held that if a state has no law permitting or requiring public institutions to bargain collectively, the institutions are not required to bargain (as state institutions are not covered by the NLRA).

[7] Prior to 1974, §2(2) of the Act excluded any corporation or association operating a hospital if no part of the net earnings inured to the benefit of any private shareholder.

[8] Pub L No.93–360 §3.88 Stat 397, 29 USC §152(2).

[9] See Rhode Island Catholic Orphan Asylum, a/k/a St Aloysius Home and Rhode Island Alliance of Social Service Employees, 224 NLRB 1344 (1976).

[10] See Rhode Island Catholic Orphan Asylum, a/k/a/ St Aloysius Home and Rhode Island Alliance of Social Service Employees, 224 NLRB 1344 (1976).

A nonprofit organization not having a sufficient impact on interstate commerce may nonetheless be subject to collective bargaining under state labor laws.

[11] Rhode Island Catholic Orphan Asylum, a/k/a/ St Aloysius Home and Rhode Island Alliance of Social Service Employees, 224 NLRB 1344 (1976).

[12] See 29 CFR §§103.1–103.3.

[13] 29 CFR §§103.1, 103.2.

[14] See Salt and Pepper Nursery School, 222 NLRB 1295 (1976).

[15] United States. See National Labor Relations Board v. Catholic Bishop of Chicago, 440 US 490, 59 L Ed2d 533, 99 S Ct 1313 (1979).

See, however, Ohio Civil Rights Commission v. Dayton Christian Schools, — US —, 91 L Ed 2d 512, 106 S Ct 2718 (1986), in which the Supreme Court ruled that the elimination of sex discrimination is a compelling state interest that would bring a religious institution within the ambit of state authorities.

See Universidad Central De Bayamon v. National Labor Relations Board, 793 F2d 383 (CA1, 1985), in which a full court was evenly divided as to whether a private nonprofit university controlled by the Dominican order of the Roman Catholic Church was subject to the jurisdiction of the National Labor Relations Board. Half of the court was of the opinion that National Labor Relations Board v. Catholic Bishop of Chicago, 440 US 490, 59 L Ed 2d 533, 99 S Ct 1313 (1979), should not be extended to a university because religion is less dominant in a university than in a religious elementary and secondary school. (The court had determined that National Labor Relations Board v. Yeshiva Faculty Ass'n, 444 US 672, 63 L Ed 2d 115, 100 S Ct 856 (1980), was not applicable because the administration responsible to the board and controlled by the president exercised far greater authority than in most major universities over specific detailed decisions that constitute university life. The faculty followed orders and did not determine curriculum, class assignment, class size or workload. Thus, faculty were more like employees than administration.)

See also Volunteers of America v. National Labor Relations Board, 777 F2d 1386 (CA9, 1985), in which the court held that the board did not exceed its jurisdictional authority. The Volunteers of America is a nonprofit, religious, charitable organization that provides alcohol treatment. The court held that the organization's religious views were not imposed upon its employees, primarily because of its funding; thus, it differed from Catholic Bishop. While its social programs were expressions of its religious philosophy, they were carried out in a secular fashion.

In Volunteers of America—Minnesota—Bar None Boys Ranch v. National Labor Relations Board, 752 F2d 345 (CA8, 1985) the court refused to extend the Catholic Bishop case to a church-run day care center. The court found that the boys' ranch resembled a secular institution in most critical aspects even though it was a vehicle for religious missionary activities. The court determined that the primary purpose of the boys' ranch was the care of children and not the propagation of faith. Similarly in National Labor Relations Board v. Salvation Army of Massachusetts Dorchester Day Care Center, 763 F2d 1 (CA5, 1985), the Fifth Circuit held that a day care center operated by a nonprofit religious organization was subject to the jurisdiction of the NLRB. The court found that the center's primary function was to care for children rather than to educate them; thus, its primary purpose was secular in nature.

[16] **United States.** National Labor Relations Board v. Yeshiva Faculty Association, 444 US 672, 63 L Ed2d 115, 100 S Ct 856 (1980).

[17] **United States.** National Labor Relations Board v. Yeshiva Faculty Association, 444 US 672, 63 L Ed2d 115, 100 S Ct 856 (1980).

§4:20. —Selection of Labor Representative.

The first step in establishing collective bargaining for a group of employees is the designation or selection of the labor representative of the employees.[1] The NLRA provides that representatives designated or selected for the purposes of collective bargaining by the majority of the employees in a unit appropriate for such purposes,[2] are the exclusive representatives of all the employees in that unit for the purpose of collective bargaining in respect to rates of pay, wages, hours of employment, or other conditions of employment.[3] An employer must recognize and bargain collectively with the representatives chosen by a majority of the workers in a bargaining unit;[4] an employer may not bargain with any other representative or representatives.[5] Thus, the will of the majority of the workers is imposed upon the minority.

A labor organization wishing to be certified as the exclusive bargaining unit must acquire authorization from a majority of the employees of that unit.[6] Union organizers often seek to enlist a majority of the workers of a particular bargaining unit through solicitation on the employer's premises. The Supreme Court has held that while an employer may not restrict its employees' right to discuss self-organization among themselves, it may prevent nonemployee organizers from using the employer's property to distribute union literature when other means are readily available.[7]

If a union can satisfy an employer that it represents a majority of the workers within a bargaining unit, the employer may voluntarily recognize the union.[8] However, the employer may require an election conducted by secret ballot or may insist that the questions of representation be settled by an NLRB election.[9]

Before an employer agrees to meet with a union, the employer should determine that the union does, in fact, represent a majority of the employees in the bargaining union.[10] The employer need not accept authorization cards from a union indicating that that union represents a majority of the employees.[11] The employer can, in fact, refuse to accept any evidence of the union's majority status other than the results of a board election[12] Further, in the absence of any agreement to permit majority status to be determined by means other than a board election, the union has the burden of taking the next step in invoking the board's election procedures.[13]

A petition to the NLRB for investigation of the question as to whether a union represents a majority of an appropriate grouping of employees can be initiated by the employer, by any person, or by a labor organization acting on behalf of a substantial number of employees (at least 30% of the workers of a particular unit).[14] The NLRB upon receipt of a petition regarding the question of union representation, will conduct an investigation to determine (a) whether the board has jurisdiction, (b) whether there is an appropriate unit of employees for the purposes of collective bargaining, (c) whether the election would reflect the free choice of employees in the appropriate unit, and (d) whether, if the petitioner is a labor organization, there is a sufficient probability that the employees have selected it to represent them (this requires a designation by 30% of the employees).[15] The NLRB makes available to the parties two types of informal consent procedures through which representation issues can be resolved without recourse to formal procedures.[16] These informal arrangements are referred to as consent election agreements.[17] A board agent will arrange the details incident to the mechanics and conduct of the election.[18] The actual polling is conducted and supervised on the employer's premises by board agents.[19]

If there is a certified or currently recognized labor representative, any employee, or group of employees or any labor organization may file decertification proceedings with the NLRB to test the question of whether the certified union still represents the employees.[20] A person seeking decertification must have the signatures of at least 30% of the employees covered by an expiring bargaining agreement in his petition.[21] However, if the employer is the petitioner, the 30% proof of representation is not needed.[22]

FOOTNOTES

[1] See procedure at 29 USC §159.

[2] Supervisors are excluded from the bargaining unit. See 29 USC §164. Three other classes of employees, professional employees, craftsmen, and

plant guards, are given special treatment. See 29 USC §159(b). Professionals are not included with nonprofessional employees in a bargaining unit unless the majority of the professionals vote for inclusion. Plant guards, those individuals employed as guards to enforce rules against employees and other persons employed to protect the property of the employer or to protect the safety of persons on the employer's premises, can only be included in a unit composed exclusively of guards.

[3] 29 USC §159(a).

[4] 29 USC §158(5).

[5] 29 USC §159(a).

[6] 29 CFR §101.17.

[7] **United States.** National Labor Relations Board v. Babcock & Wilcox Company, 351 US 105, 100 L Ed 975, 76 S Ct 679 (1956). The Court held that the private property rights of an owner prevailed over the intrusion of nonemployee organizers, even in nonworking areas of the business and during nonworking hours. The Court stated that an employer may not affirmatively interfere with organization; however, the union may not always insist that the employer aid organization. If the locations of the place of business and the living quarters of the employees place the employees beyond the reach of reasonable union efforts to communicate with the workers, then the employer must allow the union to approach its employees on the employer's property. Where these conditions do not exist, the employer may validly post its property against nonemployee distribution of union literature. According to the Court, the NLRA requires only that the employer refrain from interference, discrimination, restraint, or coercion in the employees' exercise of their own rights; it does not require that the employer permit the use of its facilities for organization when other means are available to the union.

[8] **United States.** National Labor Relations Board v. Broadmoor Lumber Company, 578 F2d 238, 241 (CA9, 1978).

[9] **United States.** See National Labor Relations Board v. Lyon & Ryan Ford Inc, 647 F2d 745 (CA7, 1981), cert den 454 US 894, 70 L Ed2d 209, 102 S Ct 3391 (1981); National Labor Relations Board v. Brown and Connolly, Inc, 593 F2d 1373 (CA1, 1979). Once the employer recognizes the union, no matter how informally, he loses the right to require an election.

[10] See 29 USC §159. Representatives of a majority of the employees are the *exclusive* representatives.
See also 29 USC §158(b)(7)(A).

[11] **United States.** See Linden Lumber Division v. National Labor Relations Board, 419 US 301, 42 L Ed 2d 465, 95 S Ct 429 (1974).

[12] **United States.** Linden Lumber Division v. National Labor Relations Board, 419 US 301, 42 L Ed 2d 465, 95 S Ct 429 (1974).
[13] **United States.** Linden Lumber Division v. National Labor Relations Board, 419 US 301, 42 L Ed 2d 465, 95 S Ct 429 (1974).
[14] See 29 USC §159(c).
[15] See 29 CFR §101.18(a).
[16] 29 CFR §101.19.
[17] 29 CFR §101.19.
[18] 29 CFR §101.19(a)(1). Prior to the date of election, the holding of the election is publicized by the posting of official notices in the establishment or by the use of other means considered appropriate. The notices reproduce a sample ballot and outline the election details as to location of polls, time of voting and eligibility rules.
[19] 29 CFR §101.19(a)(2).
[20]t29 CFR §101.17.
[21] 29 CFR §101.18(a).
[22] 29 CFR §101.18(a).

§4:21. —Duty To Bargain in Good Faith.

Once a union has been established as the representative of a bargaining unit, the employer must bargain collectively with that representative of its employees.[1] Collective bargaining is the performance of a mutual obligation on the part of the employer and the employee representative to meet at reasonable times and confer in good faith with respect to wages, hours and other terms and conditions of employment.[2] An employer is not required to make concessions or to yield any position fairly maintained but it is under an obligation to make sincere, serious efforts to adjust differences and to reach an acceptable common ground.[3] There is no duty on the employer to reach an agreement, but there is a duty to negotiate with the spirit of sincerity and cooperation.[4]

The duty to bargain in good faith assumes that the parties will meet at mutually convenient places and will be willing to devote a reasonable amount of time to the bargaining process.[5] The parties must be represented by someone who has authority to speak for the principals.[6] The parties must reply to each other's proposals within a reasonable period of time, and they must not impose unfair conditions upon bargaining, such as settlement of outstanding grievances or unfair labor practice charges.[7] The parties must not bypass each other's designated representatives and must supply each other with any reasonable information required to bargain effectively.[8]

FOOTNOTES

[1] 29 USC §158(a)(5).

[2] **United States.** Keystone Steel & Wire Division of Keystone Consolidated Industries, Inc v. National Labor Relations Board, 606 F2d 171 (CA7, 1979).

[3] **United States.** National Labor Relations Board v. Blevins Popcorn Company, 659 F2d 1173 (CA DC, 1981).

[4] **United States.** National Labor Relations Board v. West Coast Casket Company, Inc, 469 F2d 871 (CA9, 1972).

[5] **United States.** National Labor Relations Board v. White Construction & Engineering Company, 204 F2d 950 (CA5, 1953). See also 29 USC §158(d).

[6] **United States.** National Labor Relations Board v. Hibbard, 273 F2d 565 (CA7, 1960).

[7] **United States.** Fouds v. International Longshoremen's Association, 147 F Supp 103 (SD NY, 1956).

[8] **United States.** National Labor Relations Board v. Yawman & Erbe Manufacturing Company, 187 F2d 947 (CA2, 1951).

§4:22. —Subject Matter of Bargaining.

Labor and management are required to bargain as to terms and conditions of employment, such as wages, hours, and the negotiation of an agreement regarding such matters.[1] Other matters are permissive.[2] A mandatory subject of bargaining is one that materially or significantly affects the terms or conditions of employment.[3] Subject matters which have been held to affect the terms or conditions of employment and, thus, are mandatory subjects of bargaining include: insurance,[4] proposals for no-strike clauses and effective arbitration provisions,[5] union security including dues checkoff,[6] prices of food and beverage served in employer's cafeteria,[7] payment of bonuses,[8] grievance procedures,[9] health and welfare programs,[10] pension plans,[11] seniority,[12] vacation benefits,[13] and employer rules regarding coffee breaks, lunch periods, smoking, employee discipline and dress.[14]

Neither party may be required to bargain on permissive subjects.[15] Further, if the parties do bargain on permissive subjects, neither party may insist on bargaining to the point of an impasse.[16] Some subjects that have been held to be permissive include: strike benefits,[17] description of the bargaining unit,[18] decision to withdraw from business,[19] and loss of extension of seniority rights of laid off employees.[20] A party is not permitted to insist on a nonmandatory subject of bargaining as a condition or prerequisite to an agreement on a mandatory subject.[21]

Illegal subjects, such as hot cargo agreements, are not subjects of bargaining and any such agreement is unenforceable.[22]

FOOTNOTES

[1] Mandatory subjects of bargaining are those listed in 29 USC §158(d). **United States.** Clear Pine Mouldings, Inc. v. National Labor Relations Board, 632 F2d 721 (CA9, 1980).

[2] **United States.** Seattle First National Bank v. National Labor Relations Board, 444 F2d 30 (CA9, 1971).

[3] **United States.** Seattle First National Bank v. National Labor Relations Board, 444 F2d 30 (CA9, 1971).

[4] **United States.** National Labor Relations Board v. General Electric Company, 418 F2d 736 (CA2, 1969).

[5] **United States.** United Electric Radio and Machine Workers of America v. National Labor Relations Board, 409 F2d 150 (CA DC, 1969).

[6] **United States.** Carolina Forms Division of Textron, Inc v. National Labor Relations Board, 401 F2d 205 (CA4, 1968).

[7] **United States.** Westinghouse Electric Corporation v. National Labor Relations Board, 369 F2d 891 (CA4, 1966); Ford Motor Company v. National Labor Relations Board, 441 US 488, 60 L Ed2d 420, 99 S Ct 1842 (1979).

[8] **United States.** Beacon Journal Publishing Company v. National Labor Relations Board, 401 F2d 366 (CA6, 1968). Regularly paid bonuses may become a part of the total compensation and, thus, become a mandatory subject of bargaining. However, where the payment of bonuses has not been uniform in amount and has only been made intermittently depending upon the employer's financial condition, bonuses are not a mandatory bargainable matter.

[9] **United States.** Ostrofsky v. United Steelworkers of America, 171 F Supp 782 (D Md, 1959), aff'd 273 F2d 614 (CA4, 1959).

[10] **United States.** Clear Pine Mouldings Inc v. National Labor Relations Board 632 F2d 721 (CA9, 1980).

[11] **United States.** United Brick and Clay Workers of America v. International Union, United Mine Workers of America, 439 F2d 311 (CA5, 1971).

[12] **United States.** National Labor Relations Board v. Frontier Homes Corporation, 371 F2d 974 (CA8, 1967).

[13] **United States.** Adams Potato Chips Inc v. National Labor Relations Board, 430 F2d 90 (CA6, 1970).

[14] **United States.** Gallenkamp Stores Company v. National Labor Relations Board, 402 F2d 525 (CA9, 1968).

[15] **United States.** National Labor Relations Board v. Floridan Hotel of Tampa, 318 F2d 545 (CA5, 1963).

[16] **United States.** National Labor Relations Board v. Floridan Hotel of Tampa, 318 F2d 545 (CA5, 1963).

[17] **United States.** Central Florida Sheet Metal Contractors Association v. National Labor Relations Board, 664 F2d 489 (CA5, 1981).

[18] **United States.** Newport News Shipbuilding and Dry Dock Company v. National Labor Relations Board, 602 F2d 73 (CA4, 1979).

[19] **United States.** National Labor Relations Board v. North Carolina Coastal Lines, Inc, 542 F2d 637 (CA4, 1976). There is no duty to bargain over the effect of a partial closing of business as distinguished from whether or not to close.

[20] **United States.** Johnson v. Air Line Pilots in Service of Northern Airlines, Inc., 650 F2d 133 (CA5, 1981).

[21] United States. Latrobe Steel Company v. National Labor Relations Board, 630 F2d 171 (CA3, 1980).
[22] United States. Kaiser Steel Corporation v. Mullins, 455 US 72, 70 L Ed2d 833, 102 S Ct 851 (1982).

§4:23. —Unfair Labor Practices.

Certain practices on the part of management and labor are unfair labor practices; the NLRB is empowered to prevent both labor and management from engaging in unfair labor practices.[1] The NLRA lists the following as unfair labor practices of employers: (a) interfering with, restraining, or coercing employees in the exercise of their right of self-organization and to bargain collectively, (b) dominating or interfering with the formation or administration of any labor organization, (c) discriminating in regard to hire or tenure of employment, or any term or condition of employment to encourage or discourage membership in a labor organization, (d) discriminating against an employee because he has filed charges or given testimony with the NLRB, and (e) refusing to bargain collectively with the labor representative.[2] The act lists the following as unfair labor practices for a labor organization or its agents: (a) restraining or coercing employees in the exercise of their right to self-organization and to bargain collectively through representatives of their own choosing, or their right to refrain from any such activities, (b) causing or attempting to cause an employer to discriminate against an employee in violation of the act, (c) refusing to bargain collectively with an employer, (d) engaging in jurisdictional strikes or secondary boycotts, (e) charging excessive fees, (f) engaging in featherbedding (attempting to exact a payment from an employer for services which will not be performed), and (g) engaging in recognition picketing.[3]

If either management or labor is aggrieved by an unfair

labor practice of the other, it may file a complaint with the NLRB.[4] The charge is filed with the regional director for the region in which the alleged violation occurred.[5] A blank form for filing the charge is supplied by the regional office upon request.[6] A copy of the charge may be served by the NLRB upon the person against whom it was made, but it is the exclusive responsibility of the charging party to make a timely service of a copy of the charge.[7] A staff member of the NLRB will investigate the charges; after investigation, the case may be disposed of through informal methods such as withdrawal, dismissal and settlement; or the case may necessitate formal methods of disposition.[8] If efforts to dispose of the charge through informal methods fail, the regional Director will issue a notice of a hearing.[9] Following the hearing, a formal decision and recommendation are filed by the hearing judge. Either party may file exceptions to the judge's finding with the board at its Washington office.[10] The board will review the record and issue its decision. The final decision of the board may be appealed to the United States court of appeals in the circuit where the unfair labor practice in question was alleged to have occurred.[11]

If the board's decision is not appealed, the board will seek enforcement of its order, in court if required.[12] Courts can enforce, modify, or set aside an order of the board. However, findings of fact by the board are conclusive if supported by substantial evidence on the record considered as a whole.[13]

FOOTNOTES

[1] See 29 USC §§158, 160.
[2] 29 USC §158(a).
[3] 29 USC §158(b).
[4] 29 USC §160(b).
[5] 29 CFR §101.2.
[6] 29 CFR §101.2

[7] 29 CFR §101.4
[8] 29 CFR §101.4.
[9] 29 CFR §101.8.
[10] 29 CFR §101.11.
[11] 29 CFR §101.11.
[12] 29 CFR §101.14.
[13] 29 USC §160(f).
United States. Universal Camera Corporation v. National Labor Relations Board, 340 US 471, 95 L Ed 456, 71 S Ct 456 (1951). Substantial evidence is more than a mere scintilla. It means such revelvant evidence as reasonable minds might accept as adequate to support a conclusion. A court may not substitute its judgment for that of the board when the choice is between two fairly conflicting views even though the court would justifiably have made a different choice had the matter been before it de novo; it must defer to the board's areas of specialized experience and expertise.

However, it is appropriate to set aside the board's decision when the court cannot find the the evidence supporting that decision is substantial. See Soule Glass and Glazing Company v. National Labor Relations Board, 652 F2d 1055, 1073 (CA 1, 1981).

§4:24. —Strikes.

Employees have the right to strike.[1] In addition, unions may take disciplinary action against a union member who refuses to engage in protected activity that will not jeopardize his job.[2] Lawful strikes are of two types: economic strikes and unfair labor practices strikes. An economic strike generally occurs when employees cease work to achieve a labor objective classed as a mandatory subject of bargaining.[3] Such strikes most often occur after negotiations for an initial or renewal labor agreement have deadlocked. Strikes also occur to protest alleged employer unfair labor practices.

The principal distinction in the two types of strikes is the reinstatement rights of the striking employees.[4] An economic striker is entitled to reemployment after the termination of the strike if a vacancy exists for which the striker is qualified; however, an employer is permitted to replace economic strikers permanently by employing new workers.[5] On the other hand, employees who strike because management has committed an unfair labor practice are protected with respect to their reemployment even if the employer has hired replacements.[6] These strikers are entitled to unconditional reinstatement with back pay.[7]

On-the-job slowdowns designed to place economic pressure on the employer are partial economic strikes.[8] These strikers may be terminated in instances where their activities breach the employer's work rules.[9] As a result, even though a union may properly adopt rules disciplining members who refuse to engage in a full economic strike in which they do no work for the employer, a union may not force its members to engage in this type of unprotected activity.[10]

An economic strike may become an unfair labor practices strike. A strike to secure an initial labor agreement generally does not require notice to the employer or to governmental agencies.[11] Should the employer refuse to continue to bargain with the union over mandatory subjects during such a strike, the strike will be transformed from an economic to an unfair labor practice strike in which management's prerogatives will be limited.[12] However, to become an unfair labor practice strike the intervening unfair labor practice must be one that makes the strike last longer than it would otherwise.[13]

If a striker has violated an employee unfair labor practice, he may be discharged from employment lawfully on a nondiscriminatory basis.[14] In addition, an employee who engages in an illegal strike—a strike for an unlawful purpose or one that is an unfair labor practice on the part of the union—may be denied reinstatement.[15] An employer who is subjected to an unlawful strike may sue the union for damages, may file an unfair labor practice charge with the NLRB and may seek an injunction to prohibit the strike.[16] A union violates its contract with management if it strikes during the term of a labor contract which has no-strike clause.[17] The employer may seek damages and an injunction against the strike.[18]

228 Representing the Nonprofit Organization

Striking employees have the right to establish a picket line, to use arguments in support of their position, and to attempt by proper means to induce other persons not to work at jobs which they vacated by striking, or not to patronize the establishment.[19] In addition, except for health care organizations, notice of the picket need not be given the employer.[20] On the other hand, the employer and other employees have a right to be free from the harassment of illegal picketing.[21] Those who exceed the permissible scope of picket activity forfeit their right to reinstatement.[22]. In addition, an employer may be able to recover damages against the union when it engages in unlawful mass picketing.[23]

FOOTNOTES

[1] 29 USC §163. However, because public employees are not covered by the act, they do not have this right unless the state statute so provides.
United States. See National Labor Relations Board v. Erie Resistor Corporation, 373 US 221, 10 L Ed2d 308, 83 S Ct 1139 (1963); National Labor Relations Board v. Drivers, Chauffeurs, Helpers, 362 US 274, 4 L Ed2d 710, 80 S Ct 706 (1960).
Public employees are regulated by state statutes. State laws that prohibit public employees from striking have been held to be valid. See Hortonville Joint School District v. Hortonville Education Association, 426 US 482, 49 L Ed2d 1, 96 S Ct 2308 (1976).

[2] **United States.** See National Labor Relations Board v. Gaiu Local 13–B, Graphic Arts International Union, 682 F2d 304 (CA2, 1982).

[3] **United States.** See National Labor Relations Board v. Lyon & Ryan Ford, Inc, 647 F2d 745 (CA7, 1981).

[4] **United States.** National Labor Relations Board v. Lyon & Ryan Ford, Inc, 647 F2d 745 (CA7, 1981); Soule Glass and Glazing Company v. National Labor Relations Board, 652 F2d 1055 (CA1, 1981).

[5] **United States.** National Labor Relations Board v. Mackay Radio & Telegraph Company 304 US 333, 345, 82 L Ed 1381, 58 S Ct 904, 910 (1938).
Economic strikers do have a right to preferential rehiring when the departure of permanent replacements creates vacancies. See Laidlaw Corporation v. National Labor Relations Board, 414 F2d 99 (CA7, 1969);

LEGAL PROBLEMS OF NONPROFIT ENTERPRISES   229

National Labor Relations Board v. Fleetwood Trailer Company, 389 US 375, 378, 19 L Ed2d 614, 88 S Ct 543, 545 (1967).

[6] **United States.** See Mastro Plastics Corporation v. National Labor Relations Board, 350 US 270, 278, 100 L Ed 309, 76 S Ct 349, 355 (1955); Soule Glass and Glazing Company v. National Labor Relations Board, 652 F2d 1055, 1105 (CA7, 1981).

[7] **United States.** Mastro Plastics Corporation v. National Labor Relations Board, 350 US 270, 278, 100 L Ed 309, 76 S Ct 349, 355 (1955); National Labor Relations Board v. Lyon & Ryan Ford, Inc, 647 F2d 745, 754 (CA7, 1981).

[8] **United States.** National Labor Relations Board v. Gaiu Local 13–B, Graphic Arts International Union, 682 F2d 304 (CA2, 1982); National Labor Relations Board v. Blades Manufacturing Company, 344 F2d 998 (CA8, 1965).

[9] **United States.** National Labor Relations Board v. Gaiu Local 13–B, Graphic Arts International Union, 682 F2d 304 (CA2, 1982); National Labor Relations Board v. Blades Manufacturing Company, 344 F2d 998 (CA8, 1965).

[10] **United States.** National Labor Relations Board v. Gaiu Local 13–B, Graphic Arts International Union, 682 F2d 304 (CA2, 1982).

[11] **United States.** See Soule Glass and Glazing Company v. National Labor Relations Board, 652 F2d 1055 (CA1, 1981). However, 10 days' written notice must be given to a health care organization before striking or picketing it. See 29 USC §158(g).

[12] **United States.** Soule Glass and Glazing Company v. National Labor Relations Board, 652 F2d 1055 (CA1, 1981).

[13] **United States.** Soule Glass and Glazing Company v. National Labor Relations Board, 652 F2d 1055 (CA1, 1981).

[14] **United States.** National Labor Relations Board v. Fansteel Metallurgical Corporation, 306 US 240, 83 L Ed 627, 59 S Ct 490 (1939), National Labor Relations Board v. Sands Manufacturing Company, 306 US 332, 83 L Ed 682, 59 S Ct 508 (1939), and Midwest Solvents Inc v. National Labor Relations Board, 696 F2d 763 (CA10, 1982).

[15] **United States.** Complete Auto Transit, Inc v. Reis, 451 US 401, 68 L Ed2d 248, 101 S Ct 1836 (1981); National Labor Relations Board v. Fansteel Metallurgical Corporation, 306 US 240, 83 L Ed 627, 59 S Ct 490 (1939); National Labor Relations Board v. Blades Manufacturing Corporation, 344 F2d 998 (CA8, 1965).

[16] See 29 USC §§185, 187.

United States. See Complete Auto Transit, Inc. v. Reis, 451 US 40, 68 L Ed2d 248, 101 S Ct 1836 (1981). A judgment of damages may only be enforced against the union, however, and not against the individual members.

See also National Labor Relations Board v. Drivers, Chauffeurs, Helpers, Local Union No. 639, 362 US 274, 4 L Ed2d 710, 80 S Ct 706 (1960); United Mine Workers v. Osborne Mining Company, 279 F2d 716 (CA6, 1960).

[17] **United States.** Boys Markets, Inc. v. Retail Clerk's Union, 398 US 235, 26 L Ed2d 199, 90 S Ct 1583 (1970); Complete Auto Transit, Inc v. Reis, 451 US 401, 68 L Ed2d 248, 101 S Ct 1836 (1981).

[18] See 29 USC §185a.

United States. See Iodice v. Calabrese, 512 F2d 383 (CA2, 1975); Boys Market, Inc. v. Retail Clerk's Union, 398 US 235, 26 L Ed 2d 199, 90 S Ct 1583 (1970); Complete Auto Transit, Inc v. Reis, 451 US 401, 68 L Ed2d 248, 101 S Ct 1836 (1981).

[19] **United States.** National Labor Relations Board v. Visceglia, 498 F2d 43 (CA3, 1974).

[20] 29 USC §158(g).

United States. See National Labor Relations Board v. Rock Hill Convalescent Center, 585 F2d 700 (CA4, 1978) which held that the notice requirements of 29 USC §158(g) apply only to labor organizations. Because employees at the convalescent center were unrepresented, they were not required to give the 10 day notice.

[21] **United States.** Sherman Oaks Medical Arts Center v. Carpenters Local Union No. 1936, United Brotherhood of Carpenters and Joiners of America, 680 F2d 594 (CA9, 1982); Rainbow Tours, Inc. v. Hawaii Joint Council of Teamsters, 704 F2d 1443 (CA9, 1983).

[22] **United States.** Ruscoe Company v. National Labor Relations Board, 406 F2d 727 (CA6, 1969).

[23] **United States.** Rainbow Tours, Inc. v. Hawaii Joint Council of Teamsters, 704 F2d 1443 (CA9, 1983).

§4:25. —Right To Work Laws.

Section 14(b) of the National Labor Relations Act[1] permits individual states and territories to exempt themselves from the provisions of the NLRA permitting union or agency shops.[2] A union shop agreement provides that no one will be employed who does not join the union within a short time after being hired.[3] An agency shop agreement provides that while employees are not required to join the union, they are required—usually after 30 days—to pay the union a sum equal to the union initiation fee and are obligated to make periodic payments to the union equal to the union dues.[4] (These are distinguished from the closed shop agreement, which is banned by the NLRB,[5] prohibiting employers from hiring anyone who is not a member of the union at the time of hiring.[6]) The concern of Congress in permitting the union and agency shop agreements was that employees should not be entitled to the benefits of union representation without paying for them.[7]

While the NLRB permits compulsory unionism, any state can adopt so-called right-to-work laws that prohibit the union and agency shop agreements.[8] With or without right-to-work laws, most employers are free to hire whomever they choose. The concern is principally over workers' rights—whether or not a majority of workers should have the right to compel an unwilling minority to join a union after the employee has been hired.[9]

Courts in most states that have enacted right-to-work laws have prohibited a denial of an employee's right to work because of an agency shop provision that requires payment of monthly dues to a labor organization.[10] These courts have stated that such a requirement imposes a practical equivalent of compulsory membership in a labor organization as a condition of continued employment.[11]

FOOTNOTES

[1] 29 USC §164(b). Section 14(b) of the Taft-Hartley Act, 80th Cong., 1st Sess, 34 (1947).

[2] 29 USC §158(a)(3). The provision permitting the union or agency shop is §8(as)(3) of the Taft-Hartley Act, 80th Cong, 1st Sess, 6 (1947).

[3] **United States.** See Oil, Chemical and Atomic Workers v. Mobil Oil Corporation, 426 US 407, 48 L Ed2d 736, 96 S Ct 2140 (1976).

[4] **United States.** Oil, Chemical and Atomic Workers v. Mobil Oil Corporation, 426 US 407, 48 L Ed2d 736, 96 S Ct 2140 (1976). See Chicago Teachers Union, Local No. 1 v. Hudson, —US—, 89 L Ed 2d 232, 106 S Ct 1066 (1986), in which the Supreme Court held that procedural safeguards are necessary to prevent compulsory subsidization of ideological activity by nonunion employees who object to such activity, while at the same time not restricting a union's ability to require any employee to contribute to the cost of collective bargaining activities through an agency shop agreement. Because a nonunion employee's rights are protected by the First Amendment, procedures must be carefully tailored to minimize an agency shop's infringement on those rights. Nonunion employees must have a fair opportunity to identify the impact on those rights and to assert meritorious First Amendment claims. The union procedure in this case contained three constitutional defects. It failed to minimize the risk that nonunion employees' contributions might be temporarily used for impermissible purposes. It failed to provide nonmembers with adequate information about the basis for their proportionate share and it failed to provide for a reasonably prompt decision by an impartial decisionmaker. The Court held that constitutional requirements for a union's collection of agency fees include adequate explanation of the basis for the fee, a reasonably prompt opportunity to challenge the amount of the fee before an impartial decisionmaker, and escrow for the amounts reasonably in dispute while such challenges are pending.

[5] 29 USC §158(a)(3). Under the Wagner Act, enacted in 1935, closed shops, union shops and agency shops were all permitted. However, the Taft-Hartley Act, enacted in 1947, banned closed shops though still permitting union and agency shops. See S Rep No. 105, 80th Cong, 1st Sess, 6, Legislative History of the Labor Management Relations Act (1947).

[6] **United States.** See Oil, Chemical and Atomic Workers v. Mobil Oil Corporation, 426 US 407, 48 L Ed2d 736, 96 S Ct 2140 (1976).

[7] **United States.** See Oil, Chemical and Atomic Workers v. Mobil Oil Corporation, 426 US 407, 48 L Ed2d 736, 96 S Ct 2140 (1976).

[8] See 29 USC §164(b).

[9] This concern is countered with the argument that the right-to-work laws permit employees to have the benefits of union representation without paying for them.

[10] See e.g.;
United States. Retail Clerks Local 1625 v. Schermerhorn, 375 US 96, 11 L Ed 2d 179, 84 S Ct 219 (1963). The Supreme Court held that Florida courts,

LEGAL PROBLEMS OF NONPROFIT ENTERPRISES   233

rather than solely the NLRB, are tribunals with jurisdiction to enforce a state's prohibition against agency shop clauses in collective bargaining agreements.
  See also Amalgamated Association v. Las Vegas-Tonopah-Reno Stage Line, 202 F Supp 726 (D Nev, 1962), aff'd 319 F2d 783 (CA9, 1963) which held an agency shop provision was illegal under Nevada right-to-work laws.
  [11] **United States.** See, however, Oil, Chemical and Atomic Workers v. Mobil Oil Corporation, 426 US 407, 48 L Ed 2d 736, 96 S Ct 2140 (1976) in which the Supreme Court held that §14(b) of the NLRA cannot void agreements permitted by §8(b)(3) i.e., union and agency shop agreements, when the situs at which all employees covered by the agreement perform most of their work is outside of the state having a right-to-work law (even though the employees were hired in a state having the law).
  Arizona. Arizona Flame Restaurant, Inc. v. Baldwin, 82 Ariz 385, 313 P2d 759 (1954).
  Kansas. Higgins v. Cardinal Manufacturing Company, 188 Kan 88, 360 P2d 456 (1961).
  North Dakota. Blacksmiths, Forgers and Helpers, Local No. 647, 219 NW2d 860 (1974).

§4:26. Checklist of Points to Remember.

— 1. As a general rule, courts will not interfere in the internal affairs of a private association because of the public interest in maintaining an individual's freedom of association and freedom of choice in private matters. Because of the economic control possessed by professional and trade associations and by labor unions and the limited power of the individual members to control the affairs of the association, courts have exercised jurisdiction to prevent arbitrary exclusion or expulsion from these types of organizations.[1]

— 2. Without a finding of state action, courts have had no authority to compel private clubs to maintain a nondiscriminatory admission policy. However, recently courts have been more prone to find state involvement.[2] The Internal Revenue Code prohibits discrimination on the basis of race, color, or religion for social clubs that seek tax exemption.[3] The Supreme Court has also denied tax exempt status, on a public policy theory, for nonprofit educational institutions that practice race discrimination.[4]

— 3. Membership in a nonprofit organization generally may be terminated only by voluntary act of the member or by an act of the organization pursuant to authority granted it by its charter, articles of association, or bylaws.[5] If nonprofit associations establish effective nonjudicial methods of control and internal procedures, courts are less likely to hear individual and group disputes; consequently, if the constitution and bylaws of a voluntary association provide a system for trial and appeal of internal controversies between members, the court will require that members exhaust such procedures before resorting to the courts.[6]

— 4. Courts generally will not interfere in the internal affairs of religious organizations; however, occasionally courts exercise their equitable jurisdiction in church controversies for the protection and preservation of civil or property rights of the members, often to prevent an unauthorized alienation of property or the wrongful diversion of church funds.[7]

— 5. An association generally may not bring an action for damages based on harms to particular members of the association unless the association also alleges monetary damages to itself or an assignment of the damage claims of its members.[8]

— 6. Nonprofit corporations and trusts can be held liable for the torts of their agents or employees under the doctrine of respondeat superior or course of employment. Members of unincorporated associations can be individually liable for torts committed in the name of the association.[9]

— 7. In the past, charitable corporations were immune from liability for torts committed by their employees; however, the doctrine of charitable immunity has been abrogated in most states, while some still have a qualified immunity.[10]
— 8. There is a single system of statutory protection for all copyrightable works.[11] Property rights of an artist or author are protected for the artist's or author's life plus 50 years after death.[12] While the owner, or coowners, of a work are the source of copyright ownership, the employer is considered to be the author and is the initial owner of the copyright of work made for hire.[13] A work made for hire is a work prepared by an employee within the scope of employment; it includes commissioned works that are subject to a written agreement that the work is done for hire.[14]
— 9. Copyright protection is secured by placing a notice of copyright on all copies distributed to the public.; the notice is the symbol "c" in a circle, the year of first publication of the work, and the name of the copyright owner.[15] Registration of published or unpublished works is permissive; a claim can be registered by depositing copies of the work with the Copyright Office with a completed application form and a fee. While registration is not a condition to copyright, it is required if a suit for infringement is instituted.[16]
— 10. Some performances of copyrighted works by nonprofit organizations are exempt from copyright protection. In addition, the "fair use" of copyrighted work is not an infringement of the copyright. (Fair use is the use by reproduction of copyrighted works for criticism, comment, news reporting, teaching, scholarship, or research.)[17]
— 11. Unless an exempted security is involved or unless a transaction is exempt from the requirements of the securities act, no offer to sell or buy a security may be

made by the mails or in interstate commerce unless a registration statement has been filed with the SEC.[18] In addition, the states require registration of securities sold intrastate that are not otherwise exempt from state registration.[19] Debentures and memberships sold by nonprofit organizations can be securities subject to registration.[20] Securities donated to a nonprofit organization may be restricted securities and, thus, any sale will be subject to the requirements of SEC Rule 144.[21] If the donated securities have been held for more than 3 years (the donee may add the donor's holding period to its own to determine whether it has held the stock for three years), the compliance problems of Rule 144 are substantially reduced.[22]

__ 12. Nonprofit organizations can be liable under the antitrust laws. However, the unfair competition laws generally do not apply to activities of nonprofit organizations.[23]

__ 13. Nonprofit organizations involved in interstate commerce are subject to the National Labor Relations Act and, thus, may be required to engage in collective bargaining.[24]

FOOTNOTES

[1] See §4:02
[2] See §4:03.
[3] See §4:03.
[4] See §4:03.
[5] See §4:03.
[6] See §4:03.
[7] See §4:04.
[8] See §4:05.
[9] See §4:06.
[10] See §4:07.

[11] See §4:08.
[12] See §4:08.
[13] See §4:09.
[14] See §4:09.
[15] See §4:10.
[16] See §4:10.
[17] See §4:11.
[18] See §4:13.
[19] See §4:16.
[20] See §4:13.
[21] See §4:15.
[22] See §4:15.
[23] See §§4:17, 4:18.
[24] See §4:19.

CHAPTER 5

MERGER, CONSOLIDATION, AND DISSOLUTION

§ 5:01. Procedure for Merger or Consolidation.
§ 5:02. Effect of Merger or Consolidation.
§ 5:03. Articles of Merger or Consolidation.
§ 5:04. —Form of Articles of Merger.
§ 5:05. —Form of Articles of Consolidation.
§ 5:06. —Form of Articles of Merger or Consolidation of Domestic and Foreign Corporation.
§ 5:07. Withdrawal of a Foreign Corporation.
§ 5:08. Sale of Assets.
§ 5:09. Voluntary Dissolution of a Nonprofit Corporation.
§ 5:10. Distribution of Assets.
§ 5:11. —Cy Pres Doctrine.
§ 5:12. —Articles of Dissolution.
§ 5:13. —Form for Articles of Dissolution.
§ 5:14. Involuntary Dissolution.
§ 5:15. Procedures After Dissolution.
§ 5:16. Bankruptcy.
§ 5:17. Checklist of Points To Remember.

§5:01. Procedure for Merger or Consolidation.

As a general rule, the merger of two or more nonprofit corporations causes few problems. The Model Nonprofit Corporation Act provides that any two or more domestic nonprofit corporations may merge into one or may consolidate into a new corporation.[1] A plan of merger or consolidation must be adopted at a meeting of the members by a two-thirds vote of the members present or represented by proxy.[2] The board of directors must first adopt a resolution approving the proposed plan and must then direct that it be submitted to a vote of the members at an annual or special meeting.[3] For nonprofit corporations without members, a plan or merger or consolidation must be adopted at a meeting of the board of directors upon receiving a majority vote of the directors.[4]

The plan of merger or consolidation must indicate the names of the corporations proposing to merge or consolidate, the name of the corporation into which they propose to merge or the name of the new corporation into which they propose to consolidate, the terms and conditions of the proposed merger or consolidation, and a statement of any changes in the articles of incorporation for the surviving corporation in a merger, or for a consolidation, all of the statements required to be included in the articles of incorporation.[5]

Articles of merger or consolidation are executed in duplicate and delivered to the Secretary of the State.[6] The merger or consolidation is effective upon issuance of a certificate of merger or consolidation by the Secretary of State.[7] The separate existence of all corporations parties to the plan of merger or consolidation, except the surviving or new corporation, shall cease upon that date.[8]

A domestic corporation may be merged or consolidated with a foreign corporation (one not authorized to do business within the state) if the merger or consolidation is permitted by the laws of the state under which each is organized.[9] In this type of merger or consolidation, each domestic corporation must comply with the provisions of the state statutes under which each was organized.[10] Further, if the surviving or new corporation is to be governed by the laws of any other state, it must comply with the provisions of that state.[11] The surviving or new corporation must file an agreement with the Secretary of State that it may be served with process in any proceeding for the enforcement of an obligation of any domestic corporation that was a party to the merger or consolidation.[12] The Secretary of State is appointed as agent to accept service of process in such a proceeding.[13]

New York statutes provide that a merger or consolidation of Type B or Type C corporations (whether a merger or consolidation of domestic corporations or of domestic and foreign corporations) must first obtain approval of the supreme court of the state.[14] A certified copy of an order of the court approving the plan of merger or consolidation and authorizing the filing of the certificate of merger or consolidation must be annexed to the certificate.[15]

FOOTNOTES

[1] Model Nonprofit Corporation Act §§38, 39 (1964).

See Cal Corp Code §§6010, 8010 which provides that, without permission from the Attorney General, a public benefit corporation may only merge with another public benefit corporation or a religious corporation and a mutual benefit corporation may only merge with another mutual benefit corporation. If a public benefit corporation is to merge with a mutual benefit corporation, or a mutual benefit corporation with a public benefit or religious corporation, prior written consent must be obtained from the Attorney General.

See also Ohio Rev Code Ann §1702.41 which provides that a charitable corporation may merge into or may consolidate with other charitable corporations only and the surviving or new corporation must be a charitable corporation.

Pennsylvania statutes provide that every merger or consolidation must be proposed by either (a) the adoption by the board of directors of a resolution approving the plan of merger or consolidation, (b) a petition of 10% of the

242 Representing the Nonprofit Organization

voting members setting forth the proposed plan, or (c) such other method as provided for in the bylaws. See Pa Stat Ann §7922(b).

[2] Model Nonprofit Corporation Act §40 (1964). See Ohio Rev Code Ann §1702.42(B), Pa Stat Ann §7924(a) which provide for only a majority vote of the voting members. See also Ohio Rev Code Ann §1702.42(C) which provides that the merger or consolidation may be abandoned at any time prior to filing the agreement by trustees of the corporation if the power of abandonment is conferred upon the trustees either by the agreement or by the same vote of the voting members that attended the meeting at which the plan of merger or consolidation was approved.

See Cal Corp Code §§6016, 8016 which provides that the board of directors of a nonprofit corporation may, at its discretion, abandon a merger, subject to the contractual rights of third parties, including other constituent corporations, without further approval by the members.

[3] Model Nonprofit Corporation Act §40(b) (1964). The California statutes require that the proposed agreement of merger of a public benefit corporation be provided to the Attorney General at least 20 days prior to consummation. See Cal Corp Code §6010.

Some states provide that notice of the meeting must be given to both voting and nonvoting members. See Ohio Rev Code Ann §1702.42. However, a majority of the states only require notice to the voting members.

[4] Model Nonprofit Corporation Act §40(b) (1964).

[5] Model Nonprofit Corporation Act §§38 and 39 (1964). The Illinois General Not for Profit Corporation Act requires an inclusion in the plan of merger or consolidation of any provisions under which the proposed merger or consolidation may be abandoned prior to filing of the articles or merger or consolidation. See Ill Rev Stat, ch 32, par 163a37(d).

[6] Model Nonprofit Corporation Act §41(c) (1964). California statutes provide that a certificate of satisfaction of the Franchise Tax Board that all taxes have been paid by each participating corporation must be included before an agreement of merger or consolidation can be filed. See Cal Corp Code §§6014, 8014.

[7] Model Nonprofit Corporation Act §42 (1964).

[8] Model Nonprofit Corporation Act §42(b) (1964).

[9] Model Nonprofit Corporation Act §43 (1964). Ohio statutes provide that, in the merger or consolidation of a domestic and a foreign corporation, a charitable corporation may merge into or may consolidate with other charitable corporations only, and the surviving or new corporation must be a charitable corporation. See Ohio Rev Code Ann §1702.45(A).

[10] Model Nonprofit Corporation Act §43(1964).

[11] Model Nonprofit Corporation Act §43 (1964).

[12] Model Nonprofit Corporation Act §43 (1964).
[13] Model Nonprofit Corporation Act §43 (1964).
[14] NY Notfor-Profit Corp Law §907(a).
[15] NY Not-for-Profit Corp Law §907(a). Application for an order is made in the judicial district in which the principal office of the surviving or consolidated corporation is to be located, or in which the office of one of the domestic constitutent corporations is located. Upon filing of the application, the court sets a hearing and directs that notice be given to interested parties, including the attorney general and any governmental body or officer whose consent is required prior to incorporating a Type B or Type C corporation. See NY Not-for-Profit Corp Law §907(b). The court, in its discretion, may direct that any assets required to be held for a charitable purpose be transferred to the surviving corporation subject to such use or purpose, or that the assets be transferred to another corporation engaged in substantially similar activities, upon an express trust, the terms of which are approved by the court. See NY Not-for-Profit Corp Law §907(c). The court can disapprove the merger if it finds that the interests of nonconsenting members may be substantially prejudiced by the merger or consolidation. See NY Not-for-Profit Corp Law §907(d).

§5:02. Effect of Merger or Consolidation.

In either a merger or a consolidation, the surviving or the new corporation succeeds to the assets, privileges, immunities and powers of the merged or consolidated corporations.[1] The surviving or new corporation also becomes responsible and liable for all liabilities and obligations of each of the merged or consolidated corporations.[2] (This includes responsibilities regarding property held in charitable trust.) All assets pass to the surviving or new corporation as a matter of law and further act or deed is not required.[3] Any lawsuits against the merged or consolidated corporations may be prosecuted against the surviving or new corporation as if the merger or consolidation had not taken place.[4] The rights of creditors or lienholders are not impaired by the merger or consolidation.[5]

244 Representing the Nonprofit Organization

FOOTNOTES

[1] Model Nonprofit Corporation Act §42(c) (1964).
[2] Model Nonprofit Corporation Act §42(e) (1964).
[3] Model Nonprofit Corporation Act §42(d) (1964). See discussion at §4:11 regarding application of the cy pres doctrine as to assets held in a charitable trust.
Kentucky. Eitel v. Norton Memorial Infirmary, 441 SW2d 438 (Ky App, 1969). The Eitel case involved the merger of two separate hospitals in which gifts had been established solely for the benefit of one of the hospitals. The question arose regarding the status of these gifts after the donee hospital was merged with another corporation. The court held that as far as the donors were concerned, the separate institutions were considered to have survived. According to the court, neither were annihilated; they were amalgamated.
Illinois. See Estate of Fuller v. Jerseyville Community Hospital, 10 Ill App 3d 460, 294 NE2d 313 (1973) in which the court held that a bequest to a hospital passed to the surviving corporation after the donee hospital was merged into another corporation.
California statutes provide that the recordation of the merger documents evidences record ownership in the surviving corporation of all interest in real property of the disappearing corporation. See Cal Corp Code §§6021, 8021. Any bequest or gift inures to the surviving corporation. (Cal Corp Code §§6022, 8022.)
Iowa statutes also provide that any bequest or gift to or for the benefit of any of the merging or consolidating corporations inures to the benefit of the surviving or new corporation. The statute provides that so far as is necessary for that purpose, the existence of each merging or consolidating corporation is deemed to continue in and through the surviving or new corporation. See Iowa Code Ann §504A.44(5).
[4] Model Nonprofit Corporation Act §42(e) (1964).
[5] Model Nonprofit Corporation Act §42(e) (1964).

§5:03. Articles of Merger or Consolidation.

After a plan of merger or consolidation is approved by the members (or by the board of directors if the corporation has no members), articles of merger should be prepared. Such articles should include the plan of merger or consolidation, a statement indicating the date of the meeting of members at which the plan was adopted, that a quorum was present at the meeting, and that the plan received the required number of votes which the members present or represented by proxy were entitled to cast.[1] If the corporation has no members, the articles should include a statement as to the date of the meeting of the board of directors at which the plan was adopted and a statement that the plan received the vote of a majority of the directors in office.[2]

Duplicate originals of the articles should be filed with the Secretary of State who will return to the surviving or new corporation one duplicate original.[3]

FOOTNOTES

[1] Model Nonprofit Corporation Act §41 (1964).
[2] Model Nonprofit Corporation Act §41(c) (1964).
[3] Model Nonprofit Corporation Act §41 (1964).
California statutes do not require the filing of articles of merger. See Cal Corp Code §§6014, 8014 which provides that after approval of a merger, the surviving corporation must file a copy of the "agreement" of merger with an officer's certificate of each constituent corporation attached stating the total number of memberships of each class entitled to vote on the merger, identifying any other person or persons whose approval is required, and stating that the principal terms of the agreement in the form attached were approved by the required vote of the members. The merger and any amendment of the articles of the surviving corporation contained in the merger agreement become effective at that time. A copy of the agreement of merger certified by an official having custody of the agreement has the same force in evidence as the original and is conclusive evidence of the performance of all conditions precedent to the merger, the existence on the effective date of the surviving corporation, and the performance of the conditions necessary to the adoption of any amendment to the articles. See Cal Corp Code §§6017, 8017.

§5:04.   —*Form of Articles of Merger.*

ARTICLES OF MERGER[1] OF DOMESTIC CORPORATIONS INTO _____

Pursuant to article _____ of the _____ Nonprofit Corporation Act, the undersigned corporations adopt the following Articles of Merger for the purpose of merging them into one of such corporations:

FIRST: The following Plan of Merger was approved by each of the undersigned corporations;

(Insert Plan of Merger)

SECOND: As to each of the undersigned corporations, the Plan of Merger was adopted in the following manner:

(Insert one of the following statements:

a. The Plan of Merger was adopted by _____ at a meeting of its members held on _____ at which a quorum was present, and the Plan of Merger received at least two-thirds[2] of the vote which members present or represented by proxy at such meeting were entitled to cast.
b. The Plan of Merger was adopted by _____ by a consent in writing signed under date of _____ by all members entitled to vote in respect thereof.
c. The Plan of Merger was adopted by _____ at a meeting of the Board of Directors held on _____ and received the vote of a majority of the Directors in office, there being no members entitled to vote in respect thereof.
d. The Plan of Merger was adopted by _____ by a consent in writing signed under date of _____ by all

of its directors, there being no members entitled to vote in respect thereof.)

Dated_____, 19____.

_____[3]

Address _____

By _____

Its President

and _____

Its Secretary

_____[3]

Address _____

By _____

Its President

and _____

Its Secretary

FOOTNOTES

[1] Model Nonprofit Corporation Act, Official Forms §10 (1964).

[2] Check state statutes to determine the number of members required to approve a plan of merger.

[3] Use the exact corporate name of each corporation a party to the merger.

§5:05. —Form of Articles of Consolidation.

ARTICLES OF CONSOLIDATION[1] OF DOMESTIC CORPORATIONS INTO

_____

Pursuant to the provisions of Article _____ of the _____ Nonprofit Corporation Act, the undersigned corporations adopt the following Articles of Consolidation for the purpose of consolidating them into a new corporation:

FIRST: The following Plan of Consolidation was approved by each of the undersigned corporations:

(Insert Plan of Consolidation)

SECOND: As to each of the undersigned corporations, the Plan of Consolidation was adopted in the following manner:

(Insert one of the following statements:

a. The Plan of Consolidation was adopted by _____ at a meeting of its members held on _____, at which a quorum was present, and the Plan of Consolidation received at least two-thirds[2] of the votes which members present or represented by proxy at such meeting were entitled to cast.
b. The Plan of Consolidation was adopted by _____ by a consent in writing signed under date of _____ by all members entitled to vote in respect thereof.
c. The Plan of Consolidation was adopted by _____ at a meeting of the Board of Directors held on _____, and received the vote of a majority of the Directors in office, there being no members entitled to vote in respect thereof.
d. The Plan of Consolidation was adopted by _____, by a consent in writing signed under date of _____ by all of its directors, there being no members entitled to vote in respect thereof.)

Dated _____, 19_____.

_____[3]
Address _____
By _____
Its President
and _____
Its Secretary

_____[3]
Address _____
By _____
Its President
and _____
Its Secretary

FOOTNOTES

[1] Model Nonprofit Corporation Act, Official Forms §12 (1964).
[2] Check state statutes to determine the number of members required to approve a plan of consolidation.
[3] Use the exact corporate name of each corporation a party to the consolidation.

§5:06. Form of Articles of Merger or Consolidation of Domestic and Foreign Corporation.

ARTICLES OF MERGER (CONSOLIDATION)[1] OF DOMESTIC AND FOREIGN CORPORATIONS

The undersigned corporations, pursuant to Article _____ of the _____ Nonprofit Corporation Act, hereby execute the following Articles of Merger (Consolidation):

FIRST: The names of the corporations proposing to (merge) (consolidate) and the names of the states under the laws of which said corporations are organized are as follows: _____.

SECOND: The laws of _____, the state under which such foreign corporation is (corporations are) organized permit such (merger) (consolidation).

THIRD: The name of the (surviving) (new) corporation shall be _____ and it shall be governed by the laws of the state of _____.

FOURTH: The following Plan of (Merger) (Consolidation) was approved by each of the undersigned corporations.

(Insert Plan of Merger or Consolidation)

FIFTH: As to each domestic Corporation, the Plan of (Merger) (Consolidation) was adopted in the following manner:

(Insert one of the following statements:

a. The Plan was adopted by _____ at a meeting of its members, held on _____ at which a quorum was present, and said Plan received at least two-thirds[2] of the votes which members present or represented by proxy at such meeting were entitled to cast.
b. The Plan was adopted by _____ by a consent in writing signed under date of _____ by all members entitled to vote in respect thereof.
c. The Plan was adopted by _____ at a meeting of the Board of Directors held on _____ and received a vote of a majority of directors in office, there being no members entitled to vote in respect thereof.
d. The Plan was adopted by _____ by a consent in writing signed under date of _____ by all of its directors, there being no members entitled to vote in respect thereof.)

SIXTH: As to each foreign corporation, the Plan was adopted in compliance with the applicable provisions of the laws of the state under which it is organized.

It is agreed that upon and after issuance of a Certificate of (Merger) (Consolidation) by the Secretary of State of the State of _____:

1. The (surviving) (new) corporation may be served with process in the State of _____ in any proceedings for the enforcement of any obligation of any corporation organized under the laws of the State of _____ which is a party to the (merger) (consolidation):
2. The Secretary of State of the State of _____ shall be and hereby is irrevocably appointed as the agent of the (surviving) (new) corporation to accept service of process in any such proceeding.

Dated _____, 19 _____.

_____[3]
Address _____
By _____
Its President
and _____
Its Secretary

_____[3]
Address _____
By _____
Its President
and _____
Its Secretary

FOOTNOTES

[1] Model Nonprofit Corporation Act, Official Forms §14.

[2] Check state statutes to determine the number of members required to approve a plan of merger or consolidation of a foreign and domestic corporation.

[3] Use the exact corporate name of each corporation a party to the merger or consolidation.

§5:07. Withdrawal of a Foreign Corporation.

A foreign nonprofit corporation authorized to do business within a particular state[1] may withdraw from the state upon obtaining from the Secretary of State a certificate of withdrawal.[2] The application for a certificate of withdrawal should state the name of the corporation and the state under whose laws it is incorporated, that it is not conducting affairs within the state, and that it surrenders its authority to conduct affairs within the state; that it revokes the authority of its registered agent to accept service of process and consents that service of process may thereafter be made upon the Secretary of State; and the post office address to which the Secretary of State may mail a copy of any process served on him against the corporation.[3]

A certificate of authority generally may be revoked by the state if a foreign nonprofit corporation fails to file a required annual report; fails to pay any required fees when they become due and payable; fails to appoint and maintain a registered agent in the state; fails to file in the office of the Secretary of State any amendment to its articles of incorporation or any articles of merger within the time prescribed; exceeds or abuses its authority; or misrepresents any material matter in any application, report, affidavit or other document submitted by it.[4]

Upon the revocation of a certificate of authority, the Secretary of State issues a certificate of revocation at which time the authority of the foreign corporation to do business within the state ceases.[5]

FOOTNOTES

[1] See discussion on how to obtain authorization to do business in another state at §1:20.

[2] See Model Nonprofit Corporation Act §76 (1964).

Pennsylvania statutes provide that a foreign corporation must officially publish and mail a notice of its intention to withdraw from doing business within the state. See Pa Stat Ann §8129(b).

[3] Model Nonprofit Corporation Act §76 (1964).

[4] See Model Nonprofit Corporation Act §78 (1964). The Iowa statutes provide that no certificate of authority of a foreign corporation shall be revoked by the Secretary of State unless the corporation is given at least 60 days' notice by mail addressed to the principal office of the corporation in the state or country under the laws of which it is incorporated, and the corporation shall fail, prior to revocation, to file its annual report, to pay its fees or

penalties, to file the required statement of change of a registered agent or office, to file articles of amendment or merger, or to correct any misrepresentation. See Iowa Code Ann §504A.80.

Illinois statutes provide for the revocation of a certificate of authority of a foreign corporation because of acts noted in the Model Nonprofit Corporation Act §78, but also if the corporation has not conducted any affairs within the state for a period of two years. See Ill Rev Stat, ch 32, par 163a83. In addition, a foreign corporation's certificate of authority will be revoked if the corporation commits consumer fraud. See Ill Rev Stat, ch 32, par 163a83.1.

[5] Model Nonprofit Corporation Act §79 (1964).

See discussion at §1:20 of activities that are generally permitted within a state even though a corporation does not have authorization to do business within the state.

§5:08. Sale of Assets.

A nonprofit corporation may sell, lease, exchange, or mortgage all, or substantially all its property and assets if statutory requirements are followed.[1] If the corporation has members, the board of directors would direct that a resolution adopted by the board be submitted to a vote at either the regular or a special meeting of the members.[2] Written notice stating that the purpose of the meeting is to sell, lease, exchange, or mortgage all, or substantially all, the property and assets, must be given each member entitled to vote at the meeting within the time and in the manner provided by the state statute.[3] Authorization from the members generally requires a two-thirds vote of the members present at the meeting or represented by proxy.[4] If there are no members in the nonprofit corporation, the sale, lease, exchange, or mortgage must be approved by a majority vote of the directors in office.[5]

The board of directors may abandon a sale, lease, exchange, or mortgage of the corporate assets after authorization subject to the rights of third parties under any contracts entered into, without further action or approval of the members.[6]

FOOTNOTES

[1] Model Nonprofit Corporation Act §44 (1964).

California statutes require that a nonprofit public benefit corporation give written notice to the Attorney General 20 days before the corporation sells, leases, conveys, exchanges, transfers or otherwise disposes of all or substantially all of its assets unless the transaction is in the usual and regular course of its activities or unless the Attorney General has given the corporation a written waiver of the notice requirement. See Cal Corp Code §5913. A nonprofit mutual public benefit corporation must be given the same written notice to the Attorney General if it sells, leases, conveys, exchanges, transfers or otherwise disposes of any or all of its assets that are being held in trust. See Cal Corp Code §7913.

Pennsylvania statutes provide that a nonprofit corporation may not sell, lease, or exchange all or substantially all its assets unless such a plan is adopted by the corporation in the same manner as that required for adoption of a plan of merger. See Pa Stat Ann §7930(a). Articles need not be filed with the Department of State, however, but compliance with §7549(b) is required. Section 7549(b) provides that property committed to charitable purposes shall not be diverted from the objects to which it was donated unless the board of directors obtains a court order specifying the disposition of the property.

Should a nonprofit organization that is a private foundation for tax purposes transfer a significant portion of its assets to another private foundation, the transferee corporation will succeed to the tax liability of the transferor.

There can be problems in the sale of a nonprofit corporation's assets if the assets were gifts to the corporation to be used for charitable purposes. The cy pres doctrine may be applicable. See discussion at §5:11.

New York. See Lefkowitz v. Cornell University, 62 Misc 2d 95, 308 NYS2d 85 (1970), in which the court prevented Cornell University from selling research laboratory facilities donated to Cornell by Curtis-Wright Corporation. The court ruled that even though the gift was unrestricted, it was a gift subject to a charitable trust and could not be diverted to an entirely different purpose. The New York Not-for-Profit Corporation Act, adopted in 1969, has a provision providing that a nonprofit corporation holds assets for corporate purposes rather than in trust. See NY Not-for-Profit Corp Law §513. This provision provides for administration of restricted funds within the principles of corporate law rather than trust law. A nonprofit corporation acquires full ownership of charitable assets subject to the duty of the directors to follow the directions of the donor. Whether this provision would have caused the court to render a different conclusion is questionable.

[2] Model Nonprofit Corporation Act §44 (1964).

California statutes provide that a mortgage, deed of trust, or pledge of all or any part of a nonprofit corporation's assets for the purpose of securing the payment or performance of any contract or obligation may be approved by the Board of Directors. Approval of the members is not required unless the articles or bylaws provide otherwise. See Cal Corp Code §§5910, 7910.

Iowa statutes also provide that a mortgage or pledge may be made upon all or any of the assets of a nonprofit corporation upon authorization of the Board of Directors. Authorization or consent of the members is not required unless the articles of incorporation provide otherwise. See Iowa Code Ann §504A.46(3).

[3] Model Nonprofit Corporation Act §44 (1964).

[4] Model Nonprofit Corporation Act §44 (1964).

Ohio statutes provide that only a majority of the members present at the meeting is necessary (if a quorum is present) unless the articles or the regulations provide for an affirmative vote of a greater number. See Ohio Rev Code Ann §1702.39(A).

[5] Model Nonprofit Corporation Act §44 (1964).

[6] Model Nonprofit Corporation Act §44 (1964).

Ohio statutes provide that an action to set aside a conveyance by a corporation of a lease, sale, exchange, transfer or other disposition of all or substantially all the assets of the corporation on the ground that the statutes have not been complied with must be brought within 90 days after the transaction or such an action will be forever barred. See Ohio Rev Code Ann §1702.39(C).

California statutes provide that any deed or instrument conveying or otherwise transferring any assets of a nonprofit corporation may have annexed to it the certificate of the secretary of the corporation setting forth that the transaction has been validly approved by the board, that the notice required in §5913 has been given, and stating that the transfer is of less than substantially all of the assets of the corporation or that the transfer is in the usual and regular course of the business of the corporation or that, if it is of all or substantially all of the assets, that the members have approved the transfer. Such certificate will then be prima facie evidence of the existence of the facts authorizing the conveyance or other transfer of the assets and conclusive evidence in favor of any purchaser or encumbrancer, who, without notice of any trust restriction applicable to the property, parted with value. See Cal Corp Code §§5912, 7912.

§5:09. Voluntary Dissolution of a Nonprofit Corporation.

A nonprofit corporation may voluntarily dissolve if provisions of state statutes are followed.[1] The board of directors must adopt a resolution recommending that the corporation be dissolved and directing that the question of dissolution be submitted to a vote of the members at the annual meeting of the members or at a special meeting called for that purpose.[2] Written notice stating that the purpose, or one of the purposes, of the meeting is to consider the advisability of dissolving the corporation must be given to each member entitled to vote at the meeting within the time and manner provided by applicable state statute.[3] A resolution to dissolve the corporation must receive at least two-thirds votes of the members present at the meeting or represented by proxy.[4]

If the corporation has no members, or no voting members, the dissolution can be authorized at a meeting of the board of directors upon the adoption of a resolution to dissolve by the vote of a majority of the directors in office.[5]

Upon the adoption of a resolution to dissolve the corporation, the corporation must mail a notice of its dissolution to each of its known creditors and must then proceed to collect its assets and distribute them in the manner prescribed by state statute.[6]

A plan of dissolution may be revoked by the corporation at any time prior to the issuance of a certificate of dissolution by the Secretary of State.[7] A resolution to revoke the action taken to dissolve the corporation would be voted upon by the board of directors and submitted to the members. The resolution would be adopted upon a two-thirds vote of the members present at the meeting or represented by proxy.[8] If the corporation has no members, the plan to revoke the dissolution would be adopted at a meeting of the board by a majority vote of the directors in office.[9]

MERGER, CONSOLIDATION, AND DISSOLUTION 257

FOOTNOTES

[1] Model Nonprofit Corporation Act §45 (1964).

See Florida statutes which provide that a nonprofit corporation wishing to dissolve must present a petition to the circuit court of the county in which the principal office of the corporation is located. The circuit judge directs that a notice be published and, after a period of time issues a decree of dissolution, making all necessary orders and decrees for the winding up of the affairs of the corporation. The corporation is dissolved upon filing a certified copy of the decree of dissolution with the Department of State and the payment of all filing fees. See Fla Stat Ann §617.05(1).

California provides that a nonprofit corporation may voluntarily dissolve if the corporation (a) has been adjudicated a bankrupt, (b) has disposed of all of its assets and has not conducted any activity for a period of five years immediately preceding the adoption of the resolution electing to dissolve the corporation, (c) has no members, or (d) if the corporation was a subordinate corporation of a head organization and the head organization took away the subordinate's charter. See Cal Corp Code §§6610, 8610, 5132(a)(2)(i), 7132(a)(4)(i).

Ohio statutes provide that a nonprofit corporation may voluntarily dissolve (a) when the corporation has been adjudged a bankrupt or has made a general assignment for the benefit of creditors, (b) by leave of court when a receiver has been appointed in a general creditors' suit or in any suit in which the affairs of the corporation are to be wound up, (c) when substantially all of the assets have been sold, or (d) when the period of existence of the corporation specified in the articles has expired. See Ohio Rev Code Ann §1702.47.

New York statutes provide that a plan of dissolution of a Type B or Type C corporation (and any other corporation which holds assets required to be used for a particular purpose) must have been approved by a justice of the supreme court in which the office of the corporation is located. See NY Not-for-Profit Corp Law §1002(d).

[2] Model Nonprofit Corporation Act §45 (1964).

Pennsylvania statutes provide that a proposal of voluntary dissolution may be adopted by the board of directors or by petition of 10% of the voting members. The petition of the members must be directed to the board of directors and filed with the secretary of the corporation. Other methods may be provided for in the bylaws. See Pa Stat Ann §7962.

[3] Model Nonprofit Corporation Act §45 (1964).

[4] Model Nonprofit Corporation Act §45 (1964).

California, Pennsylvania and Ohio statutes provide for a majority vote of the members. See Cal Corp Code §§6611 and 8611; Pa Stat Ann §7964; Ohio Rev Code Ann §1702.47(D).

Ohio statutes require that a quorum be present at the meeting for a majority vote to be sufficient. Further, the articles or the regulations may provide or permit an affirmative vote of a greater or lesser proportion or number of the voting members. See Ohio Rev Code Ann §1702.47(D).

[5] Model Nonprofit Corporation Act §45 (1964).

[6] Model Nonprofit Corporation Act §45 (1964).

Pennsylvania statutes provide that the board of directors, or other body, at any time during the winding up proceedings may, by petition, apply to the court to have the proceedings continued under the supervision of the court. See Pa Stat Ann §7968(a). See also Cal Corp Code §§6614; 8614; NY Not-for-Profit Corp Law §1008; Ohio Rev Code Ann §1702.50.

Ohio statutes require that, following the filing of the certificate of dissolution, a notice of voluntary dissolution must be published once a week on the same day of each week for two successive weeks in a newspaper published and of general circulation in the county in which the principal office of the corporation was located. In addition, written notice of dissolution must be given to all known creditors of the dissolved corporation. See Ohio Rev Code Ann §1702.48.

[7] Model Nonprofit Corporation Act §48 (1964).

California statutes provide that the plan of distribution may be revoked prior to the distribution of assets. See Cal Corp Code §§6612, 8612.

[8] Model Nonprofit Corporation Act §48 (1964).

A vote of the majority of members is prescribed in Pennsylvania. See Pa Stat Ann §7966.

[9] Model Nonprofit Corporation Act §48 (1964).

§5:10. Distribution of Assets.

Even though a plan of dissolution has been approved by a nonprofit corporation's members and board of directors, statutory provisions regarding distribution of assets of the nonprofit corporation require that additional procedures be followed. Both state statutes and federal tax provisions (for those nonprofit corporations that are tax exempt) restrict the manner in which assets of a nonprofit corporation can be distributed.[1]

Bylaws of the corporation may not be enacted that would remove statutory restrictions.[2]

Assets held in trust, or upon certain conditions, must be returned, transferred or conveyed in accordance with the requirements of conditions imposed upon the assets.[3] Assets that are held for charitable, religious, eleemosynary, benevolent, educational, or similar purposes, but not held upon a condition requiring return, transfer or conveyance by reason of the dissolution, must be transferred or conveyed to one or more nonprofit organizations engaged in activities substantially similar to those of the dissolving corporation.[4] Other assets must be distributed in accordance with the provisions of the articles of incorporation or bylaws to the extent that the articles or bylaws determine the distributive rights of members or provide for distribution to others.[5] Any remaining assets may be distributed to those persons, societies, or organizations, whether for profit or nonprofit, as the plan of distribution specifies.[6]

A plan of distribution may be adopted by the corporation and voted upon by the voting members or, if the corporation has no members, by a majority vote of the directors in office.[7]

FOOTNOTES

[1] Upon dissolution, all assets of a §501(c)(3) organization must be distributed for one or more exempt purposes, or to the federal government, or to a state or local government, for public purposes. See Reg §1.501(c)(3)-4.

[2] **Illinois.** See Holden Hospital Corporation v. Southern Illinois Hospital Corporation, 174 NE2d 793 (1961). The Board of Directors of the Holden Hospital Corporation enacted a bylaw which would have removed the restrictions on distribution of its assets upon dissolution that were imposed by state statutes. (See Ill Rev Stat ch 32, pars 163a44, 163a45). Pursuant to its bylaw, the directors attempted to distribute the assets of the hospital corporation to Methodist Conference and Woman's Society. The court held that while a dissolution of the corporation and a sale of its assets were authorized by statute, the corporation had to follow statutory provisions relating to distribution of its assets. The assets had to be distributed to an organization

engaged in activities substantially similar to those of the dissolving corporation.

[3] See Model Nonprofit Corporation Act §46 (1964).

[4] Model Nonprofit Corporation Act §46(c) (1964). The cy pres doctrine may be applicable in these instances.

See discussion of the doctrine at §1:04 note 15, and §12:11.

See Cal Corp Code §§6716(b) and 8716(b) which provides that those assets held for charitable purposes must be disposed of on dissolution in conformity with the corporation's bylaws or articles subject to complying with the provisions of any trust under which the assets are held; however, unless a written waiver of objections to the disposition is obtained from the Attorney General, the disposition must be made by decree of the superior court of the proper county in proceedings to which the Attorney General is a party. The decree shall be made upon petition by the Attorney General or, upon 30 days' notice to the Attorney General, by any person concerned in the dissolution.

New York statutes provide that assets held for charitable purposes (Type B corporations) must be distributed to one or more domestic or foreign corporations or other organizations engaged in activities substantially similar to those of the dissolved corporation pursuant to a plan of distribution adopted by the board of directors or as ordered by the court to which the plan has been submitted for approval. The corporation or organization acquiring the assets is subject to any disposition contained in a will or other instrument, made before or after the dissolution to or for the benefit of the dissolved corporation. See NY Not-for-Profit Corp Law §1005(a)(3)(A).

Ohio statutes provide that charitable assets held in trust for specified purposes must be applied so far as feasible in accordance with the terms of the trust and any remaining assets not held in trust must be applied so far as is feasible towards carrying out the purposes stated in the corporation's articles. To the extent that it is not feasible to so apply the assets, the assets must be applied as directed by the court of common pleas of the county in which the principal office of the corporation is located, in an action brought for that purpose by the corporation or by the trustees. The attorney general of the state must be made a party to the action. See Ohio Rev Code Ann §1702.49(D)(2).

Pennsylvania statutes provide that the board of directors must apply to the court for an order specifying the distribution of any property committed to charitable purposes. See Pa Stat Ann §7968(b). For a corporation organized for the support of public worship, the court must provide for the disposition of the assets of the corporation either by vesting title in another corporation organized for public worship according to the formularies of the church or religious organization to which the dissolved corporation was in allegiance or by authorizing the sale of the assets and vesting the proceeds in a body as directed by the court, or by vesting title to the assets in any incorporated or unincorporated body designated by the petitioners for the same uses and trusts as the assets were held by the dissolved corporation. See Pa Stat Ann §7968(c).

The IRC requires that the assets must be distributed for one or more exempt purposes and may not be of charitable organizations distributed to members of the organization.

New York. See In re Green, 10 Misc 2d 557, 177 NYS2d 933 (1957), in which the court held that distribution of charitable assets to members of the corporation is improper.

[5] Model Nonprofit Corporation Act §46(d) (1964). Bylaws or articles of incorporation should provide for the distribution of assets upon dissolution. If they do not, the assets may escheat to the state.

New York statutes provide that other assets must be distributed in accordance with the specifications of a plan of distribution adopted by the board of directors, or to the extent that the certificate of incorporation prescribes the distributive rights of members. See NY Not-for-Profit Corp Law §1005(a)(3)(B). Any assets distributable to a creditor or member who is unknown or cannot be found, or who is under a disability, must be paid to the state comptroller as abandoned property within 6 months from the date fixed for payment of the final liquidating distributions and be subject to the provisions of the abandoned property law. See NY Not-for-Profit Corp Law §1005(a)(4). The plan of distribution must provide that assets will be distributed with the following order of priorities: (1) holders of certificates of subvention, (2) holders of capital certifcates, and (3) members. See NY Not-for-Profit Corp Law §1005(b).

Ohio statutes provide that if the articles or regulations have no provisions for the distribution of the remaining assets, the assets must be distributed pursuant to a plan of distribution adopted by the voting members at a meeting held for the purpose of voting on dissolution by the same affirmative vote as that required for the adoption of a resolution of dissolution. If no plan of distribution is adopted by the voting members, the remaining assets must be distributed pursuant to a plan of distribution adopted by the trustees. See Ohio Rev Code Ann §1702.49(D)(3). Any action which is authorized or approved by the voting members at a meeting held for that purpose, by the same affirmative vote as that required for the adoption of a resolution of dissolution, is conclusive for all purposes upon all members of the corporation (except that the jurisdiction of the courts is not impaired to enforce the duties of a charitable corporation in respect to the application of the assets towards charitable purposes). See Ohio Rev Code Ann §1702.49(E).

[6] Model Nonprofit Corporation Act §46(e) (1964).

California statutes provide that any person to whom assets were distributed upon dissolution may be sued in the corporate name upon any cause of action against the corporation arising prior to its dissolution. Notice of the action must be given to the Attorney General who may intervene. See Cal Corp Code §6721. Any distribution of assets may be recovered by the corporation if there has not been adequate provision for payment of any liabilities of the corporation. See Cal Corp Code §§6719, 8721.

Pennsylvania. When a corporation has no capital stock and the bylaws do not authorize the issuance of stock, distribution of assets to the members should arguably be conducted on a per capita basis. See Petition of Board of Directors of State Police Civic Ass'n, 80 Pa Commw 405, 472 A2d 731, 739 (1984).

[7] Model Nonprofit Corporation Act §47 (1964).

New York statutes provide that the board must adopt a plan for the dissolution of the corporation and the distribution of its assets. See NY Not-for-Profit Corp Law §1001. If the corporation is a Type B or Type C corporation and has no assets to distribute at the time of dissolution, the plan must include a statement to that effect, and a certified copy of the plan must be filed with the attorney general within 10 days after adoption of the plan by the board. See NY Not-for-Profit Corp Law §1001(b). For a Type B or Type C corporation that has assets, and any other corporation that holds assets at the time of dissolution which are legally required to be used for a particular purpose, the plan of dissolution and distribution of assets must have annexed thereto the approval of a justice of the supreme court in the judicial district in which the office of the corporation is located. See NY Not-for-Proft Corp Law §1002(d).

§5:11. —Cy Pres Doctrine.

The cy pres doctrine may be applicable in dissolution proceedings to determine the distribution of assets. There may be an inadequacy of funds or a failure or lapse of a particular charitable gift. The cy pres doctrine is applicable when a condition imposed by a donor has proven impracticable; the court can determine a means of using the property that will most approximately carry out the donor's intent.[1] A modified cy pres doctrine, called the doctrine of approximation, permits the court to direct the application of property to some charitable purpose which falls within the general purpose of the donor when it has become impossible or illegal to carry out the particular purpose and when the donor has manifested a more general intention to devote the property to charitable purposes.[2] The result of a too strict adherence to the words of the donors often would cause the defeat rather than the accomplishment of the donor's charitable purpose.[3] Where the issue arises because of the nonexistence, merger or dissolution of the charitable beneficiary, cy pres can be applied if the general charitable purpose is primary and the particular beneficiary is only secondary.[4]

If there is no specific gift over in the event that the charitable disposition fails, there is evidence of a general charitable purpose.[5] However, should the donor include a specific direction to pay the disposition to another charitable beneficiary, to a specified individual, or residuary donees, in the event that the gift fails, there is a specific gift and a court may not, under the cy pres doctrine, direct that the gift may be used by some other charity.[6] On the other hand, where a charitable disposition has vested and there is no specific gift over, cy pres will be applied.[7]

If the subsequent failure of a gift after vesting is because of the dissolution of a charitable corporation, there may be no necessity for an independent cy pres proceeding; state dissolution statutes which normally provide for the transfer of charitable assets to other charitable organizations will generally suffice.[8] However, if the charitable disposition has vested but is subject to be divested by a gift over, a separate cy pres proceeding may be necessary.[9]

FOOTNOTES

[1] **Connecticut.** Daggett v. Children's Center, 28 Conn Supp 468, 266 A2d 72 (1970).

[2] **Connecticut.** Daggett v. Children's Center, 28 Conn Supp 468, 266 A2d 72 (1970).

[3] **Connecticut.** Daggett v. Children's Center, 28 Conn Supp 468, 266 A2d 72 (1970).

[4] **New York.** In re Will of Goehringer, 69 Misc 2d 145, 329 NYS 2d 516, 520 (1972).

[5] **New York.** In re Will of Goehringer, 69 Misc 2d 145, 329 NYS 2d 516, 521 (1972).

[6] **New York.** In re Will of Goehringer, 69 Misc 2d 145, 329 NYS 2d 516, 522 (1972).

[7] **New York.** In re Will of Goehringer, 69 Misc 2d 145, 329 NYS 2d 516, 522 (1972).

[8] See discussion of some of the state statutes at §5:10.

[9] **New York.** In re Will of Goehringer, 69 Misc 2d 145, 329 NYS 2d 516, 522 (1972).

§5:12. —Articles of Dissolution.

After liabilities of the corporation have been discharged, or adequate provision has been made for them, and all property of the corporation has been distributed or transferred, articles of dissolution must be executed in duplicate and delivered to the Secretary of State.[1] The articles of dissolution should set forth the following: (1) name of the corporation, (2) if the corporation has members, a statement indicating the date of the meeting of the members at which a resolution was adopted, that a quorum was present at the meeting, and that the resolution received a two-thirds[2] vote of the members present at the meeting or represented by proxy, (3) if the corporation has no members or no members entitled to vote, a statement of that fact and the date of a meeting of the board of directors at which the resolution to dissolve was adopted and that it received a majority vote of the directors in office, (4) that all liabilities of the corporation have been paid or that adequate provision has been made for them, (5) a copy of the plan of distribution as adopted by the corporation or a statement that no plan was adopted, (6) a statement that all remaining property and assets have been conveyed or distributed in accordance with state statute, and (7) a statement that no suits are pending against the corporation or that adequate provision has been made for the satisfaction of any judgment, order or decree which may be entered against the corporation in a pending suit.[3]

Upon approval of the articles of dissolution by the Secretary of State, a certificate of dissolution will be issued and the existence of the corporation shall cease, except for the purpose of suits or other proceedings and appropriate corporate action by members, directors and officers.[4]

FOOTNOTES

[1] Model Nonprofit Corporation Act §§49,50 (1964).

California statutes provide that, in lieu of filing the certificate of dissolution, the board may petition the superior court of the proper county for an order declaring the corporation duly dissolved. Upon the filing of the petition, the court shall make an order requiring all interested persons, including the Attorney General, to show cause why an order should not be entered declaring the corporation dissolved. Any person claiming to be interested may appear in a proceeding at any time before the expiration of 30 days from the completion of publication of the order to show cause and contest the petition. Failure to appear will bar the claim. Thereafter, an order is entered and filed and has the same effect as an order of dissolution in an involuntary dissolution. See Cal Corp Code §§6617, 8617.

[2] Check state statutes to determine the required vote of the members.

[3] Model Nonprofit Corporation Act §49(g) (1964).

New York statutes require that an approval of the dissolution by a justice of the supreme court in the judicial district in which the office of the corporation is located in the case of a Type B or Type C corporation, and in the case of any other corporation which holds assets at the time of dissolution legally required to be used for a particular purpose, be endorsed on the certificate of dissolution. See NY Not-for-Profit Corp Law §1003(b).

[4] Model Nonprofit Corporation Act §50 (1964).

California statutes provide that before a corporation may file a certificate of dissolution, it must file a certificate of satisfaction of the Franchise Tax Board (required by §23334 of the Revenue and Taxation Code) that all taxes imposed under the Bank and Corporation Tax Law have been paid or secured. See Cal Corp Code §§6615, 8615.

New York statutes provide that a dissolved corporation, its directors, officers and members may continue to function for the purpose of winding up the affairs of the corporation in the same manner as if the dissolution had not taken place. Capital certificates may be transferred and determination of members for any purpose may be made without closing the record of members until that time. See NY Not-for-Profit Corp Law §1006. The dissolution will not affect any remedy available to or against the corporation, its directors, officers or members, for any right or claim existing or any liability incurred before the dissolution unless the corporation gave notice to all creditors to present their claims in writing and in detail at a specified place and by a specified day (not less than 6 months after the first publication of the notice). The notice must be published at least once a week for 2 successive weeks in a newspaper of general circulation in the county in which the office of the corporation was located at the time of dissolution. On or before the date of the first publication, the corporation must mail a notice to each creditor. Any claims that are not filed as provided in the notice will be barred as against the corporation. See NY Not-for-Profit Corp Law §1008.

§5:13. —Form for Articles of Dissolution.[1]

ARTICLES OF DISSOLUTION OF
_____

Pursuant to the provisions of article _____ of the _____ Nonprofit Corporation Act, the undersigned corporation adopts the following Articles of Dissolution for the purpose of dissolving the corporation:

FIRST: The name of the corporation is _____.

SECOND: A resolution to dissolve the corporation was adopted in the following manner:

(Insert one of the following statements:

a. The resolution to dissolve the corporation was adopted at a meeting of members held on _____ at which a quorum was present, and the resolution received at least two-thirds[2] of the votes which members present, or represented by proxy, at such meeting were entitled to cast.

b. The resolution to dissolve the corporation was adopted by a consent in writing signed under date of _____ by all members entitled to vote in respect thereof.

c. the resolution to dissolve the corporation was adopted at a meeting of the Board of Directors held on _____ and received the vote of a majority of the Directors in office, there being no members entitled to vote in respect thereof.

d. The resolution to dissolve the corporation was adopted by a consent in writing signed under date of _____ by all of the directors, there being no members entitled to vote in respect thereof.)

THIRD: The plan of distribution adopted by the corporation is as follows:

(Insert plan of distribution. If no plan of distribution was adopted, that fact should be stated.)

FOURTH: All debts, obligations and liabilities of the corporation have been paid and discharged, or adequate provisions have been made thereof.

FIFTH: All remaining property and assets of the corporation have been transferred, conveyed or distributed in accordance with the provisions of the _____ Nonprofit Corporation Act.

SIXTH: There are no suits pending against the corporation in any court in respect of which adequate provisions have not been made for the satisfaction of any judgment, order or decree which may be entered against it.

Dated _____, 19____.

_____[3]
Address _____
By _____
Its President
and _____
Its Secretary

FOOTNOTES

[1] This form was taken from Model Nonprofit Corporation Act, Official Forms §17.
[2] Check state statutes for number of voters required to approve a dissolution.
[3] Use the corporate name of the dissolving corporation.

§5:14. Involuntary Dissolution.

A nonprofit corporation may be involuntarily dissolved by a court decree should it fail to follow state statutes or become defunct. An action to dissolve a nonprofit corporation is filed by the Attorney General to establish that the corporation (a) failed to file its annual report within the time required, (b) procured its articles of incorporation through fraud, (c) has continued to exceed or abuse the authority conferred upon it by law, (d) has failed for 90 days to appoint and maintain a registered agent in the state, or (e) has failed for 90 days after change of its registered agent to file in the office of the Secretary of State a statement of the change.[1]

The Model Nonprofit Act provides that the Secretary of State must certify to the Attorney General the names of all corporations that have failed to file their annual reports and must certify, from time to time, the names of all corporations that have given other cause for dissolution.[2] The Attorney General must then file an action in the name of the state against each such corporation for its dissolution.[3]

A member or director may bring an action to have a court of equity liquidate the assets and affairs of a nonprofit corporation (1) when the directors are deadlocked in the management of the corporate affairs and the members are either unable to break the deadlock or there are no voting members, (2) when the acts of the directors are illegal, oppressive, or fraudulent, (3) when the members entitled to vote in the election of directors are deadlocked in voting power and have failed for at least 2 years to elect successors to directors whose terms have expired, (4) if the corporation assets are being misapplied or wasted, or (5) if the corporation is unable to carry out its purposes.[5] A creditor may bring an action to dissolve a nonprofit corporation when the claim of the creditor has been reduced to judgment and execution on the judgment has been returned unsatisfied and it is established that the corporation is insolvent, or when the corporation has admitted in writing that the claim of the creditor is due and owing and it is established that the corporation is insolvent.[6] The corporation itself may bring application that the court continue its dissolution.[7]

A court may issue injunctions and may appoint a receiver or receivers to carry on the affairs of the corporation and to preserve the corporate assets until a full hearing can be had.[8] After a hearing, the court may appoint a liquidating receiver who may sell, convey, and dispose of the assets of the corporation either at public or private sale.[9] Assets of the corporation must be distributed as follows: (1) all costs and expenses of the court proceedings and all liabilities of the corporation are paid first, (2) any assets held upon condition requiring return, transfer, or conveyance must be returned, transferred or conveyed in accordance with those requirements, (3) assets held for a charitable purpose but not upon a condition requiring return, transfer or conveyance must be conveyed to one or more domestic or foreign corporations, societies, or organizations engaged in activites substantially similar to those of the dissolving corporation, as the court directs, (4) other assets must be distributed in accordance with the provisions of the articles or bylaws to the extent that the articles or bylaws determine the distributive right of members or provide for distribution to others, and (5) any remaining assets may be distributed to those persons, societies, organizations or domestic or foreign corporations, whether for profit, or not for profit, as specified in the plan of distribution or, if no plan has been adopted, as the court directs.[10]

Any receiver appointed by the court must be a citizen of the United States or a for profit corporation.[11] The receiver must give bond and has the authority to sue and defend in his own name as receiver of the corporation.[12]

The court may require all creditors to file proofs of claim under oath in a form prescribed by the court.[13]

When all debts of the corporation have been paid, or if assets are not sufficient to satisfy the debts, and all property and assets have been applied so far as they will go to their payment, the court will enter a decree dissolving the corporation, at which time the existence of the corporation will cease.[14] A certified copy of the decree of dissolution should be filed with the Secretary of State.[15]

FOOTNOTES

[1] Model Nonprofit Corporation Act §51 (1964).

The Internal Revenue Service can terminate the existence of a nonprofit corporation that is a private foundation if the foundation has been engaged in willful and repeated acts (or failures to act) that would subject the foundation to excise taxes under §§4941–4945 of the Internal Revenue Code. One willful and flagrant act (or failure to act) that is deemed to be a gross violation of §§4941–4945 permits the IRS to terminate the foundation.

California statutes provide that the Attorney General may bring an action against any corporation in the name of the people of the state, upon the Attorney General's own information or upon complaint of a private party to procure a judgment dissolving the corporation. The grounds for such action include that the corporation: (1) has abused its corporate privileges or powers, (2) has violated any of the statutes regulating corporations, or (3) has failed to pay to the Franchise Tax Board for a period of 5 years any tax imposed upon it by the Bank and Corporation Tax Law. See Cal Corp Code §§6511 and 8511. If the ground for the action is a matter that the corporation can correct, the Attorney General must give the corporation at least 30 days' notice prior to institution of the action. See Cal Corp Code §§6511(b) and 8511(b).

Illinois statutes provide that the Attorney General may institute proceedings to dissolve a nonprofit corporation that has ceased to do business as a

LEGAL PROBLEMS OF NONPROFIT ENTERPRISES   271

corporation or that has discontinued the exercise of corporation functions. See Ill Rev Stat ch 32, par 190.

New York statutes provide that the Attorney General may bring an action for the dissolution of a corporation for the following reasons: that the corporation procured its formation through fraudulent misrepresentation or concealment of a material fact, that the corporation has exceeded the authority conferred upon it by law or has violated any provision of law whereby it has forfeited its charter or conducted business in a persistently fraudulent or illegal manner, or that it has abused its powers contrary to public policy of the state. See NY Not-for-Profit Corp Law §1101. Such an action is triable by jury as a matter of right. NY Not-for-Profit Law Corp §1101(b).

Ohio statutes provide that a corporation may be dissolved by an order of the supreme court or a court of appeals in an action in quo warranto; by an action in the court of common pleas of the county in which the corporation has its principal office brought by the voting members, by order of the common pleas of the county in which the corporation has its principal office in an action brought by a majority of the voting members, or by order of the court of common pleas in an action brought by one-half of the trustees. See Ohio Rev Code Ann §1702.52(A). If the action is brought by voting members, it must be established that (1) the articles of the corporation have been canceled or its period of existence expired, (2) that the corporation is insolvent, or (3) that the objectives of the corporation have failed or have been abandoned.

For further discussion, see Fletcher Cyc Corp §805q.1 (Perm Ed).

[2] Model Nonprofit Corporation Act §52 (1964).

[3] Model Nonprofit Corporation Act §52 (1964).

[4] Model Nonprofit Corporation Act §53 (1964).

[5] Model Nonprofit Corporation Act §54 (1964).

California statutes provide that a complaint for involuntary dissolution of a nonprofit corporation may be filed by (1) one-half or more of the directors in office, (2) a person or persons holding not less than 33$\frac{1}{3}$% of the voting power (exclusive of members who have participated in acts causing grounds for dissolution), (3) any other person expressly authorized to do so in the articles, (4) the Attorney General, or (5) the head organization under whose authority the corporation was created. See Cal Corp Code §§6510 and 8510. The grounds for involuntary dissolution include: abandonment of the corporation's activities for more than one year; deadlocked directors; internal dissension with two or more factions of members being deadlocked; members having failed to elect successors to directors whose terms have expired during any 4-year period, or when all voting power has been exercised at two consecutive meetings; management having been guilty of fraud or abuse of authority; or the period of duration having been terminated. See Cal Corp

Code §§6510 and 8510. If the ground for the complaint for involuntary dissolution is a deadlock, the court may appoint a provisional director. See Cal Corp Code §§6512, 8512.

New York statutes provide that a petition for judicial dissolution of a corporation may be presented by a majority of the directors, by the members, or the members designated for that purpose by resolution adopted by a majority vote of the members, or by 10% of the voting members (or by a lesser percentage if the certificate of incorporation or bylaws so provide). The petition may be brought by 10% of the total number of members or by any director when the directors are deadlocked, the members are deadlocked so that the votes required for the election of directors cannot be obtained, there is internal dissension, or the management has acted in an illegal or fraudulent manner or has wasted the corporate assets. See NY Not-for-Profit Corp. Law §1102.

[6] Model Nonprofit Corporation Act §54(b) (1964).
[7] Model Nonprofit Corporation Act §54(c) (1964).
[8] Model Nonprofit Corporation Act §55 (1964).
[9] Model Nonprofit Corporation Act §55 (1964).
[10] Model Nonprofit Corporation Act §55 (1964).
[11] Model Nonprofit Corporation Act §56 (1964).
[12] Model Nonprofit Corporation Act §56 (1964).
[13] Model Nonprofit Corporation Act §57 (1964).
[14] Model Nonprofit Corporation Act §59 (1964).
[15] Model Nonprofit Corporation Act §60 (1964).

§5:15. Procedures After Dissolution.

The fact of dissolution, whether voluntary or involuntary, does not impair any remedy available to or against the corporation, its directors, officers, or members, for any right or claim existing, or any liability incurred, prior to dissolution if action on the remedy is brought within a certain period of time.[1] The Model Nonprofit Corporation Act specifies 2 years after the date of the dissolution as the time limit for bringing an action.[2] Any such action or proceedings by or against the corporation may be prosecuted or defended in the corporate name.[3] If a corporation is dissolved because its period of duration expired, it may amend its articles of incorporation at any time during the period of 2 years to extend its period of duration.[4]

Any assets of a dissolved corporation that are to be distributed to a person who is unknown or cannot be found, or who is under disability and without guardian, should be sold and the cash deposited with the State Treasurer.[5] The money would be paid to the person or to the person's legal representative upon satisfactory proof of that person's right.[6]

FOOTNOTES

[1] Model Nonprofit Corporation Act §62 (1964).
[2] Model Nonprofit Corporation Act §62 (1964).
[3] Model Nonprofit Corporation Act §62 (1964).
[4] Model Nonprofit Corporation Act §62 (1964).
[5] Model Nonprofit Corporation Act §61 (1964).
[6] Model Nonprofit Corporation Act §61 (1964).

Iowa statutes provide that, upon written and verified proof of ownership or right to such a fund brought within 20 years from the date the fund was deposited, the state treasurer shall certify the owner to the state comptroller who will issue a warrant in favor of that person. If no satisfactory claim on the fund is made within 20 years from the date it was deposited, the state treasurer will publish a notice in a newspaper of general circulation in the county of the last registered office of the corporation stating the name of the person entitled to the fund, the amount of the fund, and the name of the dissolved corporation from whose assets the fund was derived. If no claimant makes satisfactory proof of right to the fund within 2 months from the time of the publication, the claim will escheat to the general fund of the state. See Iowa Code Ann §504A.63(2).

§5:16. Bankruptcy.

A nonprofit corporation may not be subjected to an involuntary action in bankruptcy commenced against it.[1] Involuntary bankruptcy may be commenced against a "person" that is a "moneyed, business, or commercial corporation."[2] Courts have held that Congress did not intend to include charitable, fraternal, educational, literary, or nonprofit corporations as those "persons" subjected to involuntary bankruptcy.[3] Even though a nonprofit organization may perform activities for profit, which standing alone would be characterized as commercial in nature, if those activities are only ancillary to the organization's exempt purpose, they will not bring the organization within the realm of a commercial organization.[4] Some courts look to state classification as a profit or nonprofit corporation in determining whether the corporation is subject to involuntary bankruptcy.[5]

A nonprofit organization may file a petition for voluntary bankruptcy.[6] The limitation on persons subject to involuntary bankruptcy is not a limitation on the benefits of voluntary bankruptcy.[7] Upon the filing of a voluntary petition in bankruptcy, the bankruptcy court may control the debtor's powers, but the debtor may continue to operate his business and to dispose of property as though the case had not commenced.[8] For those assets imposed with a charitable trust, the bankruptcy court can use the cy pres doctrine to apply the property to a similar charitable use.[9]

FOOTNOTES

[1] See 11 USC §303(a).

[2] 11 USC §303(a).

[3] **United States.** United States v. Missco Homestead Association, 185 F2d 280 (CA8, 1950).

[4] **United States.** In re Allen University, 497 F2d 346 (CA 4, 1974). The court noted that the university had no capital stock nor a return of capital to investors.

The court did hold that a cooperative was subject to involuntary bankruptcy in In re Wisconsin Cooperative Milk Pool, 119 F2d 999 (CA7, 1941). According to the court, the cooperative was like a profit corporation; it distributed its profits to its patrons. It was not an eleemosynary or charitable organization, but rather a banding together of producers for their financial advancement. The sole motive, according to the court, was pecuniary gain.

[5] **United States.** See United States v. Missco Homestead Association, 185 F2d 280 (CA 8, 1950).

[6] See 11 USC §109; 1 Norton Bankr L & Prac §8:11. Those persons excluded from filing voluntary bankruptcy are railroads, insurance companies, savings and loan associations, and municipalities. Nonprofit organizations are not excluded from the persons authorized to file voluntary bankruptcy.
United States. Highway & City Freight Drivers, Dockmen and Helpers, Local Union No. 600 v Gordon Transports Inc, 576 F2d 1285 (CA 8, 1978). The court held that a labor union, organized as an association, would qualify as a person authorized to file a petition for voluntary bankruptcy.

[7] **United States.** Highway & City Freight Drivers, Dockmen and Helpers, Local Union No. 600 v. Gordon Transports Inc, 576 F2d 1285 (CA 8, 1978).

[8] See 11 USC §303(f). This is a change from prior law where the bankruptcy court obtained possession of the bankrupt's assets and appointed a trustee in bankruptcy to operate the business and to take title to all the debtor's property.

[9] See discussion of cy pres doctrine at §5:11.

§5:17. Checklist of Points To Remember.

__ 1. Most state statutes provide for the merger or consolidation of nonprofit corporations, whether a merger or consolidation of domestic corporations or of domestic and foreign corporations.[1] In either a merger or a consolidation, the surviving or the new corporation succeeds to the assets, privileges, immunities, and powers of the merged or consolidated corporations.[2] The surviving or new corporation also becomes responsible and liable for all liabilities and obligations of the merged or consolidated corporations.

__ 2. Statutory requirements of notice and proper approval by members and/or directors must be followed to sell, lease, exchange, or mortgage all or substantially all the property of a nonprofit corporation.[3]

__ 3. A nonprofit corporation may be dissolved either voluntarily or involuntarily.[4] Statutory provisions regarding distribution of assets of the nonprofit corporation must be followed. Restrictions or conditions on the transfer of assets must be followed; assets held for charitable purposes must be transferred to other similar organizations.[5] The cy pres doctrine may be applicable to dissolution proceedings to determine the distribution of assets.[6]

__ 4. The state may bring an action in the name of the state to dissolve a nonprofit corporation that has failed to follow state statutes or that is insolvent.[7]

__ 5. The fact of dissolution, whether voluntary or involuntary, does not impair any remedy available to or against the corporation, its directors, or members, for any right or claim existing prior to dissolution if action is brought within a certain period of time.[8]

__ 6. While a nonprofit organization may file a petition for voluntary bankruptcy, it may not be subjected to an involuntary action in bankruptcy.[9] For those assets of the nonprofit corporation imposed with a charitable trust, the bankruptcy court can use the cy pres doctrine to apply the property to a similar charitable use.[10]

FOOTNOTES

[1] See §5:01.
[2] See §5:02.
[3] See §5:08.
[4] See §§5:09, 5:04.

[5] See §5:10.
[6] See §5:11.
[7] See §5:14.
[8] See §5:15.
[9] See §5:16.
[10] See §5:16.

APPENDIX

MODEL NONPROFIT CORPORATION ACT

§ 1. Short Title
§ 2. Definitions
§ 3. Applicability
§ 4. Purposes
§ 5. General Powers
§ 6. Defense of Ultra Vires
§ 7. Corporate Name
§ 8. Registered Office and Registered Agent
§ 9. Change of Registered Office or Registered Agent
§ 10. Service of Process on Corporation
§ 11. Members
§ 12. By-Laws
§ 13. Meetings of Members
§ 14. Notice of Members' Meetings
§ 15. Voting
§ 16. Quorum
§ 17. Board of Directors
§ 18. Number and Election of Directors
§ 19. Vacancies
§ 20. Quorum of Directors
§ 21. Committees
§ 22. Place and Notice of Directors' Meetings
§ 23. Officers
§ 24. Removal of Officers
§ 25. Books and Records
§ 26. Shares of Stock and Dividends Prohibited
§ 27. Loans to Directors and Officers Prohibited
§ 28. Incorporators
§ 29. Articles of Incorporation
§ 30. Filing of Articles of Incorporation

§ 31. Effect of Issuance of Certificate of Incorporation
§ 32. Organization Meetings
§ 33. Right to Amend Articles of Incorporation
§ 34. Procedure to Amend Articles of Incorporation
§ 35. Articles of Amendment
§ 36. Effectiveness of Amendment
§ 37. Restated Articles of Incorporation
§ 38. Procedure for Merger
§ 39. Procedure for Consolidation
§ 40. Approval of Merger or Consolidation
§ 41. Articles of Merger or Consolidation
§ 42. Effect of Merger or Consolidation
§ 43. Merger or Consolidation of Domestic and Foreign Corporations
§ 44. Sale, Lease, Exchange, or Mortgage of Assets
§ 45. Voluntary Dissolution
§ 46. Distribution of Assets
§ 47. Plan of Distribution
§ 48. Revocation of Voluntary Dissolution Proceedings
§ 49. Articles of Dissolution
§ 50. Filing of Articles of Dissolution
§ 51. Involuntary Dissolution
§ 52. Notification to Attorney General
§ 53. Venue and Process
§ 54. Jurisdiction of Court to Liquidate Assets and Affairs of Corporation
§ 55. Procedure in Liquidation of Corporation by Court
§ 56. Qualification of Receivers
§ 57. Filing of Claims in Liquidation Proceedings
§ 58. Discontinuance of Liquidation Proceedings
§ 59. Decree of Involuntary Dissolution
§ 60. Filing of Decree of Dissolution
§ 61. Deposits with State Treasurer
§ 62. Survival of Remedy after Dissolution
§ 63. Admission of Foreign Corporation
§ 64. Powers of Foreign Corporation
§ 65. Corporate Name of Foreign Corporation
§ 66. Change of Name by Foreign Corporation
§ 67. Application for Certificate of Authority
§ 68. Filing of Application for Certificate of Authority
§ 69. Effect of Certificate of Authority

§ 70. Registered Office and Registered Agent of Foreign Corporation
§ 71. Change of Registered Office or Registered Agent of Foreign Corporation
§ 72. Service of Process on Foreign Corporation
§ 73. Amendment to Articles of Incorporation of Foreign Corporation
§ 74. Merger of Foreign Corporation Authorized to Conduct Affairs in this State
§ 75. Amended Certificate of Authority
§ 76. Withdrawal of Foreign Corporation
§ 77. Filing of Application for Withdrawal
§ 78. Revocation of Certificate of Authority
§ 79. Issuance of Certificate of Revocation
§ 80. Conducting Affairs Without Certificate of Authority
§ 81. Annual Report of Domestic and Foreign Corporations
§ 82. Filing of Annual Report of Domestic and Foreign Corporations
§ 83. Fees for Filing Documents and Issuing Certificates
§ 84. Miscellaneous Charges
§ 85. Penalties Imposed upon Corporation
§ 86. Penalties Imposed upon Directors and Officers
§ 87. Interrogatories by Secretary of State
§ 88. Information Disclosed by Interrogatories
§ 89. Powers of Secretary of State
§ 90. Appeal from Secretary of State
§ 91. Certificates and Certified Copies to Be Received in Evidence
§ 92. Forms to Be Furnished by Secretary of State
§ 93. Greater Voting Requirements
§ 94. Waiver of Notice
§ 95. Action by Members or Directors Without a Meeting
§ 96. Unauthorized Assumption of Corporate Powers
§ 97. Reservation of Power
§ 98. Effect of Repeal of Prior Acts
§ 99. Effect of Invalidity of Part of this Act
§ 100. Repeal of Prior Acts

Appendix of Optional and Alternative Sections

*_____NONPROFIT CORPORATION ACT

Section 1. Short Title

This Act shall be known and may be cited as the "____* Nonprofit Corporation Act."

Section 2. Definitions

As used in this Act, unless the context otherwise requires, the term:

(a) "Corporation" or "domestic corporation" means a non-profit corporation subject to the provisions of this Act, except a foreign corporation.

(b) "Foreign corporation" means a non-profit corporation organized under laws other than the laws of this State.

(c) "Nonprofit corporation" means a corporation no part of the income or profit of which is distributable to its members, directors or officers.

(d) "Articles of incorporation" means the original or restated articles of incorporation or articles of consolidation and all amendments thereto, including articles of merger.**

(e) "By-laws" means the code or codes of rules adopted for the regulation or management of the affairs of the corporation irrespective of the name or names by which such rules are designated.

---

*Supply name of State.
**See optional Section 2 (p. 349) for addition of special charters or amendments.

(f) "Member" means one having membership rights in a corporation in accordance with the provisions of its articles of incorporation or by-laws.

(g) "Board of directors" means the group of persons vested with the management of the affairs of the corporation irrespective of the name by which such group is designated.

(h) "Insolvent" means inability of a corporation to pay its debts as they become due in the usual course of its affairs.

Section 3. Applicability

The provisions of this Act relating to domestic corporations shall apply to:

(a) All corporations organized hereunder; and
(b) All nonprofit corporations heretofore organized under any act hereby repealed, for a purpose or purposes for which a corporation might be organized under this Act.*

The provisions of this Act relating to foreign corporations shall apply to all foreign non-profit corporations conducting affairs in this State for a purpose or purposes for which a corporation might be organized under this Act.

Section 4. Purposes**

Corporations may be organized under this Act for any lawful purpose or purposes, including, without being limited to, any one or more of the following purposes: charitable; benevolent;

---

*See optional Sections 37A-D and 83 (pp. 350-354) for acceptance of Act by other corporations.
**See alternative Section 4 (p. 355).

eleemosynary; educational; civic; patriotic; political; religious; social; fraternal; literary; cultural; athletic; scientific; agricultural; horticultural; animal husbandry; and professional, commercial, industrial or trade association; but labor unions, cooperative organizations, and organizations subject to any of the provisions of the insurance laws of this State may not be organized under this Act.

Section 5. General Powers

Each corporation shall have power:

(a) To have perpetual succession by its corporate name unless a limited period of duration is stated in its articles of incorporation.

(b) To sue and be sued, complain and defend, in its corporate name.

(c) To have a corporate seal which may be altered at pleasure, and to use the same by causing it, or a facsimile thereof, to be impressed or affixed or in any other manner reproduced.

(d) To purchase, take, receive, lease, take by gift, devise or bequest, or otherwise acquire, own, hold, improve, use and otherwise deal in and with real or personal property, or any interest therein, wherever situated.

(e) To sell, convey, mortgage, pledge, lease, exchange, transfer and otherwise dispose of all or any part of its property and assets.

(f) To lend money to its employees other than its officers and directors and otherwise assist its employees, officers and directors.

(g) To purchase, take, receive, subscribe for, or otherwise acquire, own, hold, vote, use, employ, sell, mortgage, lend, pledge, or otherwise dispose of, and otherwise use and deal in and with, shares or other interests in, or obligations of, other domestic or for eign corporations, whether for profit or not for profit, associations, partnerships or individuals, or direct or indirect obligations of the United States, or of any other government, state, territory, governmental district or municipality or of any instrumentality thereof.

(h) To make contracts and incur liabilities, borrow money at such rates of interest as the corporation may determine, issue its notes, bonds, and other obligations, and secure any of its obligations by mortgage or pledge of all or any of its property, franchises and income.

(i) To lend money for its corporate purposes, invest and reinvest its funds, and take and hold real and personal property as security for the payment of funds so loaned or invested.

(j) To conduct its affairs, carry on its operations, and have offices and exercise the powers granted by this Act in any state, territory, district, or possession of the United States, or in any foreign country.

(k) To elect or appoint officers and agents of the corporation, who may be directors or members, and define their duties and fix their compensation.

(l) To make and alter by-laws, not inconsistent with its articles of incorporation or with the laws of this State, for the administration and regulation of the affairs of the corporation.

(m) Unless otherwise provided in the articles of incorporation, to make donations for the public welfare or for charitable, scientific or educational purposes; and in time of war to make donations in aid of war activities.

(n)* To indemnify any director or officer or former director or officer of the corporation, or any person who may have served at its request as a director or officer

---

*See alternative Section 24A (pp. 357–358).

of another corporation in which it owns shares of capital stock or of which it is a creditor, against expenses actually and reasonably incurred by him in connection with the defense of any action, suit or proceeding, civil or criminal, in which he is made a party by reason of being or having been such director or officer, except in relation to matters as to which he shall be adjudged in such action, suit or proceeding to be liable for negligence or misconduct in the performance of duty to the corporation; and to make any other indemnification that shall be authorized by the articles of incorporation or by-laws, or resolution adopted after notice by the members entitled to vote.

(o) To pay pensions and establish pension plans or pension trusts for any or all of its directors, officers and employees.

(p) To cease its corporate activities and surrender its corporate franchise.

(q) To have and exercise all powers necessary or convenient to effect any or all of the purposes for which the corporation is organized.

Section 6. Defense of Ultra Vires

No act of a corporation and no conveyance or transfer of real or personal property to or by a corporation shall be invalid by reason of the fact that the corporation was without capacity or power to do such act or to make or receive such conveyance or transfer, but such lack of capacity or power may be asserted:

(a) In a proceeding by a member or a director against the corporation to enjoin the doing or continuation of unauthorized acts, or the transfer of real or personal property by or to the corporation. If the unauthorized acts or transfer sought to be enjoined are being, or are to be, performed pursuant to any contract to which the corporation is a party, the court may, if all of the parties to the contract are parties to the proceeding and if it deems the same to be equitable, set aside and enjoin the performance of such contract, and in so doing may allow to the corporation or the other parties to the contract, as the case may be, compensation for the loss or damage sustained by either of them which may result from the action of the court in setting aside and enjoining the performance of such contract, but anticipated profits to be derived from the performance of the contract shall not be awarded by the court as a loss or damage sustained.

(b) In a proceeding by the corporation, whether acting directly or through a receiver, trustee, or other legal representative, or through members in a representative suit, against the officers or directors of the corporation for exceeding their authority.

(c) In a proceeding by the Attorney General, as provided in this Act, to dissolve the corporation, or in a proceeding by the Attorney General to enjoin the corporation from performing unauthorized acts, or in any other proceeding by the Attorney General.

Section 7. Corporate Name*

The corporate name:

(a) Shall not contain any word or phrase which indicates or implies that it is organized for any purpose other than one or more of the purposes contained in its articles of incorporation.

(b) Shall not be the same as, or deceptively similar to, the name of any corporation, whether for profit or not for

---
* See optional Sections 7A and 83 (p. 358).

profit, existing under the laws of this State, or any foreign corporation, whether for profit or not for profit, authorized to transact business or conduct affairs in this State, or a corporate name reserved or registered as permitted by the laws of this State.

(c) Shall be transliterated into letters of the English alphabet, if it is not in English.

Section 8. Registered Office and Registered Agent

Each corporation shall have and continuously maintain in this State:

(a) A registered office which may be, but need not be, the same as its principal office.

(b) A registered agent, which agent may be either an individual resident in this State whose business office is identical with such registered office, or a domestic corporation, whether for profit or not for profit, or a foreign corporation, whether for profit or not for profit, authorized to transact business or conduct affairs in this State, having an office identical with such registered office.

Section 9. Change of Registered Office or Registered Agent

A corporation may change its registered office or change its registered agent, or both, upon filing in the office of the Secretary of State a statement setting forth:

(a) The name of the corporation.
(b) The address of its then registered office.
(c) If the address of its registered office is to be changed, the address to which the registered office is to be changed.

MODEL NONPROFIT CORPORATION ACT 289

(d) The name of its then registered agent.
(e) If its registered agent be changed, the name of its successor registered agent.
(f) That the address of its registered office and the address of the office of its registered agent, as changed, will be identical.
(g) That such change was authorized by resolution duly adopted by its board of directors.

Such statement shall be executed by the corporation by its president or a vice president and delivered to the Secretary of State. If the Secretary of State finds that such statement conforms to the provisions of this Act, he shall file such statement in his office, and upon such filing, the change of address of the registered office, or the appointment of a new registered agent, or both, as the case may be, shall become effective.

Any registered agent of a corporation may resign as such agent upon filing a written notice thereof, executed in duplicate, with the Secretary of State, who shall forthwith mail a copy thereof to the corporation in care of an officer, who is not the resigning registered agent, at the address of such office as shown by the most recent annual report of the corporation. The appointment of such agent shall terminate upon the expiration of thirty days after receipt of such notice by the Secretary of State.

If a registered agent changes his or its business address to another place within the same _____*, he or it may change such address and the address of the registered office of any corporations of which he or it is registered agent by filing a statement as required above except that it need be signed only by the registered agent and need not be responsive to (e) or (g) and must recite that a copy of the statement has been mailed to each such corporation.

---

* Supply designation of jurisdiction, such as county, in accordance with local practice.

Section 10. Service of Process on Corporation

The registered agent so appointed by a corporation shall be an agent of such corporation upon whom any process, notice or demand required or permitted by law to be served upon the corporation may be served.

Whenever a corporation shall fail to appoint or maintain a registered agent in this State, or whenever its registered agent cannot with reasonable diligence be found at the registered office, then the Secretary of State shall be an agent of such corporation upon whom any such process, notice, or demand may be served. Service on the Secretary of State of any such process, notice, or demand shall be made by delivering to and leaving with him, or with any clerk having charge of the corporation department of his office, duplicate copies of such process, notice or demand. In the event any such process, notice or demand is served on the Secretary of State, he shall immediately cause one of the copies thereof to be forwarded by registered mail, addressed to the corporation at its registered office. Any service so had on the Secretary of State shall be returnable in not less than thirty days.

The Secretary of State shall keep a record of all processes, notices and demands served upon him under this section, and shall record therein the time of such service and his action with reference thereto.

Nothing herein contained shall limit or affect the right to serve any process, notice or demand required or permitted by law to be served upon a corporation in any other manner now or hereafter permitted by law.

Section 11. Members

A corporation may have one or more classes of members or may have no members. If the corporation has one or more classes of members, the designation of such class or classes, the manner of election or appointment and the qualifications and rights of the members of each class shall be set forth in the articles of incorporation or the by-laws. If the corporation has no members, that fact shall be set forth in the articles of incorporation or the by-laws. A corporation may issue certificates evidencing membership therein.

The directors, officers, employees and members of the corporation shall not, as such, be liable on its obligations.

Section 12. By-Laws*

The initial by-laws of a corporation shall be adopted by its board of directors. The power to alter, amend or repeal the by-laws or adopt new by-laws shall be vested in the board of directors unless otherwise provided in the articles of incorporation or the by-laws. The by-laws may contain any provisions for the regulation and management of the affairs of a corporation not inconsistent with law or the articles of incorporation.

Section 13. Meetings of Members

Meetings of members may be held at such place, either within or without this State, as may be provided in the by-laws. In the absence of any such provision, all meetings shall be held at the registered office of the corporation in this State.

An annual meeting of the members shall be held at such time as may be provided in the by-laws. Failure to hold the annual meeting at the designated time shall not work a forfeiture or dissolution of the corporation.

Special meetings of the members may be called by the

---

*See optional Section 12A (pp. 355–357) for emergency by-laws.

president or by the board of directors. Special meetings of the members may also be called by such other officers or persons or number or proportion of members as may be provided in the articles of incorporation or the by-laws. In the absence of a provision fixing the number or proportion of members entitled to call a meeting, a special meeting of members may be called by members having one-twentieth of the votes entitled to be cast at such meeting.

Section 14. Notice of Members' Meetings

Unless otherwise provided in the articles of incorporation or the by-laws, written notice stating the place, day and hour of the meeting and, in case of a special meeting, the purpose or purposes for which the meeting is called, shall be delivered not less than ten nor more than fifty days before the date of the meeting, either personally or by mail, by or at the direction of the president, or the secretary, or the officers or persons calling the meeting, to each member entitled to vote at such meeting. If mailed, such notice shall be deemed to be delivered when deposited in the United States mail addressed to the member at his address as it appears on the records of the corporation, with postage thereon prepaid.

Section 15. Voting

The right of the members, or any class or classes of members, to vote may be limited, enlarged or denied to the extent specified in the articles of incorporation or the by-laws. Unless so limited, enlarged or denied, each member, regardless of class, shall be entitled to one vote on each matter submitted to a vote of members.

A member entitled to vote may vote in person or, unless the articles of incorporation or the by-laws otherwise provide, may vote by proxy executed in writing by the member or by his duly authorized attorney-in-fact. No proxy shall be valid after eleven months from the date of its execution, unless otherwise provided in the proxy. Where directors or officers are to be elected by members, the by-laws may provide that such elections may be conducted by mail.

The articles of incorporation or the by-laws may provide that in all elections for directors every member entitled to vote shall have the right to cumulate his vote and to give one candidate a number of voters equal to his vote multiplied by the number of directors to be elected, or by distributing such votes on the same principle among any number of such candidates.

If a corporation has no members or its members have no right to vote, the directors shall have the sole voting power.

Section 16. Quorum

The by-laws may provide the number or percentage of members entitled to vote represented in person or by proxy, or the number or percentage of votes represented in person or by proxy, which shall constitute a quorum at a meeting of members. In the absence of any such provision, members holding one-tenth of the votes entitled to be cast on the matter to be voted upon represented in person or by proxy shall constitute a quorum. A majority of the votes entitled to be cast on a matter to be voted upon by the members present or represented by proxy at a meeting at which a quorum is present shall be necessary for the adoption thereof unless a greater proportion is required by this Act, the articles of incorporation or the by-laws.

Section 17. Board of Directors

The affairs of a corporation shall be managed by a board of directors. Directors need not be residents of this State or members of the corporation unless the articles of incorporation or the by-laws so require. The articles of incorporation or the by-laws may prescribe other qualifications for directors.

Section 18. Number and Election of Directors

The number of directors of a corporation shall be not less than three. Subject to such limitation, the number of directors shall be fixed by the by-laws, except as to the number of the first board of directors which number shall be fixed by the articles of incorporation. The number of directors may be increased or decreased from time to time by amendment to the by-laws, unless the articles of incorporation provide that a change in the number of directors shall be made only by amendment of the articles of incorporation. No decrease in number shall have the effect of shortening the term of any incumbent director. In the absence of a by-law fixing the number of directors, the number shall be the same as that stated in the articles of incorporation.

The directors constituting the first board of directors shall be named in the articles of incorporation and shall hold office until the first annual election of directors or for such other period as may be specified in the articles of incorporation or the by-laws. Thereafter, directors shall be elected or appointed in the manner and for the terms provided in the articles of incorporation or the by-laws. In the absence of a provision fixing the term of office, the term of office of a director shall be one year.

Directors may be divided into classes and the terms of office of the several classes need not be uniform. Each director shall hold office for the term which he is elected or appointed and until his successor shall have been elected or appointed and qualified.

A director may be removed from office pursuant to any procedure therefor provided in the articles of incorporation.

Section 19. Vacancies

Any vacancy occuring in the board of directors and any directorship to be filled by reason of an increase in the number of directors may be filled by the affirmative vote of a majority of the remaining directors, though less than a quorum of the board of directors, unless the articles of incorporation or the by-laws provide that a vacancy or directorship so created shall be filled in some other manner, in which case such provision shall control.

A director elected or appointed, as the case may be, to fill a vacancy shall be elected or appointed for the unexpired term of his predecessor in office.

Any directorship to be filled by reason of an increase in the number of directors may be filled by the board of directors for a term of office continuing only until the next election of directors.

Section 20. Quorum of Directors

A majority of the number of directors fixed by the by-laws, or in the absence of a by-law fixing the number of directors, then of the number stated in the articles of incorporation, shall constitute a quorum for the transaction of business, unless otherwise provided in the articles of incorporation or the by-laws; but in no event shall a quorum consist of less than one-third of the number of directors so fixed or stated. The act of the majority of the directors present at a meeting at which a quorum is present shall be the act of the board of directors, unless the act of a greater number is required by this Act, the articles of incorporation or the by-laws.

Section 21. Committees

If the articles of incorporation or the by-laws so provide, the board of directors, by resolution adopted by a majority of the directors in office, may designate and appoint one or more committees each of which shall consist of two or more directors, which committees, to the extent provided in such resolution, in the articles of incorporation or in the by-laws of the corporation, shall have and exercise all the authority of the board of directors, except that no such committee shall have the authority of the board of directors in reference to amending, altering or repealing the by-laws; electing, appointing or removing any member of any such committee or any director or officer of the corporation; amending the articles of incorporation, restating articles of incorporation adopting a plan of merger or adopting a plan of consolidation with another corporation; authorizing the sale, lease, exchange or mortgage of all or substantially all of the property and assets of the corporation; authorizing the voluntary dissolution of the corporation or revoking proceedings therefor; adopting a plan for the distribution of the assets of the corporation; or amending, altering or repealing any resolution of the board of directors which by its terms provides that it shall not be amended, altered or repealed by such committee. The designation and appointment of any such committee and the delegation thereto of authority shall not operate to relieve the board of directors, or any individual director of any responsibility imposed upon it or him by law.

Section 22. Place and Notice of Directors' Meetings

Meetings of the board of directors, regular or special, may be held either within or without this State, and upon such notice as the by-laws may prescribe. Attendance of a director at any meeting shall constitute a waiver of notice of such meeting except when a director attends a meeting for the express purpose of objecting to the transaction of any business because the meeting is not lawfully called or convened. Neither the business to be transacted at, nor the purpose of, any regular or special meeting of the board of directors need be specified in the notice or waiver of notice of such meeting.

Section 23. Officers

The officers of a corporation shall consist of a president, one or more vice presidents, a secretary, a treasurer and such other officers and assistant officers as may be deemed necessary, each of whom shall be elected or appointed at such time and in such manner and for such terms not exceeding three years as may be prescribed in the articles of incorporation or the by-laws. In the absence of any such provision, all officers shall be elected or appointed annually by the board of directors. If the by-laws so provide, any two or more offices may be held by the same person, except the offices of president and secretary.

The articles of incorporation or the by-laws may provide that any one or more officers of the corporation shall be ex officio members of the board of directors.

The officers of a corporation may be designated by such additional titles as may be provided in the articles of incorporation or the by-laws.

Section 24. Removal of Officers

Any officer elected or appointed may be removed by the persons authorized to elect or appoint such officer whenever in their judgment the best interests of the corporation will be served thereby. The removal of an officer shall be without prejudice to the contract rights, if any, of the officer so removed. Election or appointment of an officer or agent shall not of itself create contract rights.

Section 25. Books and Records

Each corporation shall keep correct and complete books and records of account and shall keep minutes of the proceedings of its members, board of directors and committees having any of the authority of the board of directors; and shall keep at its registered office or principal office in this State a record of the names and addresses of its members entitled to vote. All books and records of a corporation may be inspected by any member, or his agent or attorney, for any proper purpose at any reasonable time.

Section 26. Shares of Stock and Dividends Prohibited

A corporation shall not have or issue shares of stock. No dividend shall be paid and no part of the income or profit of a corporation shall be distributed to its members, directors or officers. A corporation may pay compensation in a reasonable amount to its members, directors, or officers for services rendered, may confer benefits upon its members in conformity with its purposes, and upon dissolution or final liquidation may make distributions to its members as permitted by this Act, and no such payment, benefit or distribution shall be deemed to be a dividend or a distribution of income or profit.

Section 27. Loans to Directors and Officers Prohibited

No loans shall be made by a corporation to its directors or officers. Any director or officer who assents to or participates in the making of any such loan shall be liable to the corporation for the amount of such loan until the repayment thereof.

Section 28. Incorporators

One or more persons may incorporate a corporation by signing and delivering articles of incorporation in duplicate to the Secretary of State.

Section 29. Articles of Incorporation

The articles of incorporation shall set forth;

(a) The name of the corporation.
(b) The period of duration, which may be perpetual.
(c) The purpose or purposes for which the corporation is organized.
(d) Any provisions, not inconsistent with law, which the incorporators elect to set forth in the articles of incorporation for the regulation of the internal affairs of the corporation, including any provision for distribution of assets on dissolution or final liquidation.
(e) The address of its initial registered office, and the name of its initial registered agent at such address.
(f) The number of directors constituting the initial board of directors, and the names and addresses of the persons who are to serve as the initial directors.
(g) The name and address of each incorporator.

It shall not be necessary to set forth in the articles of incorporation any of the corporate powers enumerated in this Act.

Unless the articles of incorporation provide that a change in the number of directors shall be made only by amendment to the articles of incorporation, a change in the number of directors made by amendment to the by-laws shall be controlling. In all other cases, whenever a provision of the articles of incorporation is inconsistent with a by-law, the provision of the articles of incorporation shall be controlling.

Section 30. Filing of Articles of Incorporation

Duplicate originals of the articles of incorporation shall be delivered to the Secretary of State. If the Secretary of State finds that the articles of incorporation conform to law, he shall, when all fees have been paid as in this Act prescribed:

(1) Endorse on each of such duplicate originals the word "Filed," and the month, day and year of the filing thereof.
(2) File one of such duplicate originals in his office.
(3) Issue a certificate of incorporation to which he shall affix the other duplicate original.

The certificate of incorporation, together with the duplicate original of the articles of incorporation affixed thereto by the Secretary of State, shall be returned to the incorporators or their representative.

Section 31. Effect of Issuance of Certificate of Incorporation

Upon the issuance of the certificate of incorporation, the corporate existence shall begin, and such certificate of incorporation shall be conclusive evidence that all conditions precedent required to be performed by the incorporators have been complied with and that the corporation has been incorporated under this Act, except as against the State in a proceeding to cancel or revoke the certificate of incorporation or for involuntary dissolution of the corporation.

Section 32. Organization Meetings

After the issuance of the certificate of incorporation an organization meeting of the board of directors named in the articles of incorporation shall be held, either within or without this State, at the call of a majority of the incorporators, for the purpose of adopting by-laws, electing officers and the transaction of such other business as may come before the meeting. The incorporators calling the meeting shall give at least three days' notice thereof by mail to each director so named, which notice shall state the time and place of the meeting.

A first meeting of the members may be held at the call of the directors, or a majority of them, upon at least three days' notice, for such purposes as shall be stated in the notice of the meeting.

Section 33. Right to Amend Articles of Incorporation

A corporation may amend its articles of incorporation, from time to time, in any and as many respects as may be desired, so long as its articles of incorporation as amended contain only such provisions as are lawful under this Act.

Section 34. Procedure to Amend Articles of Incorporation

Amendments to the articles of incorporation shall be made in the following manner:

(a) If there are members entitled to vote thereon, the board of directors shall adopt a resolution setting forth the proposed amendment and directing that it be submitted to a vote at a meeting of members entitled to vote thereon, which may be either an annual or a special meeting. Written notice setting forth the proposed amendment or a summary of the changes to be effected thereby shall be given to each member entitled to vote at such meeting within the time and in the manner provided in this Act for the giving of notice of meetings of members. The proposed amendment shall be adopted upon receiving at least two-thirds of the votes which members present at such meeting or represented by proxy are entitled to cast.

(b) If there are no members, or no members entitled to vote thereon, an amendment shall be adopted at a meeting of the board of directors upon receiving the vote of a majority of the directors in office.

Any number of amendments may be submitted and voted upon at any one meeting.

Section 35. Articles of Amendment

The articles of amendment shall be executed in duplicate by the corporation by its president or a vice president and by its secretary or an assistant secretary and shall set forth:

- (a) The name of the corporation.
- (b) The amendment so adopted.
- (c) If there are members entitled to vote thereon, (1) a statement setting forth the date of the meeting of members at which the amendment was adopted, that a quorum was present at such meeting, and that such amendment received at least two-thirds of the votes which members present at such meeting or represented by proxy were entitled to cast, or (2) a statement that such amendment was adopted by a consent in writing signed by all members entitled to vote with respect thereto.
- (d) If there are no members, or no members entitled to vote thereon, a statement of such fact, the date of the meeting of the board of directors at which the amendment was adopted, and a statement of the fact that such amendment received the vote of a majority of the directors in office.

Section 36. Effectiveness of Amendment

Duplicate originals of the articles of amendment shall be delivered to the Secretary of State. If the Secretary of State finds that the articles of amendment conform to law, he shall, when all fees have been paid as in this Act prescribed:

(1) Endorse on each of such duplicate originals the word "Filed," and the month, day and year of the filing thereof.
(2) File one of such duplicate originals in his office.
(3) Issue a certificate of amendment to which he shall affix the other duplicate original.

The certificate of amendment, together with the duplicate original of the articles of amendment affixed thereto by the Secretary of State, shall be returned to the corporation or its representative.

Upon the issuance of the certificate of amendment by the Secretary of State, the amendment shall become effective and the articles of incorporation shall be deemed to be amended accordingly.

No amendment shall affect any existing cause of action in favor of or against such corporation, or any pending action to which such corporation shall be a party, or the existing rights of persons other than members; and, in the event the corporate name shall be changed by amendment, no action brought by or against such corporation under its former name shall abate for that reason.

Section 37. Restated Articles of Incorporation

A domestic corporation may at any time restate its articles of incorporation as theretofore amended, in the following manner:

(a) If there are members entitled to vote thereon, the board of directors shall adopt a resolution setting forth the proposed restated articles of incorporation and directing that they be submitted to a vote at a meeting of members entitled to vote thereon, which may be either an annual or a special meeting.
(b) Written notice setting forth the proposed restated

articles or a summary of the provisions thereof shall be given to each member entitled to vote thereon, within the time and in the manner provided in this Act for the giving of notice of meetings of members. If the meeting be an annual meeting, the proposed restated articles or a summary of the provisions thereof may be included in the notice of such annual meeting.
(c) At such meeting a vote of the members entitled to vote thereon shall be taken on the proposed restated articles, which shall be adopted upon receiving the affirmative vote of a majority of the members entitled to vote thereon present at such meeting or represented by proxy.
(d) If there are no members, or no members entitled to vote thereon, the proposed restated articles shall be adopted at a meeting of the board of directors upon receiving the affirmative vote of a majority of the directors in office.

Upon such approval, restated articles of incorporation shall be executed in duplicate by the corporation by its president or vice president and by its secretary or assistant secretary and shall set forth:

(1) The name of the corporation.
(2) The period of its duration.
(3) The purpose or purposes which the corporation is authorized to pursue.
(4) Any other provisions, not inconsistent with law, which are then set forth in the articles of incorporation as theretofore amended, except that it shall not be necessary to set forth in the restated articles of incorporation the registered office of the corporation, its registered agent, its directors or its incorporators.

The restated articles of incorporation shall state that they correctly set forth the provisions of the articles of incorporation as theretofore amended, that they have been duly adopted as required by law and that they supersede the original articles of incorporation and all amendments thereto.

Duplicate originals of the restated articles of incorporation shall be delivered to the Secretary of State. If the Secretary of State finds that such restated articles conform to law, he shall, when all fees have been paid as in this Act prescribed:

(1) Endorse on each of such duplicate originals the word "Filed" and the month, day and year of the filing thereof.
(2) File one of such duplicate originals in his office.
(3) Issue a restated certificate of incorporation to which he shall affix the other duplicate original.

The restated certificate of incorporation, together with the duplicate original of the restated articles of incorporation affixed thereto by the Secretary of State, shall be returned to the corporation or its representative.

Upon the issuance of the restated certificate of incorporation by the Secretary of State, the restated articles of incorporation shall become effective and shall supersede the original articles of incorporation and all amendments thereto.

Section 38. Procedure for Merger

Any two or more domestic corporations may merge into one of such corporations pursuant to a plan of merger approved in the manner provided in this Act.

Each corporation shall adopt a plan of merger setting forth:

(a) The names of the corporations proposing to merge, and the name of the corporation into which they propose to merge, which is hereinafter designated as the surviving corporation.
(b) The terms and conditions of the proposed merger.

(c) A statement of any changes in the articles of incorporation of the surviving corporation to be effected by such merger.
(d) Such other provisions with respect to the proposed merger as are deemed necessary or desirable.

Section 39. Procedure for Consolidation

Any two or more domestic corporations may consolidate into a new corporation pursuant to a plan of consolidation approved in the manner provided in this Act.

Each corporation shall adopt a plan of consolidation setting forth:

(a) The names of the corporations proposing to consolidate, and the name of the new corporation into which they propose to consolidate, which is hereinafter designated as the new corporation.
(b) The terms and conditions of the proposed consolidation.
(c) With respect to the new corporation, all of the statements required to be set forth in articles of incorporation for corporations organized under this Act.
(d) Such other provisions with respect to the proposed consolidation as are deemed necessary or desirable.

Section 40. Approval of Merger or Consolidation

A plan of merger or consolidation shall be adopted in the following manner:

(a) If the members of any merging or consolidating corporation are entitled to vote thereon, the board of directors of such corporation shall adopt a resolution approving the proposed plan and directing that it be submitted to a vote at a meeting of members entitled to vote thereon, which may be either an annual or a special meeting. Written notice setting forth the proposed plan or a summary thereof shall be given to each member entitled to vote at such meeting within the time and in the manner provided in this Act for the giving of notice of meetings of members. The proposed plan shall be adopted upon receiving at least two-thirds of the votes which members present at each such meeting or represented by proxy are entitled to cast.

(b) If any merging or consolidating corporation has no members, or no members entitled to vote thereon, a plan of merger or consolidation shall be adopted at a meeting of the board of directors of such corporation upon receiving the vote of a majority of the directors in office.

After such approval, and at any time prior to the filing of the articles of merger or consolidation, the merger or consolidation may be abandoned pursuant to provisions therefor, if any, set forth in the plan of merger or consolidation.

Section 41. Articles of Merger or Consolidation

Upon such approval, articles of merger or articles of consolidation shall be executed in duplicate by each corporation by its president or a vice president and by its secretary or an assistant secretary, and shall set forth:

(a) The plan of merger or the plan of consolidation.
(b) If the members of any merging or consolidating corporation are entitled to vote thereon, then as to each such corporation (1) a statement setting forth the date of the meeting of members at which the plan was adopted, that a quorum was present at such meeting, and that such plan received at least two-thirds of the

votes which members present at such meeting or represented by proxy were entitled to cast, or (2) a statement that such amendment was adopted by a consent in writing signed by all members entitled to vote with respect thereto.

(c) If any merging or consolidating corporation has no members, or no members entitled to vote thereon, then as to each such corporation a statement of such fact, the date of the meeting of the board of directors at which the plan was adopted and a statement of the fact that such plan received the vote of a majority of the directors in office.

Duplicate originals of the articles of merger or articles of consolidation shall be delivered to the Secretary of State. If the Secretary of State finds that such articles conform to law, he shall, when all fees have been paid as in this Act prescribed:

(1) Endorse on each of such duplicate originals the word "Filed," and the month, day and year of the filing thereof.
(2) File one of such duplicate originals in his office.
(3) Issue a certificate of merger or a certificate of consolidation to which he shall affix the other duplicate original.

The certificate of merger or certificate of consolidation, together with the duplicate, original of the articles of merger or articles of consolidation affixed thereto by the Secretary of State, shall be returned to the surviving or new corporation, as the case may be, or its representative.

Section 42. Effect of Merger or Consolidation

Upon the issuance of the certificate of merger, or the certificate of consolidation by the Secretary of State, the merger or consolidation shall be effected.

When such merger or consolidation has been effected:

(a) The several corporations parties to the plan of merger or consolidation shall be a single corporation, which, in the case of a merger, shall be that corporation designated in the plan of merger as the surviving corporation, and, in the case of a consolidation, shall be the new corporation provided for in the plan of consolidation.

(b) The separate existence of all corporations parties to the plan of merger or consolidation, except the surviving or new corporation, shall cease.

(c) Such surviving or new corporation shall have all the rights, privileges, immunities and powers and shall be subject to all the duties and liabilities of a corporation organized under this Act.

(d) Such surviving or new corporation shall thereupon and thereafter possess all the rights, privileges, immunities, and franchises, as well of a public as of a private nature, of each of the merging or consolidating corporations; and all property, real, personal and mixed, and all debts due on whatever account, and all other choses in action, and all and every other interest, of or belonging to or due to each of the corporations so merged or consolidated, shall be taken and deemed to be transferred to and vested in such single corporation without further act or deed; and the title to any real estate, or any interest therein, vested in any of such corporations shall not revert or be in any way impaired by reason of such merger or consolidation.

(e) Such surviving or new corporation shall thenceforth be responsible and liable for all the liabilities and obligations of each of the corporations so merged or consolidated; and any claim existing or action or proceeding pending by or against any of such corporations may be prosecuted as if such merger or consolidation had not taken place, or such surviving or new corporation may be substituted in its place. Neither the rights of creditors nor any liens upon the property of any such corporation shall be impaired by such merger or consolidation.

(f) In the case of a merger, the articles of incorporation of the surviving corporation shall be deemed to be amended to the extent, if any, that changes in its articles of incorporation are stated in the plan of merger; and, in the case of a consolidation, the statements set forth in the articles of consolidation and which are required or permitted to be set forth in the articles of incorporation of corporations organized under this Act shall be deemed to be the articles of incorporation of the new corporation.

Section 43. Merger or Consolidation of Domestic and Foreign Corporations

One or more foreign corporations and one or more domestic corporations may be merged or consolidated in the following manner, if such merger or consolidation is permitted by the laws of the state under which each such foreign corporation is organized:

(a) Each domestic corporation shall comply with the provisions of this Act with respect to the merger of consolidation, as the case may be, of domestic corporations and each foreign corporation shall comply with the applicable provisions of the laws of the state under which it is organized.

(b) If the surviving or new corporation, as the case may be, is to be governed by the laws of any state other than this State, it shall comply with the provisions of this Act with respect to foreign corporations if it is to conduct affairs in this State, and in every case it shall file with the Secretary of State of this State:

(1) an agreement that it may be served with process in this State in any proceeding for the enforcement of any obligation of any domestic corporation which is a party to such merger or consolidation; and

(2) an irrevocable appointment of the Secretary of State of this State as its agent to accept service of process in any such proceeding.

The effect of such merger or consolidation shall be the same as in the case of the merger or consolidation of domestic corporations, if the surviving or new corporation is to be governed by the laws of this State. If the surviving or new corporation is to be governed by the laws of any state other than this State, the effect of such merger or consolidation shall be the same as in the case of the merger or consolidation of domestic corporations except in so far as the laws of the other state provide otherwise.

After approval by the members or, if there be no members entitled to vote thereon, by the board of directors, and at any time prior to the filing of the articles of merger or consolidation, the merger or consolidation may be abandoned pursuant to provisions therefor, if any, set forth in the plan of merger or consolidation.

Section 44. Sale, Lease, Exchange, or Mortgage of Assets

A sale, lease, exchange, mortgage, pledge or other disposition of all, or substantially all, the property and assets of a corporation may be made upon such terms and conditions and for such consideration, which may consist in whole or in part of money or property, real or personal, including shares of any corporation for profit, domestic or foreign, as may be authorized in the following manner:

(a) If there are members entitled to vote thereon, the board of directors shall adopt a resolution recommending such sale, lease, exchange, mortgage, pledge or other disposition and directing that it be submitted to a vote at a meeting of members entitled to vote thereon, which may be either an annual or a special meeting. Written notice stating that the purpose, or one of the purposes, of such meeting is to consider the sale, lease, exchange, mortgage, pledge or other disposition of all, or substantially all, the property and assets of the corporation shall be given to each member entitled to vote at such meeting, within the time and in the manner provided by this Act for the giving of notice of meetings of members. At such meeting the members may authorize such sale, lease, exchange, mortgage, pledge or other disposition and may fix, or may authorize the board of directors to fix, any or all of the terms and conditions thereof and the consideration to be received by the corporation therefor. Such authorization shall require at least two-thirds of the votes which members present at such meeting or represented by proxy are entitled to cast. After such authorization by a vote of members, the board of directors, nevertheless, in its discretion, may abandon such sale, lease, exchange, mortgage, pledge or other disposition of assets, subject to the rights of third parties under any contracts relating thereto, without further action or approval by members.

(b) If there are no members, or no members entitled to vote thereon, a sale, lease, exchange, mortgage, pledge or other disposition of all, or substantially all, the property and assets of a corporation shall be authorized upon receiving the vote of a majority of the directors in office.

Section 45. Voluntary Dissolution

A corporation may dissolve and wind up its affairs in the following manner:

(a) If there are members entitled to vote thereon, the board of directors shall adopt a resolution recommending that the corporation be dissolved, and directing that the question of such dissolution be submitted to a vote at a meeting of members entitled to vote thereon, which may be either an annual or a special meeting. Written notice stating that the purpose, or one of the purposes, of such meeting is to consider the advisability of dissolving the corporation, shall be given to each member entitled to vote at such meeting, within the time and in the manner provided in this Act for the giving of notice of meetings of members. A resolution to dissolve the corporation shall be adopted upon receiving at least two-thirds of the votes which members present at such meeting or represented by proxy are entitled to cast.

(b) If there are no members, or no members entitled to vote thereon, the dissolution of the corporation shall be authorized at a meeting of the board of directors upon the adoption of a resolution to dissolve by the vote of a majority of the directors in office.

Upon the adoption of such resolution by the members, or by the board of directors if there are no members or no members entitled to vote thereon, the corporation shall cease to conduct its affairs except in so far as may be necessary for the winding up thereof, shall immediately cause a notice of the proposed dissolution to be mailed to each known creditor of the corporation, and shall proceed to collect its assets and apply and distribute them as provided in this Act.

Section 46. Distribution of Assets

The assets of a corporation in the process of dissolution shall be applied and distributed as follows:

(a) All liabilities and obligations of the corporation shall be paid and discharged, or adequate provision shall be made therefor;
(b) Assets held by the corporation upon condition requiring return, transfer or conveyance, which condition occurs by reason of the dissolution, shall be returned, transferred or conveyed in accordance with such requirements;
(c) Assets received and held by the corporation subject to limitations permitting their use only for charitable, religious, eleemosynary, benevolent, educational or similar purposes, but not held upon a condition requiring return, transfer or conveyance by reason of the dissolution, shall be transferred or conveyed to one or more domestic or foreign corporations, societies or organizations engaged in activities substantially similar to those of the dissolving corporation, pursuant to a plan of distribution adopted as provided in this Act;
(d) Other assets, if any, shall be distributed in accordance with the provisions of the articles of incorporation or the bylaws to the extent that the articles of incorporation or bylaws determine the distributive rights of members, or any class or classes of members, or provide for distribution to others;
(e) Any remaining assets may be distributed to such persons, societies, organizations or domestic or foreign corporations, whether for profit or non-profit, as may be specified in a plan of distribution adopted as provided in this Act.

Section 47. Plan of Distribution

A plan providing for the distribution of assets, not inconsistent with the provisions of this Act, may be adopted by a corporation in the process of dissolution and shall be adopted by a corporation for the purpose of authorizing any transfer or conveyance of assets for which this Act requires a plan of distribution, in the following manner:

(a) If there are members entitled to vote thereon, the board of directors shall adopt a resolution recommending a plan of distribution and directing the submission thereof to a vote at a meeting of members entitled to vote thereon, which may be either an annual or a special meeting. Written notice setting forth the proposed plan of distribution or a summary thereof shall be given to each member entitled to vote at such meeting, within the time and in the manner provided in this Act for the giving of notice of meetings of members. Such plan of distribution shall be adopted upon receiving at least two-thirds of the votes which members present at such meeting or represented by proxy are entitled to cast.

(b) If there are no members, or no members entitled to vote thereon, a plan of distribution shall be adopted at a meeting of the board of directors upon receiving a vote of a majority of the directors in office.

Section 48. Revocation of Voluntary Dissolution Proceedings

A corporation may, at any time prior to the issuance of a certificate of dissolution by the Secretary of State, revoke the action theretofore taken to dissolve the corporation, in the following manner:

(a) If there are members entitled to vote thereon, the board of directors shall adopt a resolution recommending that the voluntary dissolution proceedings be revoked, and directing that the question of such revocation be submitted to a vote at a meeting of members entitled to vote thereon, which may be either an annual or a special meeting. Written notice stating that the purpose, or one of the purposes, of such meeting is to consider the advisability of revoking the voluntary dissolution proceedings, shall be given to each member entitled to vote at such meeting, within the time and in the manner provided in this Act for the giving of notice of meetings of members. A resolution to revoke the voluntary dissolution proceedings shall be adopted upon receiving at least two-thirds of the votes which members present at such meeting or represented by proxy are entitled to cast.

(b) If there are no members, or no members entitled to vote thereon, a resolution to revoke the voluntary dissolution proceedings shall be adopted at a meeting of the board of directors upon receiving the vote of a majority of the directors in office.

Upon the adoption of such resolution by the members, or by the board of directors where there are no members or no members entitled to vote thereon, the corporation may thereupon again conduct its affairs.

Section 49. Articles of Dissolution

If voluntary dissolution proceedings have not been revoked, then when all debts, liabilities and obligations of the corporation shall have been paid and discharged, or adequate provision shall have been made therefor, and all of the remaining property and assets of the corporation shall have been transferred, conveyed or distributed in accordance with the provisions of this Act, articles of dissolution shall be executed in duplicate by the corporation by its president or a vice president, and by its secretary or an assistant secretary, which statement shall set forth:

(a) The name of the corporation.
(b) If there are members entitled to vote thereon, (1) a statement setting forth the date of the meeting of members at which the resolution to dissolve was adopted, that a quorum was present at such meeting, and that such resolution received at least two-thirds of the votes which members present at such meeting or represented by proxy were entitled to cast, or (2) a statement that such resolution was adopted by a consent in writing signed by all members entitled to vote with respect thereto.
(c) If there are no members, or no members entitled to vote thereon, a statement of such fact, the date of the meeting of the board of directors at which the resolution to dissolve was adopted and a statement of the fact that such resolution received the vote of a majority of the directors in office.
(d) That all debts, obligations, and liabilities of the corporation have been paid and discharged or that adequate provision has been made therefor.
(e) A copy of the plan of distribution, if any, as adopted by the corporation, or a statement that no plan was so adopted.
(f) That all the remaining property and assets of the corporation have been transferred, conveyed or distributed in accordance with the provisions of this Act.
(g) That there are no suits pending against the corporation in any court, or that adequate provision has been made for the satisfaction of any judgment, order or

decree which may be entered against it in any pending suit.

Section 50. Filing of Articles of Dissolution

Duplicate originals of such articles of dissolution shall be delivered to the Secretary of State. If the Secretary of State finds that such articles of dissolution conform to law, he shall, when all fees have been paid as in this Act prescribed:

(1) Endorse on each of such duplicate originals the word "Filed," and the month, day and year of the filing thereof.
(2) File one of such duplicate originals in his office.
(3) Issue a certificate of dissolution to which he shall affix the other duplicate original.

The certificate of dissolution, together with the duplicate original of the articles of dissolution affixed thereto by the Secretary of State, shall be returned to the representative of the dissolved corporation. Upon the issuance of such certificate of dissolution the existence of the corporation shall cease, except for the purpose of suits, other proceedings and appropriate corporate action by members, directors and officers as provided in this Act.

Section 51. Involuntary Dissolution

A corporation may be dissolved involuntarily by a decree of the _____* court in an action filed by the Attorney General when it is established that:

(a) The corporation has failed to file its annual report within the time required by this Act; or

---

*Supply name of court.

(b) The corporation procured its articles of incorporation through fraud; or
(c) The corporation has continued to exceed or abuse the authority conferred upon it by law; or
(d) The corporation has failed for ninety days to appoint and maintain a registered agent in this State; or
(c) The corporation has failed for ninety days after change of its registered agent to file in the office of the Secretary of State a statement of such change.

Section 52. Notification to Attorney General

The Secretary of State, on or before the last day of December of each year, shall certify to the Attorney General the names of all corporations which have failed to file their annual reports in accordance with the provisions of this Act. He shall also certify, from time to time, the names of all corporations which have given other cause for dissolution as provided in this Act, together with the facts pertinent thereto. Whenever the Secretary of State shall concurrently mail to the corporation at its registered office a notice that such certification has been made. Upon the receipt of such ceritfication, the Attorney General shall file an action in the name of the State against such corporation for its dissolution. Every such certificate from the Secretary of State to the Attorney General pertaining to the failure of a corporation to file an annual report shall be taken and received in all courts as prima facie evidence of the facts therein stated. If, before action is filed, the corporation shall file its annual report, or shall appoint or maintain a registered agent as provided in this Act, or shall file with the Secretary of State the required statement of change of registered agent, such fact shall be forthwith certified by the Secretary of State to the Attorney General and he shall not file an action against such corporation for such cause. If, after action is filed, the corporation shall file its annual report, or shall appoint or maintain a registered agent as provided in this Act, or shall file with the Secretary of State the required statement of change of registered agent, and shall pay the costs of such action, the action for such cause shall abate.

Section 53. Venue and Process

Every action for the involuntary dissolution of a corporation shall be commenced by the Attorney General either in the _____* court of the county in which the registered office of the corporation is situated, or in the _____ court of _____ county. Summons shall issue and be served as in other civil action. If process is returned not found, the Attorney General shall cause publication to be made as in other civil cases in some newspaper published in the county where the registered office of the corporation is situated, containing a notice of the pendency of such action, the title of the court, the title of the action, and the date on or after which default may be entered. The Attorney General may include in one notice the names of any number of corporations against which actions are then pending in the same court. The Attorney General shall cause a copy of such notice to be mailed to the corporation at its registered office within ten days after the first publication thereof. The certificate of the Attorney General of the mailing of such notice shall be prima facie evidence thereof. Such notice shall be published at least once each week for two successive weeks, and the first publication thereof may begin at any time after the summons has been returned. Unless a corporation shall have been served with summons, no default shall be taken against it earlier than thirty days after the first publication of such notice.

---

*Supply name of court.

Section 54. Jurisdiction of Court to Liquidate Assets and Affairs of Corporation

Courts of equity shall have full power to liquidate the assets and affairs of a corporation.

(a) In an action by a member or director when it is made to appear:
  (1) That the directors are deadlocked in the management of the corporate affairs and that irreparable injury to the corporation is being suffered or is threatened by reason thereof, and either that the members are unable to break the deadlock or there are no members having voting rights; or
  (2) That the acts of the directors or those in control of the corporation are illegal, oppressive or fraudulent; or
  (3) That the members entitled to vote in the election of directors are deadlocked in voting power and have failed for at least two years to elect successors to directors whose terms have expired or would have expired upon the election of their successors;
  (4) That the corporate assets are being misapplied or wasted; or
  (5) That the corporation is unable to carry out its purposes.
(b) In an action by a creditor:
  (1) When the claim of the creditor has been reduced to judgment and an execution thereon has been returned unsatisfied and it is established that the corporation is insolvent; or
  (2) When the corporation has admitted in writing that the claim of the creditor is due and owing and it is established that the corporation is insolvent.
(c) Upon application by a corporation to have its dissolution continued under the supervision of the court.
(d) When an action has been filed by the Attorney General

to dissolve a corporation and it is established that liquidation of its affairs should precede the entry of a decree of dissolution.

Proceedings under this section shall be brought in the _____* in which the registered office or the principal office of the corporation is situated.

It shall not be necessary to make directors or members parties to any such action or proceedings unless relief is sought against them personally.

Section 55. Procedure in Liquidation of Corporation by Court

In proceedings to liquidate the assets and affairs of a corporation the court shall have the power to issue injunctions, to appoint a receiver or receivers pendente lite, with such powers and duties as the court, from time to time, may direct, and to take such other proceedings as may be requisite to preserve the corporate assets wherever situated, and carry on the affairs of the corporation until a full hearing can be had.

After a hearing had upon such notice as the court may direct to be given to all parties to the proceedings and to any other parties in interest designated by the court, the court may appoint a liquidating receiver or receivers with authority to collect the assets of the corporation. Such liquidating receiver or receivers shall have authority, subject to the order of the court, to sell, convey and dispose of all or any part of the assets of the corporation wherever situated, either at public or private sale. The order appointing such liquidating receiver or receivers shall state their powers and duties. Such powers and duties may be increased or diminished at any time during the proceedings.

The assets of the corporation or the proceeds resulting from

---

*Supply designation of jurisdiction, such as county, in accordance with local practice.

a sale, conveyance, or other disposition thereof shall be applied and distributed as follows:

  (a) All costs and expenses of the court proceedings and all liabilities and obligations of the corporation shall be paid, satisfied and discharged, or adequate provision shall be made therefor;
  (b) Assets held by the corporation upon condition requiring return, transfer or conveyance, which condition occurs by reason of the dissolution or liquidation, shall be returned, transferred or conveyed in accordance with such requirements;
  (c) Assets received and held by the corporation subject to limitations permitting their use only for charitable, religious, eleemosynary, benevolent, educational or similar purposes, but not held upon a condition requiring return, transfer or conveyance by reason of the dissolution or liquidation, shall be transferred or conveyed to one or more domestic or foreign corporations, societies or organizations engaged in activities substantially similar to those of the dissolving or liquidating corporation as the court may direct;
  (d) Other assets, if any, shall be distributed in accordance with the provisions of the articles of incorporation or the by-laws to the extent that the articles of incorporation or by-laws determine the distributive right of members, or any class or classes of members, or provide for distribution to others;
  (e) Any remaining assets may be distributed to such persons, societies, organizations or domestic or foreign corporations, whether for profit or not for profit, specified in the plan of distribution adopted as provided in this Act, or where no plan of distribution has been adopted, as the court may direct.

The court shall have power to allow, from time to time, as expenses of the liquidation compensation to the receiver or receivers and to attorneys in the proceeding, and to direct the payment thereof out of the assets of the corporation or the proceeds of any sale or disposition of such assets.

A receiver of a corporation appointed under the provisions of this section shall have authority to sue and defend in all courts in his own name as receiver of such corporation. The court appointing such receiver shall have exclusive jurisdiction of the corporation and its property, wherever situated.

Section 56. Qualification of Receivers

A receiver shall in all cases be a citizen of the United States or a corporation for profit authorized to act as receiver, which corporation may be a domestic corporation or a foreign corporation authorized to transact business in this State, and shall in all cases give such bond as the court may direct with such sureties as the court may require.

Section 57. Filing of Claims in Liquidation Proceedings

In proceedings to liquidate the assets and affairs of a corporation the court may require all creditors of the corporation to file with the clerk of the court or with the receiver, in such form as the court may prescribe, proofs under oath of their respective claims. If the court requires the filing of claims it shall fix a date, which shall be not less than four months from the date of the order, as the last day for the filing of claims, and shall prescribe the notice that shall be given to creditors and claimants of the date so fixed. Prior to the date so fixed, the court may extend the time for the filing of claims. Creditors and claimants failing to file proofs of claim on or before the date so fixed may be barred, by order of court, from participating in the distribution of the assets of the corporation.

Section 58. Discontinuance of Liquidation Proceedings

The liquidation of the assets and affairs of a corporation may be discontinued at any time during the liquidation proceedings when it is established that cause for liquidation no longer exists. In such event the court shall dismiss the proceedings and direct the receiver to redeliver to the corporation all its remaining property and assets.

Section 59. Decree of Involuntary Dissolution

In proceedings to liquidate the assets and affairs of a corporation, when the costs and expenses of such proceedings and all debts, obligations, and liabilities of the corporation shall have been paid and discharged and all of its remaining property and assets distributed in accordance with the provisions of this Act, or in case its property and assets are not sufficient to satisfy and discharge such costs, expenses, debts, and obligations, and all the property and assets have been applied so far as they will go to their payment, the court shall enter a decree dissolving the corporation, whereupon the existence of the corporation shall cease.

Section 60. Filing of Decree of Dissolution

In case the court shall enter a decree dissolving a corporation, it shall be the duty of the clerk of such court to cause a certified copy of the decree to be filed with the Secretary of State. No fee shall be charged by the Secretary of State for the filing thereof.

Section 61. Deposits with State Treasurer

Upon the voluntary or involuntary dissolution of a corporation, the portion of the assets distributable to any person who is unknown or cannot be found, or who is under disability and there is no person legally competent to receive such distributive portion, shall be reduced to cash and deposited with the State Treasurer and shall be paid over to such person or to his legal representative upon proof satisfactory to the State Treasurer of his right thereto.

Section 62. Survival of Remedy after Dissolution

The dissolution of a corporation either (1) by the issuance of a certificate of dissolution by the Secretary of State, or (2) by a decree of court when the court has not liquidated the assets and affairs of the corporation as provided in this Act, or (3) by expiration of its period of duration, shall not take away or impair any remedy available to or against such corporation, its directors, officers, or members, for any right or claim existing, or any liability incurred, prior to such dissolution if action or other proceeding thereon is commenced within two years after the date of such dissolution. Any such action or proceeding by or against the corporation may be prosecuted or defended by the corporation in its corporate name. The members, directors and officers shall have power to take such corporate or other action as shall be appropriate to protect such remedy, right or claim. If such corporation was dissolved by the expiration of its period of duration, such corporation may amend its articles of incorporation at any time during such period of two years so as to extend its period of duration.

Section 63. Admission of Foreign Corporation

No foreign corporation shall have the right to conduct affairs in this State until it shall have procured a certificate of authority so to do from the Secretary of State. No foreign corporation shall be entitled to procure a certificate of authority under this Act to conduct in this State any affairs which a corporation organized under this Act is prohibited from conducting. A foreign corporation shall not be denied a certificate of authority by reason of the fact that the laws of the state or country under which such corporation is organized governing its organization and internal affairs differ from the laws of this State, and nothing in this Act contained shall be construed to authorize this State to regulate the organization or the internal affairs of such corporation.

Without excluding other activities which may not constitute conducting affairs in this State, a foreign corporation shall not be considered to be conducting affairs in this State, for the purposes of this Act, by reason of carrying on in this State any one or more of the following activities:

(a) Maintaining or defending any action or suit or any administrative or arbitration proceeding, or effecting the settlement thereof or the settlement of claims or disputes.
(b) Holding meetings of its directors or members or carrying on other activities concerning its internal affairs.
(c) Maintaining bank accounts.
(d) Creating evidences of debt, mortgages or liens on real or personal property.
(e) Securing or collecting debts due to it or enforcing any rights in property securing the same.
(f) Conducting its affairs in interstate commerce.
(g) Granting funds.
(h) Distributing information to its members.
(i) Conducting an isolated transaction completed within a period of thirty days and not in the course of a number of repeated transactions of like nature.

Section 64. Powers of Foreign Corporation

A foreign corporation which shall have received a certificate of authority under this Act shall, until a certificate of revocation or of withdrawal shall have been issued as provided in this Act, enjoy the same, but no greater, rights and privileges as a domestic corporation organized for the purposes set forth in the application pursuant to which such certificate of authorization is issued; and, except as in this Act otherwise provided, shall be subject to the same duties, restrictions, penalties and liabilities now or hereafter imposed upon a domestic corporation of like character.

Section 65. Corporate Name of Foreign Corporation

No certificate of authority shall be issued to a foreign corporation unless the corporate name of such corporation:
(a) Shall not contain any word or phrase which indicates or implies that it is organized for any purpose other than one or more of the purposes contained in its articles of incorporation.
(b) Shall not be the same as, or deceptively similar to, the name of any corporation, whether for profit or not for profit, existing under the laws of this State, or any foreign corporation, whether for profit or not for profit, authorized to transact business or conduct affairs in this State, or a corporate name reserved or registered as permitted by the laws of this State.
(c) Shall be transliterated into letters of the English alphabet, if it is not in English.

Section 66. Change of Name by Foreign Corporation

Whenever a foreign corporation which is authorized to conduct affairs in this State shall change its name to one under which a certificate of authority would not be granted to it on application therefor, the certificate of authority of such corporation shall be suspended and it shall not thereafter conduct any affairs in this State until it has changed its name to a name which is available to it under the laws of this State.

Section 67. Application for Certificate of Authority

A foreign corporation, in order to procure a certificate of authority to conduct affairs in this State, shall make application therefor to the Secretary of State, which application shall set forth:

(a) The name of the corporation and the state or country under the laws of which it is incorporated.
(b) The date of incorporation and the period of duration of the corporation.
(c) The address of the principal office of the corporation in the state or country under the laws of which it is incorporated.
(d) The address of the proposed registered office of the corporation in this State, and the name of its proposed registered agent in this State at such address.
(e) The purpose or purposes of the corporation which it proposes to pursue in conducting its affairs in this State.
(f) The names and respective addresses of the directors and officers of the corporation.
(g) Such additional information as may be necessary or appropriate in order to enable the Secretary of State to determine whether such corporation is entitled to a certificate of authority to conduct affairs in this State.

Such application shall be made on forms prescribed and furnished by the Secretary of State and shall be executed in duplicate by the corporation by its president or a vice president and by its secretary or an assistant secretary.

Section 68. Filing of Application for Certificate of Authority

Duplicate originals of the application of the corporation for a certificate of authority shall be delivered to the Secretary of State, together with a copy of its articles of incorporation and all amendments thereto, duly certified by the proper officer of the state or country under the laws of which it is incorporated.

If the Secretary of State finds that such application conforms to law, he shall, when all fees have been paid as in this Act prescribed:

(1) Endorse on each of such documents the word "Filed," and the month, day and year of the filing thereof.
(2) File in his office one of such duplicate originals of the application and the copy of the articles of incorporation and amendments thereto.
(3) Issue a certificate of authority to conduct affairs in this State to which he shall affix the other duplicate original application.

The certificate of authority, together with the duplicate original of the application affixed thereto by the Secretary of State, shall be returned to the corporation or its representative.

Section 69. Effect of Certificate of Authority

Upon the issuance of a certificate of authority by the Secretary of State, the corporation shall be authorized to conduct affairs in this State for those purposes set forth in its application, subject, however, to the right of this State to suspend or to revoke such authority as provided in this Act.

Section 70. Registered Office and Registered Agent of Foreign Corporation

Each foreign corporation authorized to conduct affairs in this State shall have and continuously maintain in this State;

(a) A registered office which may be, but need not be, the same as its principal office.
(b) A registered agent, which agent may be either an individual resident in this State whose business office is identical with such registered office, or a domestic corporation, whether for profit or not for profit, or a foreign corporation, whether for profit or not for profit, authorized to transact business or conduct affairs in this State, having an office identical with such registered office.

Section 71. Change of Registered Office or Registered Agent of Foreign Corporation

A foreign corporation authorized to conduct affairs in this State may change its registered office or change its registered agent, or both, upon filing in the office of the Secretary of State a statement setting forth:

(a) The name of the corporation.
(b) The address of its then registered office.
(c) If the address of its registered office be changed, the address to which the registered office is to be changed.
(d) The name of its registered agent.
(e) If its registered agent be changed, the name of its successor registered agent.
(f) That the address of its registered office and the address of the office of its registered agent, as changed, will be identical.
(g) That such change was authorized by resolution duly adopted by its board of directors.

Such statement shall be executed by the corporation by its president or a vice president and delivered to the Secretary of

State. If the Secretary of State finds that such statement conforms to the provisions of this Act, he shall file such statement in his office, and upon such filing the change of address of the registered office, or the appointment of a new registered agent, or both, as the case may be, shall become effective.

Any registered agent in this State appointed by a foreign corporation may resign as such agent upon filing a written notice thereof, executed in duplicate, with the Secretary of State who shall forthwith mail a copy thereof to the foreign corporation at its principal office in the state or country under the laws of which it is incorporated as shown by its most recent annual report. The appointment of such agent shall terminate upon the expiration of 30 days after receipt of such notice by the Secretary of State.

If a registered agent changes his or its business address to another place within the same _____ *, he or it may change such address and the address of the registered office of any corporations of which he or it is registered agent by filing a statement as required above except that it need be signed only by the registered agent and need not be responsive to (e) or (g) and must recite that a copy of the statement has been mailed to each such corporation.

Section 72. Service of Process on Foreign Corporation

The registered agent so appointed by a foreign corporation authorized to conduct affairs in this State shall be an agent of such corporation upon whom any process, notice or demand required or permitted by law to be served upon the corporation may be served.

Whenever a foreign corporation authorized to conduct affairs in this State shall fail to appoint or maintain a registered

---

*Supply designation of jurisdiction, such as county, in accordance with local practice.

agent in this State, or whenever any such registered agent cannot with reasonable diligence be found at the registered office, or whenever the certificate of authority of a foreign corporation shall be suspended or revoked, then the Secretary of State shall be an agent of such corporation upon whom any such process, notice, or demand may be served. Service on the Secretary of State of any such process, notice, or demand shall be made by delivering to and leaving with him, or with any clerk having charge of the corporation department of his office, duplicate copies of such process, notice or demand. In the event any such process, notice or demand is served on the Secretary of State, he shall immediately cause one of the copies thereof to be forwarded by registered or certified mail, addressed to the corporation at its principal office in the state or country under the laws of which it is incorporated. Any service so had on the Secretary of State shall be returnable in not less than thirty days.

The Secretary of State shall keep a record of all processes, notices and demands served upon him under this Section, and shall record therein the time of such service and his action with reference thereto.

Nothing herein contained shall limit or affect the right to serve any process, notice or demand, required or permitted by law to be served upon a corporation in any other manner now or hereafter permitted by law.

Section 73. Amendment to Articles of Incorporation of Foreign Corporation

Whenever the articles of incorporation of a foreign corporation authorized to conduct affairs in this State are amended, such foreign corporation shall, within thirty days after such amendment becomes effective, file in the office of the Secretary of State a copy of such amendment duly certified by the proper officer of the state or country under the laws of which it is incorporated; but the filing thereof shall not of itself enlarge or alter the purpose or purposes which such corporation is authorized to pursue in conducting its affairs in this State, nor authorize such corporation to conduct affairs in this State under any other name than the name set forth in its certificate of authority.

Section 74. Merger of Foreign Corporation Authorized to Conduct Affairs in this State

Whenever a foreign corporation authorized to conduct affairs in this State shall be a party to a statutory merger permitted by the laws of the state or country under the laws of which it is incorporated, and such corporation shall be the surviving corporation, it shall, within thirty days after such merger becomes effective, file with the Secretary of State a copy of the articles of merger duly certified by the proper officer of the state or country under the laws of which such statutory merger was effected; and it shall not be necessary for such corporation to procure either a new or amended certificate of authority to conduct affairs in this State unless the name of such corporation be changed thereby or unless the corporation desires to pursue in this State other or additional purposes than those which it is then authorized to pursue in this State.

Section 75. Amended Certificate of Authority

A foreign corporation authorized to conduct affairs in this State shall procure an amended certificate of authority in the event it changes its corporate name, or desires to pursue in this State other or additional purposes than those set forth in its prior application for a certificate of authority, by making application therefor to the Secretary of State.

The requirements in respect to the form and contents of such application, the manner of its execution, the filing of duplicate originals thereof with the Secretary of State, the issuance of an amended certificate of authority and the effect thereof, shall be the same as in the case of an original application for a certificate of authority.

Section 76. Withdrawal of Foreign Corporation

A foreign corporation authorized to conduct affairs in this State may withdraw from this State upon procuring from the Secretary of State a certificate of withdrawal. In order to procure such certificate of withdrawal, such foreign corporation shall deliver to the Secretary of State an application for withdrawal, which shall set forth:

(a) The name of the corporation and the state or country under the laws of which it is incorporated.
(b) That the corporation is not conducting affairs in this State.
(c) That the corporation surrenders its authority to conduct affairs in this State.
(d) That the corporation revokes the authority of its registered agent in this State to accept service of process and consents that service of process in any action, suit or proceeding based upon any cause of action arising in this State during the time the corporation was authorized to conduct affairs in this State may thereafter be made on such corporation by service thereof on the Secretary of State.
(e) A post-office address to which the Secretary of State may mail a copy of any process against the corporation that may be served on him.

The application for withdrawal shall be made on forms prescribed and furnished by the Secretary of State and shall be executed by the corporation by its president or a vice president and by its secretary or an assistant secretary, or, if the corporation is in the hands of a receiver or trustee, shall be executed on behalf of the corporation by such receiver or trustee.

Section 77. Filing of Application for Withdrawal

Duplicate originals of such application for withdrawal shall be delivered to the Secretary of State. If the Secretary of State finds that such application conforms to the provisions of this Act, he shall, when all fees have been paid as in this Act prescribed:

(1) Endorse on each of such duplicate originals the word "Filed," and the month, day and year of the filing thereof.
(2) File one of such duplicate originals in his office.
(3) Issue a certificate of withdrawal to which he shall affix the other duplicate original.

The certificate of withdrawal, together with the duplicate original of the application for withdrawal affixed thereto by the Secretary of State, shall be returned to the corporation or its representative. Upon the issuance of such certificate of withdrawal, the authority of the corporation to conduct affairs in this State shall cease.

Section 78. Revocation of Certificate of Authority

The certificate of authority of a foreign corporation to conduct affairs in this State may be revoked by the Secretary of State upon the conditions prescribed in this Section when:

(a) The corporation has failed to file its annual report within the time required by this Act, or has failed to pay any fees or penalties prescribed by this Act when they have become due and payable; or

(b) The corporation has failed to appoint and maintain a registered agent in this State as required by this Act; or

(c) The corporation has failed, after change of its registered agent, to file in the office of the Secretary of State a statement of such change as required by this Act; or

(d) The corporation has failed to file in the office of the Secretary of State any amendment to its articles of incorporation or any articles of merger within the time prescribed by this Act; or

(e) The certificate of authority of the corporation was procured through fraud practiced upon the State; or

(f) The corporation has continued to exceed or abuse the authority conferred upon it by this Act; or

(g) A misrepresentation has been made of any material matter in any application, report, affidavit, or other document submitted by such corporation pursuant to this Act.

No certificate of authority of a foreign corporation shall be revoked by the Secretary of State unless (1) he shall have given the corporation not less than sixty days' notice thereof by mail addressed to its registered office in this State, and (2) the corporation shall fail prior to revocation to file such annual report, or pay such fees or penalties, or file the required statement of change of registered agent, or file such articles of amendment or articles of merger, or correct such misrepresentation.

Section 79. Issuance of Certificate of Revocation

Upon revoking any such certificate of authority, the Secretary of State shall:

(1) Issue a certificate of revocation in duplicate.
(2) File one of such certificates in his office.
(3) Mail to such corporation at its registered office in this State a notice of such revocation accompanied by one of such certificates.

Upon the issuance of such certificate of revocation, the authority of the corporation to conduct affairs in this State shall cease.

Section 80. Conducting Affairs Without Certificate of Authority

No foreign corporation which is conducting affairs in this State without a certificate of authority shall be permitted to maintain any action, suit or proceeding in any court of this State until such corporation shall have obtained a certificate of authority. Nor shall any action, suit or proceeding be maintained in any court of this State by any successor or assignee of such corporation on any right, claim or demand arising out of the conduct of affairs by such corporation in this State, until a certificate of authority shall have been obtained by such corporation or by a corporation which has acquired all or substantially all of its assets.

The failure of a foreign corporation to obtain a certificate of authority to conduct affairs in this State shall not impair the validity of any contract or act of such corporation, and shall not prevent such corporation from defending any action, suit or proceeding in any court of this State.

A foreign corporation which conducts affairs in this State without a certificate of authority shall be liable to this State, for the years or parts thereof during which it conducted affairs in this State without a certificate of authority, in an amount equal to all fees which would have been imposed by this Act upon such corporation had it duly applied for and received a certifiate of authority to conduct affairs in this State as required by this Act and thereafter filed all reports required by this Act, plus all interest and penalties imposed by this Act for failure to pay such fees. The Attorney General shall bring proceedings to recover all amounts due this State under the provisions of this section.

Section 81. Annual Report of Domestic and Foreign Corporations

Each domestic corporation, and each foreign corporation authorized to conduct affairs in this State, shall file, within the time prescribed by this Act, an annual report setting forth:

(a) The name of the corporation and the state or country under the laws of which it is incorporated.
(b) The address of the registered office of the corporation in this State, and the name of its registered agent in this State at such address, and, in the case of a foreign corporation, the address of its principal office in the state or country under the laws of which it is incorporated.
(c) A brief statement of the character of the affairs which the corporation is actually conducting, or, in the case of a foreign corporation, which the corporation is actually conducting in this State.
(d) The names and respective addresses of the directors and officers of the corporation.

Such annual report shall be made on forms prescribed and furnished by the Secretary of State, and the information therein contained shall be given as of the date of the execution of the report. It shall be executed by the corporation by its president, a vice president, secretary, an assistant secretary, or treasurer, or, if the corporation is in the hands of a receiver or trustee, it shall be executed on behalf of the corporation by such receiver or trustee.

Section 82. Filing of Annual Report of Domestic and Foreign Corporations

Such annual report of a domestic or foreign corporation shall be delivered to the Secretary of State between the first day of January and the first day of March of each year, except that the first annual report of a domestic or foreign corporation shall be filed between the first day of January and the first day of March of the year next succeeding the calendar year in which its certificate of incorporation or its certificate of authority, as the case may be, was issued by the Secretary of State. Proof to the satisfaction of the Secretary of State that prior to the first day of March such report was deposited in the United States mail in a sealed envelope, properly addressed, with postage prepaid, shall be deemed a compliance with this requirement. If the Secretary of State finds that such report conforms to the requirements of this Act, he shall file the same. If he finds that it does not so conform, he shall promptly return the same to the corporation for any necessary corrections, in which event the penalties hereinafter prescribed for failure to file such report within the time hereinabove provided shall not apply, if such report is corrected to conform to the requirements of this Act and returned to the Secretary of State within thirty days from the date on which it was mailed to the corporation by the Secretary of State.

Section 83. Fees for Filing Documents and Issuing Certificates

The Secretary of State shall charge and collect for:

(a) Filing articles of incorporation and issuing a certificate of incorporation, ten dollars.

(b) Filing articles of amendment and issuing a certificate of amendment, five dollars.
(c) Filing Restated Articles of Incorporation and issuing Restated Certificate of Incorporation, five dollars.
(d) Filing articles of merger or consolidation and issuing a certificate of merger or consolidation, five dollars.
(e) Filing a statement of change of address of registered office or change of registered agent, or both, one dollar.
(f) Filing articles of dissolution, one dollar.
(g) Filing an application of a foreign corporation for a certificate of authority to conduct affairs in this State and issuing a certificate of authority, ten dollars.
(h) Filing an application of a foreign corporation for an amended certificate of authority to conduct affairs in this State and issuing an amended certificate of authority, five dollars.
(i) Filing a copy of an amendment to the articles of incorporation of a foreign corporation holding a certificate of authority to conduct affairs in this State, five dollars.
(j) Filing a copy of articles of merger of a foreign corporation holding a certificate of authority to conduct affairs in this State, five dollars.
(k) Filing an application for withdrawal of a foreign corporation and issuing a certificate of withdrawal, one dollar.
(l) Filing any other statement or report, including an annual report, of a domestic or foreign corporation, one dollar.

Section 84. Miscellaneous Charges

The Secretary of State shall charge and collect:
(a) For furnishing a certified copy of any document, instrument, or paper relating to a corporation, thirty-

five cents per page and one dollar for the certificate and affixing the seal thereto.

(b) At the time of any service of process on him as resident agent of a corporation, five dollars, which amount may be recovered as taxable costs by the party to the suit or action causing such service to be made if such party prevails in the suit or action.

Section 85. Penalties Imposed upon Corporation

Each corporation, domestic or foreign, that fails or refuses to file its annual report for any year within the time prescribed by this Act shall be subject to a penalty of fifty dollars to be assessed by the Secretary of State.

Each corporation, domestic or foreign, that fails or refuses to answer truthfully and fully within the time prescribed by this Act interrogatories propounded by the Secretary of State in accordance with the provisions of this Act, shall be deemed to be guilty of a misdemeanor and upon conviction thereof may be fined in any amount not exceeding five hundred dollars.

Section 86. Penalties Imposed upon Directors and Officers

Each director and officer of a corporation, domestic or foreign, who fails or refuses within the time prescribed by this Act or answer truthfully and fully interrogatories propounded to him by the Secretary of State in accordance with the provisions of this Act, or who signs any articles, statement, report, application or other document filed with the Secretary of State which is known to such officer or director to be false in any material respect, shall be deemed to be guilty of a misdemeanor, and upon conviction thereof may be fined in any amount not exceeding five hundred dollars.

Section 87. Interrogatories by Secretary of State

The Secretary of State may propound to any corporation, domestic or foreign, subject to the provisions of this Act, and to any officer or director thereof, such interrogatories as may be reasonably necessary and proper to enable him to ascertain whether such corporation has complied with all the provisions of this Act applicable to such corporation. Such interrogatories shall be answered within thirty days after the mailing thereof, or within such additional time as shall be fixed by the Secretary of State, and the answers thereto shall be full and complete and shall be made in writing and under oath. If such interrogatories be directed to an individual they shall be answered by him, and if directed to a corporation they shall be answered by the president, vice president, secretary or assistant secretary, or treasurer or assistant treasurer thereof. The Secretary of State need not file any document to which such interrogatories relate until such interrogatories be answered as herein provided, and not then if the answers thereto disclose that such document is not in conformity with the provisions of this Act. The Secretary of State shall certify to the Attorney General, for such action as the Attorney General may deem appropriate, all interrogatories and answers thereto which disclose a violation of any of the provisions of this Act.

Section 88. Information Disclosed by Interrogatories

Interrogatories propounded by the Secretary of State and the answers thereto shall not be open to public inspection nor shall the Secretary of State disclose any facts or information obtained therefrom except in so far as his official duty may require the same to be made public or in the event such interrogatories or the answers thereto are required for evidence in any criminal proceedings or in any other action by this State.

Section 89. Powers of Secretary of State

The Secretary of State shall have the power and authority reasonably necessary to enable him to administer this Act efficiently and to perform the duties therein imposed upon him

Section 90. Appeal from Secretary of State

If the Secretary of State shall fail to approve any articles of incorporation, amendment, merger, consolidation or dissolution, or any other document required by this Act to be approved by the Secretary of State before the same shall be filed in his office, he shall, within ten days after the delivery thereof to him, give written notice of his disapproval to the person or corporation, domestic or foreign, delivering the same, specifying the reasons therefor. From such disapproval such person or corporation may appeal to the _____* court of the county in which the registered office of such corporation is, or is proposed to be, situated by filing with the clerk of such court a petition setting forth a copy of the articles or other document sought to be filed and a copy of the written disapproval thereof by the Secretary of State; whereupon the matter shall be tried de novo by the court, and the court shall either sustain the action of the Secretary of State or direct him to take such action as the court may deem proper.

If the Secretary of State shall revoke the certificate of authority to conduct affairs in this State of any foreign corporation, pursuant to the provisions of this Act, such foreign corporation

---

*Supply name of court.

may likewise appeal to the _____* court of the county where the registered office of such corporation in this State is situated, by filing with the clerk of such court a petition setting forth a copy of its certificate of authority to conduct affairs in this State and a copy of the notice of revocation given by the Secretary of State; whereupon the matter shall be tried de novo by the court, and the court shall either sustain the action of the Secretary of State or direct him to take such action as the court may deem proper.

Appeals from all final orders and judgments entered by the _____* court under this Section in review of any ruling or decision of the Secretary of State may be taken as in other civil actions.

Section 91. Certificates and Certified Copies to Be Received in Evidence

All certificates issued by the Secretary of State in accordance with the provisions of this Act, and all copies of documents filed in his office in accordance with the provisions of this Act when certified by him, shall be taken and received in all courts, public offices, and official bodies as prima facie evidence of the facts therein stated. A certificate by the Secretary of State under the great seal of this State, as to the existence or non-existence of the facts relating to corporations which would not appear from a certified copy of any of the foregoing documents or certificates shall be taken and received in all courts, public offices, and official bodies as prima facie evidence of the existence or non-existence of the facts therein stated.

---

*Supply name of court.

Section 92. Forms to Be Furnished by Secretary of State

All reports required by this Act to be filed in the office of the Secretary of State shall be made on forms which shall be prescribed and furnished by the Secretary of State. Forms for all other documents to be filed in the office of the Secretary of State shall be furnished by the Secretary of State on request therefor, but the use thereof, unless otherwise specifically prescribed in this Act, shall not be mandatory.

Section 93. Greater Voting Requirements

Whenever, with respect to any action to be taken by the members or directors of a corporation, the articles of incorporation or by-laws require the vote or concurrence of a greater proportion of the directors or members or any class of members than required by this Act, the provisions of the articles of incorporation or by-laws shall control.

Section 94. Waiver of Notice

Whenever any notice is required to be given to any member or director of a corporation under the provisions of this Act or under the provisions of the articles of incorporation or by-laws of the corporation, a waiver thereof in writing signed by the person or persons entitled to such notice, whether before or after the time stated therein, shall be equivalent to the giving of such notice.

Section 95. Action by Members or Directors Without a Meeting

Any action required by this Act to be taken at a meeting of the members or directors of a corporation, or any action which may be taken at a meeting of the members or directors, may be taken without a meeting if a consent in writing, setting forth the action so taken, shall be signed by all of the members entitled to vote with respect to the subject matter thereof, or all of the directors, as the case may be.

Such consent shall have the same force and effect as a unanimous vote, and may be stated as such in any articles or document filed with the Secretary of State under this Act.

Section 96. Unauthorized Assumption of Corporate Powers

All persons who assume to act as a corporation without authority so to do shall be jointly and severally liable for all debts and liabilities incurred or arising as a result thereof.

Section 97. Reservation of Power

The _____.* shall at all times have power to prescribe such regulations, provisions and limitations as it may deem advisable,
which regulations, provisions and limitations shall be binding upon any and all corporations subject to the provisions of this Act, and the _____* shall have power to amend, repeal or modify this Act at pleasure.

Section 98. Effect of Repeal of Prior Acts

The repeal of a prior act by this Act shall not affect any right accrued or established, or any liability or penalty incurred, under the provisions of such act, prior to the repeal thereof.

---

*Supply name of legislative body.

Section 99. Effect of Invalidity of Part of this Act

If a court of competent jurisdiction shall adjudge to be invalid or unconstitutional any clause, sentence, paragraph, section or part of this Act, such judgment or decree shall not affect, impair, invalidate or nullify the remainder of this Act, but the effect thereof shall be confined to the clause, sentence, paragraph, section or part of this Act so adjudged to be invalid or unconstitutional.

Section 100. Repeal of Prior Acts

(Insert appropriate provisions)

APPENDIX

OPTIONAL AND ALTERNATIVE SECTIONS

DIVISION 1. Election to Accept the Act. (Optional Sections)

In many states the laws governing corporations non-profit presently in effect permit such corporations to issue stock. This is forbidden under Section 26 of the Model Act. The following provisions covering the revisions of the Act which would be required to meet this situation have been combined with mechanics for election to accept the Act by a corporation which would not automatically become subject to its terms because, for example, the law under which it was organized contained no reservation of power to amend or repeal. Since there will be no need for these provisions in some states, they have been added as optional sections

Section 2. Definitions

As used in this Act, unless the context otherwise requires, the term * * * (d) "Articles of incorporation" includes the original or restated articles of incorporation or articles of consolidation and all amendments thereto including articles of merger, and, in the case of a corporation created by special act of the legislature, includes the special charter and any amendments thereto made by special act of the legislature or pursuant to general law. * * *

Section 3. Applicability

The provisions of this Act relating to domestic corporations shall apply to

(a) all corporations organized hereunder;
(b) All non-profit corporations heretofore organized under any act hereby repealed, without shares or capital stock and for a purpose or purposes for which a corporation might be organized under this Act; and
(c) each non-profit corporation having shares or capital stock organized under any act hereby repealed and each non-profit corporation whether with or without shares or capital stock heretofore organized under any general law or created by special act of the legislature of this State in each case for a purpose or purposes for which a corporation may be organized under this Act, but not otherwise entitled to the rights, privileges, immunities and franchises provided by this Act, which shall elect to accept this Act as hereinafter provided.

The provisions of this Act relating to foreign corporations shall apply to all foreign non-profit corporations conducting affairs in this State for a purpose or purposes for which a corporation might be organized under this Act.

Section 37A. Procedure to Elect to Accept Act

Any non-profit corporation with shares or capital stock heretofore organized under any act hereby repealed, and any non-profit corporation whether with or without shares or capital stock heretofore, organized under any general law or created

OPTIONAL AND ALTERNATIVE SECTIONS 351

by any special act of the legislature of this State for a purpose or purposes for which a corporation may be organized under this Act, may elect to accept this Act in the following manner:

(a) If there are members or stockholders entitled to vote thereon, the board of directors shall adopt a resolution recommending that the corporation accept this Act and directing that the question of such acceptance be submitted to a vote at a meeting of the members or stockholders entitled to vote thereon, which may be either an annual or a special meeting. Written notice stating that the purpose, or one of the purposes, of such meeting is to consider electing to accept this Act, shall be given to each member and stockholder entitled to vote at such meeting, within the time and in the manner provided in this Act for the giving of notice of meetings of members. Such election to accept the Act shall require for adoption at least two-thirds of the votes which members or stockholders present at such meeting in person or by proxy are entitled to cast.

(b) If there are no members or stockholders entitled to vote thereon, election to accept this Act may be made at a meeting of the board of directors pursuant to majority vote of the directors in office.

In effecting such acceptance the corporation shall in addition follow the requirements of the law under which it was organized, its articles of incorporation and by-laws so far as applicable.

If the corporation does not have a registered office and a registered agent in this State registered in the office of the Secretary of State, it shall designate a registered office and appoint a registered agent having an office identical with such registered office.

Section 37B. Statement of Election to Accept the Act

A statement of election to accept the Act shall be executed in duplicate by the corporation by its president or a vice president and by its secretary or an assistant secretary and shall set forth:

(a) The name of the corporation.
(b) A statement by the corporation that it has elected to accept this Act and that all reports have been filed and all fees, taxes and penalties due to the State accruing under any act to which the corporation has heretofore been subject have been paid.
(c) If there are members or stockholders entitled to vote thereon, a statement setting forth the date of the meeting of such members or stockholders at which the election to accept this Act was made, that a quorum was present at such meeting and that such acceptance was authorized by at least two-thirds of the votes which members or stockholders present at such meeting in person or by proxy were entitled to cast.
(d) If there are no members or stockholders entitled to vote thereon, a statement of such fact, the date of the meeting of the board of directors at which election to accept this Act was made, that a quorum was present at such meeting and that such acceptance was authorized by a majority vote of the directors present at such meeting.
(e) A statement that, in addition, the corporation followed the requirements of the law under which it was organized, its articles of incorporation and by-laws so far as applicable in effecting such acceptance.
(f) The address of the registered office of the corporation

in this State and the name of the registered agent at such address.

(g) The names and respective addresses of its officers and directors.

(h) A statement that the attached copy, if any, of the articles of incorporation of the corporation is true and correct.

(i) If the corporation has issued shares of stock, a statement of such fact including the number of shares theretofore authorized, the number issued and outstanding, and a statement that all issued and outstanding shares of stock have been delivered to the corporation to be cancelled upon the acceptance of this Act by the corporation becoming effective and that from and after the effective date of said acceptance the authority of the corporation to issue shares of stock shall be thereby terminated.

Section 37C. Filing Statement of Election to Accept Act

Duplicate originals of the statement of election to accept this Act shall be delivered to the Secretary of State. If the Secretary of State finds that said statement conforms to law, he shall, when all fees have been paid, as in this Act prescribed:

(1) Endorse on each of such duplicate originals the word "Filed" and the month, day and year of the filing thereof;
(2) file one of such duplicate originals in his office;
(3) issue a certificate of acceptance to which he shall affix the other duplicate original.

The certificate of acceptance, together with the duplicate original of the statement of election to accept this Act affixed thereto by the Secretary of State, shall be returned to the corporation or its representative.

Section 37D. Effect of Certificate of Acceptance

Upon the issuance of a certificate of acceptance, the election of the corporation to accept this Act shall become effective and such corporation shall have the same powers and privileges and be subject to the same duties, restrictions, penalties and liabilities as though such corporation had been originally organized hereunder and shall also be subject to any duties or obligations expressly imposed upon such corporation by its special charter, provided, however, (a) that the first annual report of the corporation so accepting the benefits of this Act shall be filed between the first day of January and the first day of March of the year next succeeding the calendar year in which the certificate of acceptance shall have been issued; (b) that if no period of duration shall be expressly fixed in the articles of incorporation of such corporation, its period of duration shall be deemed to be perpetual; (c) that no amendment to the articles of incorporation adopted after such election to accept this Act shall release or terminate any duty or obligation expressly imposed upon any such corporation under and by virtue of a special charter or enlarge any right, power or privilege granted to any such corporation under a special charter except to the extent that such right, power or privilege might have been included in the articles of incorporation of a corporation organized under this Act; and (d) that in the case of any corporation with issued shares of stock, the holders of such issued shares who surrender them to the corporation to be cancelled upon the acceptance of this Act by the corporation becoming effective, shall be and become members of the corporation with one vote for each share of stock so surrendered until such time as the corporation by proper corporate action relative to the election, qualification, terms and voting power of members shall otherwise prescribe.

Section 83. Fees for Filing Documents and Issuing Certificates

The Secretary of State shall charge and collect for: * * *
(a-1) Filing statement of election to accept the Act, five dollars. * * *

DIVISION 2. Purposes. (Alternative Section)

Section 4. Purposes

Corporations may be organized under this Act for any lawful purpose or purposes except . . . [list, if any]. . . . .

DIVISION 3. Emergency By-laws. (Optional Section)

Section 12A. By-Laws and Other Powers in Emergency

The board of directors of any corporation may adopt emergency by-laws, which shall, notwithstanding any different provision elsewhere in this Act or in the articles of incorporation or by-laws, be operative during any emergency in the conduct of the affairs of the corporation resulting from an attack on the United States or any nuclear or atomic disaster. The emergency by-laws may make any provision that may be practical and necessary for the circumstances of the emergency, including provisions that:

(a) A meeting of the board of directors may be called by any officer or director in such manner and under such conditions as shall be prescribed in the emergency by-laws;

(b) The director or directors in attendance at the meeting, or any greater number fixed by the emergency by-laws, shall constitute a quorum; and

(c) The officers or other persons designated on a list approved by the board of directors before the emergency, all in such order of priority and subject to such conditions and for such period of time (not longer than reasonably necessary after the termination of the emergency) as may be provided in the emergency by-laws or in the resolution approving the list, shall, to the extent required to provide a quorum at any meeting of the board of directors be deemed directors for such meeting.

The board of directors, either before or during any such emergency, may provide, and from time to time modify, lines of succession in the event that during any such emergency any or all officers or agents of the corporation shall for any reason be rendered incapable of discharging their duties.

The board of directors, either before or during any such emergency, may, effective in the emergency, change the head office or designate several alternative head offices or regional offices, or authorize the officers so to do.

To the extent not inconsistent with any emergency by-laws so adopted, the by-laws of the corporation shall remain in effect during any such emergency and upon its termination the emergency by-laws shall cease to be operative.

Unless otherwise provided in emergency by-laws, notice of any meeting of the board of directors during any such emergency may be given only to such of the directors as it may be feasible to reach at the time and by such means as may be feasible at the time, including publication or radio.

To the extent required to constitute a quorum at any meeting of the board of directors during any such emergency, the officers of the corporation who are present shall, unless otherwise provided in emergency by-laws, be deemed, in order of rank and within the same rank in order of seniority, directors for such meeting.

No officer, director or employee acting in accordance with any emergency by-laws shall be liable except for willful misconduct. No officer, director or employee shall be liable for any action taken by him in good faith in any such emergency in furtherance of the ordinary affairs of the corporation even though not authorized by the by-laws then in effect.

DIVISION 4. Indemnification of Directors. (Alternative Section)

Strike Section 5(n) and use in the alternative the following section which requires court approval of payments by way of indemnification under certain circumstances:

Section 24A. Indemnification of Officers and Directors

When any claim is asserted, whether by action in court or otherwise, against any person by reason of his being or having been a director or officer of a corporation, the court in the proceeding in which such claim has been asserted, or any court having the requisite jurisdiction of an action instituted by such director or officer on his claim for indemnity, may assess indemnity against the corporation, its receiver or trustee, for the amount paid by such director or officer in satisfaction of any judgment on or in compromise of any such claim (exclusive in either case of any amount paid to the corporation), and any expenses and costs (including attorneys' fees) actually and necessarily incurred by him in connection therewith to the extent that the court shall deem reasonable and equitable, provided, nevertheless, that indemnity may be assessed under this Section only if the court finds that the person indemnified was not guilty of actual negligence or misconduct in the performance of his duties as such director or officer. The right and remedy provided by this Section shall be exclusive when any action brought on such claim has resulted in judgment against the person claiming indemnity, or when the person claiming indemnity has paid or agreed to pay any sum in settlement of any such claim or action, and in such case indemnity shall be awarded only upon order of court pursuant to the provision of this Section.

In all other cases the right and remedy provided by this Section shall not be exclusive, but each corporation shall have power to indemnify any director or officer or former director or officer of such corporation against expenses and costs (including attorney's fees) actually and necessarily incurred by him in connection with any claim asserted against him, by action in court or otherwise, by reason of his being or having been such director or officer, except in relation to matters as to which he shall have been guilty of actual negligence or misconduct in the performance of his duties as such director or officer.

DIVISION 5. Reserved Name. (Optional Sections)

The following provisions are suggested to provide mechanics for reserving a corporate name:

Section 7A. Reserved Name

The exclusive right to the use of a corporate name may be reserved by filing in the office of the Secretary of State an application to reserve a specified corporate name, executed by the applicant. If the Secretary of State finds that such name is available for corporate use, he shall reserve the same for the exclusive use of such applicant for a period of one hundred twenty days.

The right to the exclusive use of a specified corporate name so reserved may be assigned by filing in the office of the Secretary of State a notice of such assignment, executed by the person for whom such name was reserved and specifying the name and address of the transferee.

Section 83. Fees for Filing Documents and Issuing Certificates

The Secretary of State shall charge and collect for: * * *

- (c-1) Filing and application to reserve a corporate name, five dollars.
- (c-2) Filing a notice of transfer of a reserved corporate name, five dollars: * * *

INDEX

A

Age Discrimination in Employment Act, 3.10
Antitrust laws, application to nonprofit enterprises of, 4:17
Application for reservation of corporate name, 1:05
    form for the, 1:06
Articles of amendment, 1:18
    form of the, 1:19
Articles of consolidation, form for, 5:05
Articles of dissolution, 5:12
    form for, 5:13
Articles of incorporation, 1:02
    amending, 1:18–1:19
    form for, 1:03
    procedures to amend, 1:17
Articles of merger, form of, 5:04
Articles of merger or consolidation of domestic and foreign corporation, form of, 5:06
Assets
    distribution by a nonprofit corporation of, 5:10
    sale by a nonprofit corporation of, 5:08
Association, judicial relief based on the standing of an, 4:05
Authorization to do business in another state by a nonprofit corporation, 1:20

B

Board of directors. See Directors of nonprofit corporations
Bylaws
    defined, 1:11
    forms for, 1:12

C

California
    removal of officers under the statutes of, 3:06
    right of members to inspect books and records under the statutes of, 2:09
Certificate of authority for authorization to do business in another state, 1:21
    form for application for, 1:22
Change of registered office or registered agent, or both, form for, 1:08
Charitable immunity, 4:07

Checklist of points to remember in organizing a nonprofit corporation, 1:28
Civil Rights Act of 1964. See Title VII
Collective bargaining
  "good faith" duty covering, 4:21
  selection of labor representative(s) for the establishment of, 4:20
  subject matter of, 4:22
Copyright
  application for, 4:10
  protection, 4:08–4:10
  fair use of works protected by, 4:12
  sources of ownership of, 4:09
Corporate minutes, 1:13
  form for, 1:14
Creation of a nonprofit corporation, 1:01–1:28
Cy pres doctrine, 5:11

D

Defense of Ultra Vires, 1:16
Directors of nonprofit corporations, 2:12
  action of the board of, 2:16
  election of, 2:13
  meetings of, 2:14
  removal of, 2:17
Discriminatory practices of private associations, 4:03
Dissolution of a nonprofit corporation
  involuntary, 5:14
  voluntary, 5:09

E

Employees of nonprofit organizations, 3:07. See also Collective bargaining and Union organizations
  collective bargaining for, 4:20
  coverage under the Equal Pay Act of, 3:09
  retirement plans of, 3:13
  strikes by, 4:24
  unfair labor practices by members to, 4:23
Employment discrimination under Title VII, 3:08–3:09
The Equal Pay Act administered under the Equal Employment Opportunity Commission, 3:09

F

Federal Insurance Contributions Act (FICA), 3:18
Federal Securities Act, 4:16
Federal tax exempt status under 501(c)(3) of the Internal Revenue Code, 1:02
Federal Trade Commission, monitoring of nonprofit organizations by the, 4:18
Feoffees of Heriot's Hospital v. Ross, 4:07
Foreign nonprofit corporation, withdrawal of a, 5:07
Form 5305 or 5305-A, for the creation of an Individual Retirement Account, 3:22
401(k) plans, 3:24
　nonprofit corporations' qualified, 3:14
403(b) plans, 3:24

I

Incorporators of nonprofit organizations, requirements for the number and qualification of, 1:09
Individual Retirement Accounts, 3:22
Internal Revenue Service
　annual reporting of qualified retirement plans with the, 3:19
　Form 4972 of the, 3:21
　Form 5310 of the, 3:20
　Form 5500, 5500-C, 5500-R of the, 3:19
　notification of retirement plan termination given to the, 3:20
　ruling on a corporate director as an employee by the, 3:04
　waiving of the minimum funding requirements of a retirement plan by the, 3:16

L

Labor laws, compliance of nonprofit organizations with, 4:19
Litigation involving nonprofit enterprises, 4:01
　checklist of points to remember concerning, 4:26

M

McDonnell Douglas Corporation v. Green, 3:08
Meetings, 2:02
　form of notice of member, 2:04

Meetings (*Cont.*)
 form of notice of special member, 2:05
 notice of member, 2:03
Members and directors of a nonprofit corporation, 2:01–2:18
Members of nonprofit corporations
 benefits to, 1:24
 checklist of points to remember for, 2:18
 derivative actions of, 2:10
 meetings of, 2:02
 numbers of, 2:01
 right to inspect books and records by, 2:09
Merger or consolidation of nonprofit corporations
 articles of, 5:03
 checklist of points to remember concerning, 5:17
 effect of, 5:02
 procedure for, 5:01
Model Nonprofit Corporation Act, 1:02, 1:16
 bylaws as provided for under the, 1:11
 derivative actions of members covered by the, 2:10
 director(s) as defined under the, 2:12–2:13
 incorporators of nonprofit corporations specified by the, 1:09
 listing of the powers of a nonprofit corporation in the, 1:15
 management of affairs of a nonprofit corporation covered by the, 2:15
 merger provisions under the, 5:01
 notice of member meeting specified by the, 2:03
 organizational meeting requirements specified by the, 1:10
 powers of a nonprofit corporation proscribed by the, 1:15
 proscriptions for names of nonprofit corporations by the, 1:05
 proxy voting provisions covered under the, 2:07
 registered office and agent as specified by the, 1:07
 removal of director under the, 2:17
 removal of officers as specified by the, 3:06
 right to inspect books and records by members under the, 2:09
 selection of officers of nonprofit corporations under the, 3:01

N

National Labor Relations Act, 4:19, 4:23, 4:25
National Labor Relations Board, 4:19–4:20, 4:23
 permission of right to work laws by the, 4:24
New York state
 provisions for merger under the statutes of, 5:01
 proxy voting statutes in, 2:07

purposes for which nonprofit corporations may be formed in, 1:04
removal of officers under the statutes of, 3:06
1947 Copyright Act, 4:11
1976 Copyright Act, 4:11–4:12
1986 Revised Model Nonprofit Corporation Act, 2:01
Nonprofit corporation(s). See also Litigation
   articles of incorporation for, 1:02, 1:18–1:19
   authorization to do business in another state by a, 1:20–1:22
   bankruptcy proceedings involving, 5:16
   books and records required of, 1:23
   checklist of requirements for organizing, 1:28
   classifications under the law of, 2:01
   creation of a, 1:01–1:28
   directors of, 2:12
   distribution of assets of, 5:10
   involuntary dissolution of, 5:14
   licenses and permits required of, 1:25
   management of affairs of a, 2:15
   members of, 1:24, 2:01
   names provided under the Model Act for, 1:05
   organization of a, 1:01
   powers of a, 1:15
   procedures after dissolution of, 5:15
   registered office and agent required of, 1:07
   sale of assets of, 5:08
   statement or purpose required by, 1:04
   withdrawal of a foreign, 5:07
   voluntary dissolution of, 5:09
Nonprofit enterprises
   antitrust laws applied to, 4:17
   application of the Copyright Act to, 4:08
   labor law compliance of, 4:19
   legal problems of, 4:01–4:26
   public performances of copyrighted music by, 4:11
   tort liability of, 4:06
   unfair competition laws applied to, 4:18

O

Officers and employees of nonprofit corporations, 3:01–3:25
Officers of nonprofit corporations
   authority of, 3:03

Officers of nonprofit corporations (*Cont.*)
    checklist of points to remember for, 3:25
    duties of, 3:02
    as employees, 3:04
    liability of, 3:05
    removal of, 3:06
    selection of, 3:01
Organizational meeting, 1:10

P

Pension Benefit Guaranty Corporation, 3:19–3:20
Pension plans, simplified employee, 3:23. See also 401 plans
Permits for charitable solicitations, 1:26
Proxy voting, 2:07
    form for, 2:08

R

Registered office and agent, requirement of nonprofit corporations concerning a, 1:07
Religious associations, judicial intervention in, 4:04
Retirement plans. See also 401(k) plans
    for employees of nonprofit enterprises, 3:13
    funding for qualified, 3:16
    integration with Social Security of, 3:18
    limitations on contributions to, 3:17
    reporting requirements for qualified, 3:19
    sample calculations of the taxation of benefits from, 3:21
    termination of, 3:20
    test requirements for, 3:15
    vesting and participation of employees in, 3:15
Right of association, 4:02
Right to work laws, 4:25

S

SEC Rule 144, 4:15
Secretary of State of Maryland v. Joseph Munson Co., 1:25
Securities Act of 1933, 4:13–4:15

Securities
  compliance with state laws concerning, 4:16
  donations to nonprofit organizations from the sale of, 4:15
  exemptions from registration of, 4:14
  laws, 4:13
Sherman Act, 4:17
Simplified employee pension plan, 3:23
Statement of Change of Registered Office or Registered Agent, or Both, form for the, 1:08
Statutory requirements generally applied to nonprofit corporations. See also Model Nonprofit Corporation Act
  books and records specified by the, 1:23
  corporate minutes specified by the, 1:13
  licenses and permits specified by the, 1:25
  number and qualification of the incorporators specified by the, 1:09
  permits for charitable solicitations under the, 1:26
  statement of purpose or purposes generally specified by the, 1:04
Strikes, 4:24

T

Tax exempt status, obtaining, 1:27
Tax-sheltered annuities for employees of 501(c)(3) organizations, 3:24
Title VII (Civil Rights Act of 1964)
  discrimination in employment subject to, 3:08
  enforcement by the Equal Employment Opportunity Commission under, 3:08
  nonprofit organizations' coverage under, 3:08
  standards applied to charges of age discrimination, 3:10
  violation of the Equal Pay Act under, 3:09

U

Unfair competition laws, 4:18
Uniform Securities Act, 4:16
Union organizations
  duty to bargain in good faith by members of, 4:21
  regulations covering, 4:19–20

V

Vietnam Era Veterans' Readjustment Assistance Act, 3:12
Vocational Rehabilitation Act, 3.11
Voting
  by proxy, 2:07
  rights, 2:06